The End of the Refugee Cycle?

REFUGEE AND FORCED MIGRATION STUDIES

General Editors: Dawn Chatty, Refugee Studies Programme, International Development Centre, University of Oxford, *and* Chaloka Beyani, Law Department, London School of Economics

THE END OF
THE REFUGEE CYCLE?

Refugee Repatriation and Reconstruction

Edited by

Richard Black and *Khalid Koser*

Berghahn Books
New York • Oxford

First published in 1999 by

Berghahn Books

©1999 Richard Black and Khalid Koser

Library of Congress Cataloging-in-Publication Data

The end of the refugee cycle? : refugee repatriation and
reconstruction / edited by Richard Black and Khalid Koser.
    p.cm. -- (Refugee and forced migration studies ; v. 4)
    Includes bibliographical references and index.
    ISBN 1-57181-987-8 (alk. paper). -- ISBN 1-57181-987-8 (pbk.:
alk. paper)
    1. Refugees. 2. Repatriation 3. Reverse migration. I. Black,
Richard, 1964-   . II. Koser, Khalid. III. Series.
HV640.E5 1998
362.87--dc21

98-50558
CIP

British Library Cataloguing in Publication Data

Contents

List of Tables

List of Figures

Acknowledgements

Several papers from this volume were first presented at the 5th International Research and Advisory Panel (IRAP) Conference on Forced Migration, organised by the International Association for the Study of Forced Migration at Moi University, Eldoret, 9–12 April 1996, whilst others were specially commissioned for this volume. The IRAP meeting was generously supported by the United Nations High Commissioner for Refugees (UNHCR), and the governments of Sweden, the Netherlands and Switzerland. The editors would like to thank an anonymous referee for useful comments on a first draft, and Hazel Lintott for producing the maps.

List of Abbreviations

Africa Educational Trust (AET)
Alliance of Democratic Forces for the Liberation of Congo-Zaire (ADFL)
Cable News Network (CNN)
Cambodian People's Party (CPP)
Cambodian Resettlement and Reintegration (CARERE)
Coalition Government of Democractic Kampuchea (CGDK)
Commission for Eritrean Refugee Affairs (CERA)
Commonwealth of Independent States (CIS)
Coordinating Council for Assistance to Refugees and Forced Migrants
     (CCARFM)
Demobilisation and Rehabilitation Programme (DRP)
Development Project for Refugees, Displaced and Returnees (PRODERE)
Eritrean Liberation Front (ELF)
Eritrean People's Liberation Front (EPLF)
European Community Monitoring Mission (ECMM)
European Economic Area (EEA)
European Free Trade Area (EFTA)
European Union (EU)
Extremely Vulnerable Individual (EVI)
Federal Migration Service (FMS)
Food and Agriculture Organisation of the United Nations (FAO)
Forças Armadas Angolanas (FAA)
Forces Armées Rwandaises (FAR)
Forces Armées Zairoises (FAZ)
German Assisted Return Programme (GARP)
Internally Displaced Person (IDP)
International Committee of the Red Cross (ICRC)
International Conference on Refugees in Central America (CIREFCA)
International Council for Voluntary Agencies (ICVA)
International Organisation for Migration (IOM)
International Refugee Law Project (IRLP)
International Resource Group on Disarmament and Security in the Horn
     of Africa (IRG)
Khmer People's National Liberation Front (KPNLF)

La Unidad Revolucionara Nacional de Guatemala (URNG)
Liberation Tigers for Tamil Eelam (LTTE)
Médecins sans Frontières (MSF)
Nongovernmental Organisation (NGO)
Nucleo de Apoio para os Refugiados (NAR)
Organisation of African Unity (OAU)
Overseas Development Administration (ODA)
People's Revolutionary Party of Kampuchea (PRPK)
People's Revolution Party (PRP) (Zaire)
Programme for Refuge Reintegration and Rehabilitation of Resettlement
    Areas in Eritrea (PROFERI)
Provisional Government of Eritrea (PGE)
Quick Impact Project (QIP)
Repatriation Information Centre (RIC)
Repatriation Information Reports (RIR)
Republika Srpska (RS)
Resistência Nacional de Moçambique (RENAMO)
Rwandese Patriotic Army (RPA)
Rwandese Patriotic Front (RPF)
South African Catholic Bishops Conference (SACBC)
Southern Africa Development Council (SADC)
Special Emergency Programme for the Horn of Africa (SEPHA)
Swedish International Development Agency (SIDA)
Tigrayan People's Liberation Front (TPLF)
Uganda People's Defence Forces (UPDF)
União para a Independência Total de Angola (UNITA)
United Nations Logistical and Transport Operations (UNILOG)
United Nations (UN)
United Nations Childrens Fund (UNICEF)
United Nations Coordinating Unit for Humanitarian Assistance in Angola
    (UCAH)
United Nations Department for Humanitarian Affairs (DHA)
United Nations Development Programme (UNDP)
United Nations High Commissioner for Refugees (UNHCR)
United Nations Office for the Coordination of Humanitarian and
    Economic Assistance Programmes Relating to Afghanistan (UNOCA)
United Nations Research Institute for Social Development (UNRISD)
United Nations Special Programme for Economic Assistance to Central
    America (PEC)
United Nations Transitional Authority in Cambodia (UNTAC)
United Nations Institute in Nambia (UNIN)
United States Agency for International Development (USAID)
Voluntary Repatriation Programme (VRP)
War-Affected People (WAP)
World Food Programme (WFP)

PART ONE
REFUGEE REPATRIATION
AND RECONSTRUCTION

1

The End of the Refugee Cycle?

Khalid Koser and *Richard Black*

A t the beginning of the 1990s there was great optimism that the end of the Cold War might also result in the end of the global 'refugee cycle'. Cold War analyses of refugee displacements often highlighted the 'escape' from communism as the principal motive for refugee movements in the North. They tended to explain refugee-generating conflicts in the South in terms of wars conducted by proxy by the two superpowers (Suhrke and Zolberg 1989). In reality, though, the global refugee population increased substantially immediately after the end of the Cold War, from about 14.9 million in 1990 to 17.2 million in 1991 (UNHCR 1995a). The collapse of the former Soviet Union was a particularly significant event, which led to a wave of ethnic conflicts in the former Republics. As many as two million refugees have fled conflicts in Nagorno-Karabakh, Georgia, Moldova, Tajikistan and in the Russian Caucasus (Codagnone 1997). In the South, it became clear that many of the conflicts which perhaps started as proxy wars had taken on their own momentum, and refugees continued to flee Angola and Afghanistan, for example. In addition, new conflicts have emerged in the new geopolitical environment (Sword 1992). Up to two million people were displaced by the war in the former Yugoslavia, and perhaps one million from Liberia. New battle lines have been drawn between local protagonists and a range of international sponsors.

Along with initial optimism about the number of refugees in a post-Cold War 'new world order', there were also hopes amongst many academics and policy makers that the individual 'refugee cycle' might come to an end for many. These hopes for an enhanced environment for repatriation appear to have been better founded. During the 1990s, repatriation has occurred on a scale far more substantial than during previous decades. It is estimated that up to 12 million refugees have returned to their countries of origin during the 1990s, either independently or under organised programmes. Major organised repatriations of over half a million people took place in both Cambodia and Mozambique. In these countries, as well as in countries such as Namibia, Angola, Eritrea and Liberia, policies to assist repatriation have been linked to attempts to support political reform, democratisation and economic reconstruction – although not always successfully. The 'refugee cycle' itself meanwhile seems to have accelerated, and repatriation has already occurred to some countries where conflicts have evolved since the end of the Cold War, for example to Rwanda, and to Bosnia, the latter representing the largest repatriation movement in Europe since the Second World War.

One of the effects of the increased and accelerated rates of repatriation during this decade has been to lend weight and popular legitimacy to a discourse that has come to dominate refugee policy, namely that repatriation is the optimum and most feasible 'durable solution' to the refugee crisis (Harrell-Bond 1989). Another effect, however, has been to engender closer academic research, which has begun to interrogate this discourse of repatriation. Just as the refugee crisis has risen on political agendas, so repatriation has become a political issue. There is a need to scrutinise the motivations of host and home governments, of the international community in general, and specifically of the Office of the United Nations High Commissioner for Refugees (UNHCR), which has become a major 'player' in repatriation as well as refugee protection and assistance. There is equally a need to understand the priorities of refugees in exile, for many of whom repatriation is not a desired outcome, and for whom 'home' has come to mean something quite different from the meaning often ascribed by policy makers. Even where return has occurred, there is a need to pay much closer attention to relations after return, and to recognise that even if repatriation is the end of one cycle, it is also usually the beginning of a new cycle which can challenge and expose some returnees to vulnerability.

These changing constructions and realities of refugee repatriation provide the backdrop for this book, which presents new empirical research on examples of refugee repatriation and reconstruction worldwide, and throughout the 1990s. Most of the cases highlighted are still ongoing and remain poorly documented beyond internal agency and government reports. The contributions to this book ask how the discourses of repatriation and especially return 'home' have evolved; they examine whether these discourses are accurate or appropriate, and point towards alternative perspectives on repatriation. In the rest of this introductory chapter we address some of the conceptual themes and arguments which are central to the volume as a whole. In raising these issues, we also attempt to highlight questions which need to be placed on the political and research agendas of those concerned with the role and impact of repatriation.

The politics of repatriation

It is impossible to understand the current repatriation discourse in isolation from the changing political context affecting attitudes towards refugees. In the industrialised democracies, the clear tendency is towards controlling immigration (Cornelius et al. 1994), in a period of high unemployment, retrenchment and of fear of importing 'ethnic' and other conflicts. The tendency to exclude migrants has been extended to refugees as well. Most asylum seekers now fail to obtain formal refugee status because they are not seen as meeting the criteria for refugee definition laid down in the 1951 Geneva Convention. In turn, these criteria are interpreted by states in an increasingly strict manner. A range of policies have been developed by Northern countries to limit or prevent the arrival of asylum seekers (normally termed 'bogus refugees') in the first place (Koser 1996a). There is a justifiable fear that such restrictions 'impinge on *bona fide* refugees as much as, or more than, other categories of asylum-seekers' (Collinson 1993: 25). Refugee status is too often seen by policy makers as something 'exploited' by individual migrants to circumvent normal immigration rules (and one which provides much greater security and social welfare benefits), rather than an important safety net of protection for those genuinely suffering persecution.

Such an attitude of policy makers is not surprising, given the state of 'public opinion' and the influence of the media; but it also provides an essential backdrop for increasing interest in repatriation as the preferred durable solution at the end of a refugee crisis. For example, refugee status tends to confer permanent residence rights upon recipients, whereas the return of all other categories of displaced person, including asylum seekers and those granted 'temporary protection', is perceived to be much easier. Thus even though some good reasons may exist to reform international law as it relates to asylum and refugees, and seek an alternative paradigm for refugee protection (Hathaway 1995a), the reality is that increasing political interest in repatriation has gone hand in hand with increasing restrictions on the granting of refugee status. If one is talking about 'temporary protection' status, whether in European countries or in North America, it is difficult to disentangle the extent to which such status is genuinely about keeping options for repatriation open on the one hand, or whether it is about undermining the rights and security of 'genuine' refugees on the other.

Repatriation has similarly become a preferred solution in many African states, as they too have begun to pull away from the level of protection of refugees guaranteed by the 1951 Geneva Convention, and more particularly the Organisation of African Unity (OAU) Convention on Refugees. During the 1960s and 1970s relatively few organised repatriation movements took place in Africa (an important exception was the return of some 200,000 people to Algeria in 1962). Those refugees who did not repatriate independently were often locally integrated in their host state, in some cases, as in Tanzania and Zaire, even achieving full citizenship. When numbers are perceived as manageable and there is a high degree of certainty that return will not be possible, then local integration is still an option which some African governments are prepared to entertain, especially if assistance for the process is available from the international community. However, where refugee displacements are substantial, where they are seen to impact negatively upon resources that may already be severely constrained, and where social and political tensions are exacerbated by the refugees' presence, a political push for the repatriation of refugees has often evolved (Rogge 1994). Of course, this often has much to do too with the initial political stance of the host government towards the conflict or regime from which refugees are fleeing, such that local integration of a quarter of a million Liberian refugees has been largely acceptable to neighbouring Côte d'Ivoire.

In contrast to that of host governments, the role of home governments in the repatriation process has tended to be underestimated. Limited research, however, indicates that their priorities can also politicise and affect the repatriation process. In a case study of the involuntary repatriation of Ethiopian refugees from Djibouti between 1977 and 1983, Crisp (1984) demonstrated how the Ethiopian government brought pressure to bear on the government of Djibouti to repatriate refugees, the absence of whom was seen as damaging the legitimacy of the state in Ethiopia. Similar forces were at work in Rwanda after the victory of the Rwandan Patriotic Front (RPF) in 1994, as the maintenance of large refugee populations outside the country constituted both a potential military, and public relations threat to the new regime. Johan Pottier, in this volume, describes how repatriation emerged as the only acceptable solution in the new 'Democratic Republic of the Congo' for host government, home government and UNHCR, effectively becoming part of a military carve-up of the region. In contrast, Lucia Ann McSpadden, also in this volume, demonstrates how the government in Eritrea has resisted UNHCR efforts to repatriate refugees from Sudan. Her analysis demonstrates divergent perspectives: a short-term focus on physical return by UNHCR, and a longer-term focus on reintegration and development by the Eritrean government.

The case of repatriation to Eritrea highlights the priorities of UNHCR in the contemporary politics of repatriation. In response to financial and political pressures imposed by donor states, UNHCR has been perceived by many commentators as actively promoting the repatriation option in the short term, rather than facilitating voluntary repatriation when conditions have become conducive (Coles 1989; Harrell-Bond 1989; Allen and Morsink 1994a). It is striking that antagonism towards refugees in host countries has coincided with the politicisation of – or at least politicisation of discussion within – UNHCR, the primary international actor charged with independently and non politically representing the interests of refugees. What is clear is that UNHCR finds itself in an increasingly difficult position with regards to respecting the sovereignty of both host and home states, and their insistence upon the right to manage migration. In particular, as the political pressure to return refugees from host states rises, there is concern that repatriation may at times not be completely voluntary, and that it may be encouraged before conditions in the country of origin are genuinely conducive to secure and dignified return. The guarantee of voluntariness; the definition of security, and promotion of lasting return and reintegration in peoples' 'homes' (rather than simply their 'homelands') are all repatriation priorities which UNHCR is increasingly perceived as unable to deliver in the new political environment (Human Rights Watch 1997). The need for the international community to develop a protocol to specify the role and mandate of UNHCR in repatriation situations is becoming a pressing agenda, highlighted in several contributions to this volume.

Going home?

One of the points of reference in the discourse of repatriation is that return is the favoured option for refugees, for whom the refugee cycle can at last end when they 'go home'. For many refugees, however, repatriation does not represent a homecoming; nor is there agreement in the literature on what 'going home' actually means. The notion of a return 'home' can be viewed in a number of ways. At its simplest, it can represent a return to the refugee's country of origin; but more generally, it is seen as more specific than that, involving the place of origin, perhaps the refugee's own house or land that was abandoned at the time of flight. This place called 'home' may have both cultural or spiritual meaning for the returnee, as well as being the returnee's own property, imbuing it with an economic significance. For Warner (1994: 162), 'home' is 'the association of an individual within a homogeneous group and the association of that group with a particular physical place'. There is often an implicit assumption that at the end of conflict, a return to a place called 'home' is both possible and desirable. However, such an assumption can be questioned in both its aspects: return 'home' may be impossible.

The case studies examined in this volume provide varying perspectives on the process of returning home. First, if an essentialist view of 'home' is not appropriate, it may still be possible for return to be combined with the construction of a new home as part of a wider community or nation-building process. For example, in the case of Eritrea, Lucia Ann McSpadden argues that the physical destruction associated with war, and the fact that many refugees were born in exile, have made a speedy return to places of origin highly problematic. Yet for the Eritrean authorities, a broader notion of home has been seen as appropriate, with return 'home' potentially representing a return to the national process of reconstruction in the country as a whole. 'Home' is thus constituted as a viable and sustainable national economic base in the homeland, rather than being tied to a particular place. In the case of Cambodia, considered by Marita Eastmond and Joakim Öjendal, returnees themselves prioritised return to areas of the country that were perceived as the most fertile, and with the greatest economic potential, rather than necessarily to their original place of origin.

Nonetheless, some of the difficulties of this approach, which has seen returnees moving, not to a stable and revitalised 'home', but to a province in which low-level conflict has continued, and their position has proved precarious, highlight the dangers of a wider conception of the return 'home'. Indeed, in some other repatriations, a return to place of origin can be seen as desirable, but not possible. A dilemma then arises as to whether return should be prioritised at all if a more strict definition of 'home' as original place of origin cannot be met. For example, in an increasing number of organised repatriations, refugees have returned to areas which, for some of them at least, are not those from which they fled, and where their 'ethnic' or 'tribal' identity may mark them out for discrimination by the local population or local authorities. In this volume, Christopher McDowell highlights the generalised return of failed asylum seekers from Switzerland to the south of Sri Lanka, irrespective of their ethnic and regional origin in the Tamil north. Similarly, Bosnians in Germany, who are originally from what is now the 'Republika Srpska' (RS), have been returned since the Dayton Peace Accord to areas within the Bosnian Federation, not their original 'homes'. Although they do not form an ethnic minority, and are unlikely to suffer *ethnic* persecution, their insecurity is manifested in a lack of secure housing rights and prospects for 'reintegration'. Of course, in this situation, 'minority return' of ethnic minorities to their places of original residence is much more problematic than 'majority return'. However, the point is that the latter flow has occurred despite UNHCR guidelines to the contrary (and despite a more or less exclusive focus on 'majority returns' to 'places of origin' in every other EU country), and the organisation, and the 'international refugee regime', have been powerless to stop it (Black et al. 1997).

In both Sri Lanka and Bosnia, the expectation of governments promoting repatriation is that returnees will relocate internally once their 'home' areas are secure. However, the policy of accepting an 'internal flight alternative' – particularly after a period of quasi-refugee status – has been criticised as simply transforming refugees into internally displaced persons, and therefore in no way offering a 'durable' solution. In some cases, it may be encouraged by local authorities wishing to strengthen government-held, as opposed to rebel-held, areas (and as such arguably represents one of the 'weapons' of war); whilst in the case of Bosnia, it has clearly contributed to a tacit, and in some cases overt consolidation of the process of ethnic cleansing. For example, a brochure published by Croatian authorities encouraging Bosnian Croats to return to areas under Bosnian Croat control in exchange for a new house, employment and other privileges has been circulated by Croatian embassies in Europe to Bosnian Croat refugee communities (Black et al. 1997). Participants in such 'assisted return schemes' are likely to become dependent on the authorities and hence to play a significant role in protests against minority return (i.e. return of minority groups to their *own* homes). Similarly, Bosniak communities-in-exile have been established along the Bosnian Federation's border with the RS, and Serb refugees from Croatia settled as a buffer within the RS against the Federation. Such cases represent one example of why repatriation does not necessarily bring the refugee cycle to an end for refugees themselves, and may be manipulated as part of the cycle of conflict.

Further complexity is added to the intersections between 'home' and 'ethnic' identities where they do not correspond with 'national' identities. It has often been observed of refugees in Africa, for example, that they may flee and repatriate across political boundaries which do not coincide with ethnic or tribal boundaries which are much more meaningful to them (Rogge 1994). Hilary Pilkington and Moya Flynn, in this volume, illustrate this confrontation of identities in the former Soviet Union. 'Ethnic Russians' here are involuntarily leaving states of the former Soviet Union to 'return' to the Russian homeland where they have never lived and where many actually consider themselves to be refugees. In this case, paradoxically, 'repatriation' might be considered to be the *beginning* of a refugee cycle. There are clear parallels with the 'return' of ethnic Greeks (Pontians) from the former Soviet Union to modern Greece (Voutira 1991), or of the *Aussiedler* to Germany, although these cases can be more clearly seen as 'voluntary' movements. However, there are also parallels, for example, with the case of Rwanda, where many of those 'returning' to Rwanda from Uganda and Tanzania in 1994 as the Rwandan Patriotic Front took control had never lived in Rwanda before. In such situations, notions of 'home', 'nationality' and 'identity' become critically blurred.

At a more conceptual level, repatriation initiatives have consistently tended to underemphasise the concept of 'home' in the minds of refugees. Literature on Cypriot and Afghan refugees suggests that the duration of refugeehood can influence the definition of home, such that people may feel more 'at home' in the countries in which they may have been in exile for the whole, or the majority of their lives (Zetter 1988). In situations such as Eritrea and former Yugoslavia, return is to a country which has not formally existed during the lifetime of most refugees, other than as a level of regional government or as an 'imagined' state. In the extreme situation of involuntary repatriation, and sometimes when repatriation is prematurely promoted, people can also be returned to a country where they are deprived of the basic rights which might be expected in a place called 'home' (Shacknove 1985). Even when voluntary return is the ultimate intended outcome for refugees themselves, the mere removal of war and conflict may not be a sufficient condition to guarantee returnees full rights as 'citizens' on return, as Chris Dolan argues in this volume.

A challenge to policy makers is to incorporate in repatriation initiatives refugees' own meanings of repatriation, and their perceptions and expectations of 'home'. In a practical sense, the disparities which can occur between different actors in defining where and what is 'home' translate into the imperative of consulting and involving refugees in the negotiations over repatriation. For example, although the removal of the 'root causes' of flight is usually considered the single most important requisite condition for return by the international community, refugees themselves may return under conditions of conflict (Larkin et al. 1992), and may develop in exile a new set of priorities for return which are essentially unrelated to their motives for flight (Koser 1997a). The chapter by Martha Walsh, Richard Black and Khalid Koser, in this volume, suggests that campaigns aimed at informing refugees of conditions at home should perhaps stop being developed *for* refugees, and start being developed *by* refugees.

Repatriation and reconstruction

One reason that the predominant discourse perceives repatriation as the best solution for refugees has been the lack of attention paid to the experiences of refugees after return, although in some respects this represents as much a symptom as a cause of this discourse. For example, even though its Executive Committee confirmed as early as 1985 that UNHCR should have a legitimate interest in the consequences of return and should have access to returnees, the organisation has been unable formally to extend its mandate to include returnees (Allen and Morsink 1994a). Many states have resisted systems for the long-term monitoring of returnees, and there are perhaps justifiable concerns that the extension of protection by the international community to returnees might simply legitimise the premature repatriation of refugees by host countries. To a large extent, a continuing policy vacuum at an international level has also been reflected in the literature, although in some respects, both 'policy' and 'literature' on 'repatriation' has existed, but has been described under a different name – 'post-conflict reconstruction', 'rebuilding of war-torn societies', or even just 'development', with actors such as the United Nations Development Programme (UNDP) and the World Bank at the helm.

A wide range of challenges faced by returnees are described in the contributions to this volume. Recurring physical problems include the presence of land-mines and the destruction of housing; economic activity is shown to depend on access to key resources such as land, labour, working capital and skills, and social confrontation can often arise in the context of the reintegration of returnees with the internally displaced, with those who never fled, and also with demobilised soldiers. One of the most important variables which can influence the reintegration process is demonstrated to be conditions in refugee settlements in exile, and specifically the extent to which refugees have been allowed to gain a degree of self-reliance. Other variables which are highlighted include the type and management of settlements for returnees (where these are formally constructed), and the extent and type of assistance made available to returnees.

Beyond the detailed nature of the reintegration process described in the various case studies in this volume, three more systematic issues are prominent. First, the existence and extent of social networks are clearly paramount in the reintegration process. As Marita Eastmond and Joakim Öjendal demonstrate in their case study on return to Cambodia, household economic viability can be largely dependent on the existence of a local community, and livelihood strategies are intimately related to the structure of social relations and an individual's or household's position within that structure. The case study in this volume by Laura Hammond of return to Tigray demonstrates the evolutionary nature of social networks, and how in the return context social structures often reveal an ambiguity between old and new patterns of ownership, authority and control.

A second theme which is found to characterise many of the post-return situations covered in this volume concerns the creation or exacerbation of vulnerability amongst certain groups. Vulnerability may coincide with gender: women's traditional roles, responsibilities and supportive networks can be dramatically altered during the 'refugee cycle' (Rogge 1994), although traditional roles of men (especially as the household's 'breadwinner') may also be negatively affected by refugee flight and return. Vulnerability may also coincide with other preexisting analytical categories, such as ethnicity or social class; but also with new social categories, developed in exile and often revolving around degrees of economic self-reliance or community power structures. A particularly important implication from several studies, however, is that vulnerability can effectively be created after return, as a result, for example, of the allocation of inappropriate settlement sites, or the unequal distribution of land. In this context, the role of the home state can be crucial, in some cases in institutionalising vulnerability, and in others in mediating the effects of sources of vulnerability.

What is clear from all of these studies is that return for most refugees is to a new and challenging environment. If repatriation brings to an end the 'refugee cycle', it also coincides with the beginning of a new cycle. In this context, a third theme to emerge from the contributions concerns the 'language' of repatriation. Laura Hammond poses the challenge to rethink the 'repatriation equals homecoming' equation. She suggests that the vocabulary of return, which emphasises 'reintegration', 'reconstruction' and 'rehabilitation' should be translated to focus on 'construction', 'creativity', 'innovation' and 'improvisation'. Seen in this light, the experience of returnees can teach lessons about culture change, the construction of communities, and changing meanings of identity, culture, home and geographical place. From a more practical perspective, Finn Stepputat suggests that assistance programmes which recognise this dynamic character of returnees can enhance their potential contribution to the construction of peace and to postconflict state formation and consolidation.

Conceptual themes and arguments

Unlike other volumes on the subject of refugee repatriation (Allen and Morsink 1994a; Allen 1996; Larkin et al. 1992), this book is deliberately global in perspective. This orientation reflects the changing realities of the global refugee crisis, the impact of which is arguably less localised now than at any time previously. Refugees from the South are a 'live' political issue in countries of the North, both directly through their arrival as 'spontaneous' asylum seekers, and indirectly through media coverage and the funding crisis between UNHCR and donor governments. At the same time, one of the characteristics of the range of empirical case studies included in this volume is a series of shared systematic issues. The intersections between 'ethnic' identity and home are as complex in Bosnia and Russia as they are in Rwanda. The political negotiations over repatriation are as complicated between Switzerland and Sri Lanka as they are between Sudan and Eritrea, and in both cases the role of UNHCR has been criticised. And the operational and socioeconomic challenges associated with repatriation are great whether the country concerned is Afghanistan, Cambodia or Guatemala.

Another distinguishing characteristic of this volume as a whole is that it combines studies of various 'types' of forced migrants, including refugees, asylum seekers and those offered 'temporary protection'. While we recognise the political arguments for maintaining the distinct label 'refugee' as a form of international protection for those suffering from persecution, a more inclusive approach to forced migration is arguably both academically justified, and reflects the changing political realities of the global refugee regime. Thus not only has the distinction between voluntary and involuntary migrants, or economic and political migrants, become increasingly blurred in practice, but, as argued above, increasing limitations on the conferral of refugee status by governments clearly represents a strategy to *promote* repatriation, and vice versa. Meanwhile, the case for an analytical distinction between refugees and other migrants is looking increasingly less robust (Koser 1997b), especially at the margin of explaining behaviour of different migrant groups, their reliance on social networks, and their relationship with host country institutions. In the same spirit of rejecting the study of refugee populations in isolation, the contributions in this volume which concern the experience of returnees recognise that this experience is embedded in relations with other populations, including the internally displaced and demobilising soldiers.

The chapters in this volume are organised into four distinct but interrelated parts, and it may be useful here to say something about the rationale and content of each part. Part One, of which this chapter is the first, aims to describe the dominant 'discourse' of repatriation and to explain how it has evolved. Thus in chapter 2 Rosemary Preston goes on to ask the questions, 'who is researching repatriation, and why?'. She concludes that an increasing body of research on the repatriation process itself, and on postrepatriation 'reconstruction' initiatives, is being stimulated by organisations concerned to facilitate repatriation, but that there are powerful reasons why the impact of this research on policy is itself limited. In this case, illustrative material is drawn from return to Namibia, as well as a global survey of what it might mean to return in 'safety' and in 'dignity'.

In Part Two, attention is turned to four 'mass' voluntary repatriations that occurred, to a greater or lesser degree, in the early 1990s, immediately after the end of the Cold War. Thus chapters 3-6 focus on repatriation to Cambodia, Afghanistan, Eritrea and Mozambique respectively, highlighting complications in large-scale repatriation exercises that were either expected to be, or are even still seen in hindsight as largely unproblematic. Thus Marita Eastmond and Joakim Öjendal's study of return from Thailand to Cambodia concerns one of the first major repatriations supervised by the international community in what the UN High Commissioner for Refugees, Sadako Ogota was later to describe as the 'decade of repatriation'. One of their conclusions is that while the repatriation exercise was highly successful in physically moving refugees across the border in a short period of time and providing initial support upon return, many returnees are now virtually destitute. In focusing on return from Pakistan and Iran to Afghanistan, Peter Marsden analyses the largest attempted repatriation since the Second World War. His chapter focuses on operational aspects of repatriation and reconstruction assistance, and asks critical questions about the premises upon which these exercises were based. Meanwhile, Lucia Ann McSpadden's chapter highlights the political context for repatriation, detailing the way that the negotiations for the mass return of Eritrean refugees from Sudan stalled, and showing that the majority of these refugees are still in exile. In the case of return to Mozambique, the chapter by Chris Dolan emphasises how, in spite of generally positive (internal) reviews of the repatriation operation from other neighbouring countries, the specific process of return from South Africa suffered a number of practical problems in its implementation, especially relating to perhaps an over-eagerness of UNHCR and other agencies to accomplish the repatriation as quickly as possible.

In Part Three, the book turns to more recent, and in many respects, more complex repatriation movements, with chapters 7-10 examining return to Bosnia-Herzegovina, Sri Lanka, Rwanda and the Russian Federation respectively. In chapter 7, Martha Walsh, Richard Black and Khalid Koser focus on the dissemination of information to prospective Bosnian returnees in the European Union, highlighting a number of flaws in this process which reflect concerns to 'sell' the repatriation option. Christopher McDowell is concerned with a more overtly 'forced' repatriation, of failed Tamil asylum seekers in Switzerland, who have been returned to Sri Lanka under the terms of an agreement between the Swiss and Sri Lankan authorities. In chapter 9, Johan Pottier considers perhaps the most contentious repatriation of the decade – of Rwandans living in the North Kivu region of the Democratic Republic of the Congo, which has been hailed by some as an 'African solution' to the problems faced by the region since the Rwandan genocide in 1994. Pottier challenges this view, suggesting that the military solution of forced repatriation will not bring stability to the region. Hilary Pilkington and Moya Flynn focus attention on the 'return' of ethnic Russians from states of the former Soviet Union to the Russian 'homeland'. Analysis of the social constructions of this return by the Russian state, combined with the social realities experienced by the repatriates, demonstrates how this movement defies the neat categories typically applied to repatriations.

The final part of the book extends the coverage further by focusing attention on the postrepatriation experience. A study by Art

Hansen and David Tavares in chapter 11 focuses on one important aspect of reconstruction – the demobilisation of soldiers – in Angola, a country which has prepared for repatriation a number of times, but has yet to witness large-scale returns. The chapter argues that international agency personnel's perceptions of the background and aspirations of demobilised soldiers do not always fit the reality – whilst these aspirations may themselves be unrealistic. In chapter 12 Finn Stepputat focuses on the relationship between returnees and the 'state' in Guatemala. Repatriation is demonstrated to have contributed to the social construction of peace and 'state formation' in Guatemala. Finally in chapter 13, Laura Hammond draws on case study material from returnee communities in Tigray, Ethiopia to pose a series of specific challenges to the 'discourse' of repatriation, and suggests new directions for the discourse of policy makers and academics alike.

New research agendas

The contributions to this volume identify a range of research gaps in the study of refugee repatriation and reconstruction. While it is beyond the scope of this introductory chapter to provide a systematic overview of all of these gaps, it is worth drawing attention to a number of recurring themes. As a general comment, research gaps are particularly obvious in the postreturn context. More specifically, the need for further research is repeatedly identified as needed on the motivations of governments in countries of origin in negotiations for return; from the perspective of returnees on the definition and evolution of social networks in postreturn environments, and from a more conceptual perspective on the rewriting of the 'language' of return. The way that such research is conducted also needs to be reappraised, to include a search for links between different return situations, and for interrelationships between returnees and other migrant as well as nonmigrant populations. More generally, in a field of study as emotive and applied as 'refugee studies', the purposes of research and its relationship to the political agenda need to be foremost in researchers' minds.

A series of more direct policy implications also recur. Perhaps foremost among these is the need on the part of the international community to clarify the role of UNHCR based on a clear assessment of the agency's ability to secure lasting, voluntary repatriation. Possible areas of reform might include the financial and political relationship between UNHCR and donor governments; the role of UNHCR in identifying potential returnees, and on reassessing divisions of responsibility between UNHCR and other international and non-governmental organisations. The case studies stress that potential returnees and returnees themselves are conspicuously missing from consultation on most policy developments, and demonstrate how as a consequence it is frequently the case that their views and suggestions are not prioritised. A related theme is that assistance to returnees should recognise and enhance their potential, not only for self-reliance after return, but also for contributing to the wider challenges of state formation and national reconstruction.

From a more holistic perspective, the message of this book is that the predominant discourse that repatriation is the 'end of the refugee cycle', and that voluntary repatriation implies a return 'home', deserves to be scrutinised and reformulated. Despite the aims of many host states that repatriation should be the principal solution to the refugee crisis, it is worth remembering that there are two other potential 'durable' solutions, namely third country resettlement and local integration. It is salutary to note that most countries in Europe no longer even publish an annual quota for the resettlement of refugees (Troeller 1991). In contrast, a certain amount of optimism is perhaps justified in recognising that the countries of the European Union have offered what is effectively permanent residence to over 100,000 Bosnians who were originally accepted there under 'temporary protection' and on the understanding that they would repatriate (Black et al. 1997).

It is equally important to understand that repatriation at the end of conflict or persecution is by no means always the preferred option of refugees themselves, although it has often transpired to be their only feasible option. For many refugees, however, a lack of desire to return in the short-term does not necessarily imply a loss of interest in, or a betrayal of, their country of origin. How refugee communities can participate in postconflict reconstruction without physically returning is an important research question; and research on this subject could be used to demonstrate to countries of origin (and asylum) how a different end to the refugee cycle might still be of benefit to national reconstruction efforts. Such links between refugees and their countries of origin during the postconflict 'reconstruction' phase may represent a maintained long-term or even symbolic aspiration to return to a spiritual or cultural 'home', whether this is a specific place of origin, a country, or even a former way of life. Yet this is tempered by a realisation that remaining in the asylum country may be socially, economically, or even politically the 'best' solution for those involved, in the short term at least – that their practical 'home' remains elsewhere. In particular, return before conditions are 'right' for it to occur safely and with the consent of all concerned risks leading to conflict, for example between returnees and those who stayed, especially where substantial 'incentives' are provided by international actors to speed up the return process. Such conflict in turn risks undermining not only the security of those who return, but in some cases the process of peace building itself in countries emerging from war and generalised violence.

At the same time, repatriation as soon as it can be achieved in 'safety' and in 'dignity' clearly is the preferred option of many other refugees, and has been occurring at a substantial rate during this decade. Furthermore it is probably realistic in the current political climate to recognise that repatriation is bound to continue to be promoted. In this context, perhaps the most important message of this book is that even when repatriation does bring to an end the 'refugee cycle', it also marks the beginning of a new cycle for returnees, as a new notion of 'home' is explored and created. It is essential that the discourse of repatriation extends beyond the border of the country of origin, to recognise the potential of returnees; to incorporate the challenges faced by returnees, and to understand that both social and physical reconstruction are part of the return process.

2

Researching Repatriation And Reconstruction: Who Is Researching What And Why?

Rosemary Preston

In various parts of the world, and throughout the twentieth century, the transition from conflict to peace has led to the repatriation of exiles to their countries of origin (Coles 1985). Over recent decades, increases in the world's refugee and asylum-seeking populations have led to an increase in the number of people going back to their countries of origin at the end of war and conflict.[1] The visibility of such moves is also growing. The laws of migration are such that every outward movement generates a back flow and there is research which suggests that this might be proportional, varying with flows of different magnitude and under different circumstances. This logic means that increases in returns from coercive war-related migration will also be associated with earlier increases in outward movements.

To observe trends, a long-term overview of reliable statistics is required. Observations of subtle change over periods of a few years (Table 2.1) provide an inadequate basis for generalisation. Nonetheless, from Table 2.1, it can be seen that in the year ending December 1994, there were 2.9 million organised repatriations recorded at a time when there were, worldwide, some 16.3 million

---

1. 'Going back' and 'country of origin' for some are misnomers. They include those with citizenship or other long-term residence entitlements who were born outside the country and who have never lived there.

Table 2.1. *World refugee statistics*

	Dec 92	Dec 94	Dec 96
Refugees and asylum seekers	millions	millions	millions
Africa	5.7	5.8	3.7
Europe and North America	3.4	2.6	2.6
Latin America and the Caribbean	0.1	0.1	0.1
East Asia and the Pacific	0.4	0.4	0.5
Middle East	5.6	5.5	5.8
South and Central Asia	2.3	1.8	1.8
Total	**17.6**	**16.3**	**14.5**
Significant voluntary repatriations	2.4	2.7	0.5
Involuntary returns and expulsions	0.1	0.2	0.2
Total returnees	**2.5**	**2.9**	**0.7**
Ratio returnees to refugees	**14%**	**18%**	**5%**
Ratio involuntary to voluntary returnees	**4%**	**7%**	**40%**

Source: United States Committee for Refugees, World Refugee Surveys, 1993, 1995, 1997.

refugees, a ratio of less than one in four. Among those returning, about six percent are thought to have returned involuntarily. By the year ending December 1996, the number of refugees and asylum seekers had fallen to 14.5 million. There were 700,000 returns, amounting to about one in twenty of those in exile. Of these, nearly 30 percent were involuntary (USCR 1997). Bascom (1995) describes the relationship of the number of official repatriations to the number of refugees in Africa, for the twenty years from 1973 to 1993. His data show the sharp increase of refugees in Africa from 1980, with a visible, if low, increase in the number of repatriations through the 1980s and early 1990s. Bascom suggests that the increasing difficulty of return may explain this. However, his data suggest an increasing rate of return subsequently, as a ratio of 3.57 million refugees to 200,000 returnees (1 in 18) in 1980 has changed to one of 4.6 million refugees and 1.5 million returnees (1 in 3) in 1989. In spite of its increasing incidence, Bascom (1995) and other writers (Allen and Morsink 1994b) continue to make frequent reference to the paucity of research on repatriation and reconstruction, in general, or in respect of specialist subject areas (Parker 1996). However, this chapter suggests that a large number of studies are being done for different purposes. Their scope and number, for various reasons, have remained elusive.

From taboo to norm

If there is a lack of published material on repatriation, this may be attributable to the difficulties associated with discussing, let alone studying, return, postreturn integration and reconstruction (Allen and Morsink 1994a: 2). With notable exceptions, from 1947 until the 1970s, repatriation was unlikely to be perceived as the long-term plan for refuge-seeking groups. Larkin (1992: ix) refers to a post-Second World War reticence to recommend repatriation as the conclusion to exile, since it was feared that legitimate repatriation would quickly facilitate *refoulement.* Today, repatriation is no longer taboo. It is the valid outcome of exile preferred in many circumstances (but not necessarily simultaneously) by refugees and asylum seekers, involved governments and the international organisations. Moreover, it does not necessarily presuppose the cessation of conflict or changed political structures in the country of destination (Larkin 1992; Cuny et al. 1992).

The 1992 declaration by UNHCR that the 1990s would be the decade of repatriation confirms the changed long-term settlement priority at an international level. It has been accompanied by increased pressures on source states to facilitate return and to prevent secondary exodus. Policy, indicated in *The State of the World's Refugees, 1993* (UNHCR 1993a), has included action to resolve conflict so as to enable return; action to prevent renewed conflict and subsequent exit; and action to prevent the development of conditions of new conflict and disintegration. Accompanying these measures, but less publicised, has been more or less coercive action, in many parts of the world, to pressure refugee groups to repatriate (McDowell 1996).

Chronologies of research

The evolution of research into involuntary war-related migration places the 1970s as the decade for the study of the parameters of flight and the 1980s as the period of study of asylum and resettlement. The 1990s, not entirely coincident with changing policy and practice, have become the time to research repatriation. However, just as a chronology of exile explains the changing emphasis of this theorising across decades, so within the study of repatriation, researchers are mapping a temporal path of analysis. From different stakeholder perspectives, studies have accounted for orientations towards and preparations for return (Makanya 1993a; Bascom 1994), the process of return and its effects (Akol 1994; Stein 1994) and finally, post-arrival integration and reconstruction (Allen and Turton 1996). Analysts have differentiated the processes of return at each of these stages, taking account of the ways in which they are influenced by a range of micro, meso, macro and meta-level factors. These include the characteristics of the groups involved; their community, organisational, national and international policy environments; global, legal, social and economic trends; and language, ideology and theory.

Associated with country to country moves, under whatever circumstances, quantities of policy and operational research have been commissioned by UNHCR and other government and nongovernmental organisations (NGOs) providing aid. At different stages of the project cycle, they include, for example: surveys of refugee preferences in respect of the long-term settlement options said to be open to them (Preston 1992; Hansen and Tavares, this volume); needs analyses relating either to specific subgroups or groups as a whole (Thorn 1992), and logistical planning (Schulz and Wöhnung 1989; UNHCR 1990; Blaeser 1990; Doherty 1990; Mebtouche 1990). Journalists and academics have provided overviews and commentaries and, in time, detailed disciplinary and cross-disciplinary field-based studies have begun to emerge. Recent examples include research into: the macroeconomic analysis of war and development (Stewart 1993; Fitzgerald 1994); the economics of disarmament, demobilisation and rehabilitation of fighters (World Bank 1993; Collier 1994; Colletta et al. 1996a; 1996b); the sociology of labour market reintegration (Tamas and Gleichmann 1993; Preston 1994a); the anthropology of repatriation and community integration (Allen 1993; Bascom 1994; Stepputat, this volume); the psychology of integration after return (Brett 1996; Endale 1996; Parker 1996); and geographical perspectives on return and reconstruction (Simon and Preston 1992; Koser 1993). Focused on the experience of particular social groups, there are cross-disciplinary case studies of the experience of women (Dupree 1989; Thorn 1992; Watson 1996), children (Comisión Nacional de Derechos Humanos 1993; O'Donnell 1994), the disabled (Mollica 1992; Zinkin 1993) former prisoners (Brown and Dix 1993) and fighters (Mills 1992; Kingma 1995; Preston 1997).

Normally a plethora of documentation becomes available within a relatively short period after a major repatriation, which taken together, reflects on the whole experience and its aftermath from multiple points of view. Although each is generally locally specific, such studies are often used by funding and implementing organisations, as well as by other researchers, to infer implications for practice and experience elsewhere, when similar research is not available.[2] If in the first instance this material is disparate, produced to meet very specific organisational needs, it gradually becomes synthesised, from pieces of grey literature into more generalised studies, and acquires more durable form. The task for later researchers becomes one of finding and reviewing the collection, before gathering yet more information on the same or related topics. The Namibian study described below attempted to do this systematically through a comparative study of the Zimbabwean experience ten years earlier (Makanya 1993b), accounts of the role of international organisations in the transition to peace in postconflict reconstruction (Brown 1993) and the reanalysis of data bases (LeBeau and Pemberton 1993).

Taking a more panoramic view, in their introduction to *When Refugees Go Home*, a collection of case studies in east and southern Africa, Allen and Morsink (1994a: 2) suggest that the initial focus of research on organised repatriation was on the legal and political parameters of return,[3] as well as on the operational aspects of specific moves. They claim that analyses of the politics of different moves have served largely to promote the cause of particular interested parties. They draw attention to cross-national comparative studies on repatriation. These include Coles's (1985) accounts of voluntary repatriations, from 1918 to 1985, which serve as an inventory of experience decade by decade. In a work written for UNHCR and the Institute of Humanitarian Law, San Remo, Coles draws upon secondary sources to describe, sometimes in detail, those aspects of the process of voluntary return for which documentation was available. From the report, it is possible to trace changing trends in the legal and political principles guiding repatriation in different parts of the world. At a general level, the study allows a clear understanding of the history of different exile experiences and the way these affect repatriation. However, it does not include enough information to comment at a micro level on individuals and their preparation for return, the move itself or what happened to them on arrival.

Whilst Coles's study provides the most comprehensive, long-term assessment of the legal implications of voluntary repatriation in the twentieth century, an unpublished thesis by Reid (1992) provides a substantial political analysis of selected moves. Based on six case studies constructed from secondary data, Reid sets out to explain the repatriation process in terms of change in the wider political environment, and the extent to which the local political climate at the

---

2. An example of this would be the ways in which the World Bank is reacting to Paul Collier's peace dividend study of the social costs and benefits of the disarmament and demobilisation of fighters in Uganda (Collier, 1994).
3. Some would argue that the crux of research in refugee law lies in the conditions under which people in refugee-like situations might return to their country of origin.

moment of return was conducive to a more or less hospitable reception. Like Coles, Reid is unable to comment on the individual experiences of return or on individual integration after arrival at destination.

This does not mean that such work was not being done. By the late 1980s, the United Nations Research Institute for Social Development (UNRISD) was sponsoring studies on mass involuntary return in Zimbabwe, Uganda and Chad and in 1991 and 1992 commissioned papers on the experiences of different returnee groups and the roles of government and NGOs elsewhere in Africa. These were presented at international conferences in Harare, N'Djamena and Addis Ababa attended by members of the research community, policy makers and staff of the national and international agencies concerned with refugee and repatriation affairs. As well as a report (Turton and Ghai 1993), two collections of papers presented to these conferences have now been published (Allen and Morsink 1994a; Allen 1996), making a valuable contribution to the social and anthropological studies of repatriation in Africa. They include analyses of the influences of policy and project environments within which organised repatriations occur (Stein 1994; Wilson and Nunes 1994) and analyses of the social and community dynamics of integration in more or less favourable contexts (Kabera and Muyanja 1994; Tapscott 1994). Meanwhile, micro- and meso-level studies conducted in 1992-93 of postwar integration in a single country, Namibia, (Preston 1993b), were developed within an overarching conceptual framework from the literature on integration following return from labour-related migration. This was supplemented by literature on coercive war-related moves, where models have recently been developed to facilitate the study of integration in countries of asylum. The latter were themselves constructed from psychological, economic and social frameworks of analysis applicable to migrant labour. By 1994-95, in a study of the social implications of possible proposals for the reformulation of refugee law (Quick et al. 1995), reference was made to seventeen of what were a significantly greater number of largely unpublished case studies, from all parts of the world, and relevant to the analysis of return in safety and dignity. These provide insights into both individual and group experiences of voluntary and involuntary return (Chingono 1995; McDowell 1995; Quick 1995a; 1995b). By 1993 there was more or less coordinated research into repatriation and reconstruction at universities in Europe, North America and Africa. A group at the Centre for Refugee Studies at York University (Ontario) was working on different aspects of postreturn integration (CRS 1993), while at the Refugee Studies Programme (Oxford), staff and fellows were completing significant primary research (Wilson 1994) and unpublished overviews based on some of the growing literature available (Frechette 1994; Schaffer 1995).

Along with all this has come an increased problematisation of concepts relating to repatriation, integration and reconstruction. Stein and Cuny (1990) were instrumental in drawing attention to the distinction between people who return as part of an organised move arranged through tripartite agreements and those who, in greater number, return independently of such initiatives. They emphasised, also through cross-national and cross-regional comparison, the incidence of relative peace and conflict at destination after return and the ways in which this variously influences the quality of life that can be sustained (Larkin et al. 1992). In like manner, but closer to Reid in that they develop a more sophisticated model of the post-conflict state, Colletta and colleagues (World Bank 1993) seek to explain the development and effectiveness of fighter demobilisation and rehabilitation programmes in different countries. In time, studies such as these, which have created frameworks of analysis, will lend themselves to more general writing on the reconstruction process. In the case of Namibia, for example, there was considerable anticipatory research projecting the process of national reconstruction, based largely on institutional planning strategies oriented at modernisation (UNIN 1986), as well as studies of what has happened in the event (Cliffe et al. 1994; Leys and Saul 1995). In addition to their concern with post-conflict integration, these describe the reconstruction of instruments of state and other social institutions.

All of this and much more suggests that research into repatriation and its consequences is thriving. It may be that the lags between the completion of initial primary research and its publication and review have been significant in keeping out of sight what will in time prove to have been a considerable 1990s endeavour. Certainly, as well as the gradual appearance of published articles, there are now bibliographies (Crisp 1987; Fosseldorf and Medson 1994; Weiss Fagen 1995), edited volumes (Allen and Morsink 1994a; Allen 1996) and single author reports, theses and books (Coles 1985; Mollica 1992; Reid 1992; Watson 1996). This further confirms the growth of research interest in repatriation, integration and reconstruction, so that it is emerging as a comprehensive body of literature on return from involuntary conflict and war-related migration.

Definitions

Before moving any further, it is important to provide a working definition of some critical terms. According to Coles (1985), the term 'refugee' includes all persons who may be deemed to have been coerced for one reason or another to leave their country and/or stay in another country. Following Quick et al. (1995:2), and as is apparent from the foregoing paragraphs, this chapter takes the 'repatriation' of such refugees to refer to the preparation for return, the process of return, and the reception and arrangements for integration made immediately after arrival in the country of destination. Meanwhile, from the Namibian project, but building on several definitions, 'integration' refers to the ability of individuals and groups to interact cohesively, overcoming differences without a breakdown of social relationships and conflict (Preston 1993b).

This leaves the question of 'reconstruction'. While reconstruction might be assumed to be predicated on social cohesion resulting from integration, there are shifting views about how this end state might be described. For example, given the view in some quarters that the term 'development' is increasingly redundant, and that it needs to be replaced with concepts of 'economic stability' and 'social cohesion', there is a need to examine the political, economic and social conditions which make these different end states possible, without prioritising state economic growth as a prerequisite. In practice, goals of stability and cohesion under the present economic system would seem to legitimise increasing economic disparities between rich and poor states, and between rich and poor groups within them, to the point that marginal and excluded categories do not rebel. Further, they legitimise the development of social institutions within marginal and excluded categories which serve to foster their internal cohesion, at least to the point that their growing strength maintains them at the periphery and poses no threat to the mainstream. In the meantime, talk of reconstruction as opposed to integration, seems typically to refer to top-down development initiatives in postwar societies. In the context of the present chapter, questions arise in the first instance about how this works in the context of repatriation and postconflict integration. Secondly, there is the question of the role of research in the process.

Rather than attempt another panoramic overview, I refer now to three examples of research which provide some insight into some contemporary thinking among the research community into these processes. They have been chosen for several reasons. Among them is the fact that each includes a cluster of case studies to illustrate their theme, whilst each has achieved outcomes beyond those indicated in its publicised statement of purpose. They are presented in the order in which they would occur in chronologically staged repatriation, which is not the order in which they were undertaken.

Case Study 1: The social side of return 'in safety and dignity'

Over several years, the International Refugee Law Unit at York University (Ontario) has been working on proposals for the possible reformulation of refugee law (Hathaway 1995b). In March 1993, a seminar was held at which people with expertise in the field discussed the legal considerations that would have to be taken on board if this idea were to be pursued. During 1994, the 'International Refugee Law Project' (IRLP) commissioned papers from six teams of social scientists to propose ways in which different elements of these proposals might be planned and implemented, so as to optimise the effectiveness of their implementation, including their acceptability. The rationale for the proposals was the worldwide disregard of the principles of voluntary repatriation and non-*refoulement*, and so the inferred redundancy of current law. The crux of the IRLP proposals was for a system of guaranteed, preset, fixed-term 'temporary protection', to be administered through cross-national burden-sharing systems. On expiry, assuming conditions of safety and dignity prevail, those granted temporary protection will be required to exercise their right of return to their own country, under the auspices of an international supervisory authority.

One team of researchers worked on the study of repatriation in safety and dignity, and undertook four tasks as the terms of reference for their study which were found in the background materials provided (Quick et al. 1995). They were to:

- define what constitutes return in safety and dignity;
- appraise the feasibility of defining and applying criteria for terminating temporary protection;
- discuss the feasibility of creating a supra-national authority competent to apply criteria which will terminate temporary protection and ensure return in safety and dignity;
- assess the case for maintaining formal procedures which will oblige agencies to address the needs of individuals and sub-groups, in addition to the needs of the returning group as a whole.

This study referred to legal instruments and documents, accounts of the application of refugee and human rights law and to seventeen case studies, to which reference has already been made. They were chosen in part to represent the globality of contemporary practice and to include studies within richer and poorer countries in most of the world's regions. These included western and eastern Europe, North America, the Horn of Africa and southern African countries, Latin America and the South Pacific.

The researchers stressed that they were social and not legal scientists, before positioning themselves in terms of international refugee and human rights law and other instruments and related concepts, such as voluntariness and non-*refoulement*. Contextualising the proposals in terms of change in the global political economy, they went on to discuss the intention underlying and the outcomes of (a) the preference for repatriation to countries of long-term residential status; (b) the use of increasingly restrictive alternative forms of residential status in respect of people admitted to states in which they request asylum and (c) trends to prevent people either from leaving their country of origin or entering the country in which they would wish to request asylum.

It was argued that the intentions underlying (a), (b) and (c) could be such as to achieve a reduction in the number of refugees with entitlements specified by the Geneva Convention of 1951 and Protocol of 1967. At best, it was felt that the language of temporary residence might serve to equalise the treatment of all those applying for residence in states other than their own. In this way, entitlements would be granted according to the activity to be pursued during residence, not necessarily with reference to the reasons for leaving the territory of belonging. Such a procedure would not require the denaturalisation and depoliticisation that is a prerequisite of refugee status. At worst, in the present climate, temporary residential status would discriminate against would-be seekers of international asylum in favour of those admitted as students or for specified work. For increasingly brief periods, their permits may disallow employment, mobility or registration for any course of study. Prospects of renewal on expiry would be minimal. Residence after expiry or other infringements would be likely to lead to the ascription of the status of illegal immigrant, followed by deportation, regardless of events in the country of origin. In such contexts, it was concluded that while the IRLP desire to ensure at least minimal protection was in itself laudable, the setting of its operational parameters would be beset by difficulty.

This position hung on a challenge to what the IRLP claimed to be the neutrality of the term return with which it was proposed to replace the term repatriation. The researchers spent much time, in the library and with one or two lawyers, seeking to differentiate the commonly tied concepts, 'safety' and 'dignity'. Safety as the principle of asylum is familiar and used in all refugee contexts to refer to physical security and the entitlement to human rights, including protection from forced return (Quick et al. 1995: 25). The term 'dignity' does not appear in refugee terminology until the late 1980s (ibid.: 26). IRLP (Tab 7, 4: 12) suggested that dignity is to be measured in terms of the quality of life on return. With reference to Vincent (1986: 14, 17), Quick et al. (1995: 28) augmented this and took dignity to indicate the right of individuals to achieve human potential in ways that are determined by themselves and free from coercion. In practice, this would imply definitions of conditions of safety by any stakeholder with an interest in the repatriation of specific refugee groups. Assessment of whether the return could take place with dignity would need to be determined by the people themselves.

Quick and colleagues suggested a series of obstacles to the feasibility of identifying and applying criteria for return in safety and dignity. Among others, these included: the lack of mechanisms which would ensure the provision of reliable information about conditions in the country of return and at the proposed destination; and the impossibility, without coercion, of preventing the movement of individuals or groups or of bringing it about, against the will of those to whom it is proposed, regardless of the prevailing conditions in either place. On these grounds, attempts to preset fixed periods of temporary protection would prove irrelevant. Also, and in the light of decades of experience with analogous organisations, it was felt improbable that any international supervisory authority would have the capacity to guarantee the safety of a proposed return or of conditions after arrival. Supported by a specific argument in respect of major subgroups and individuals whose interests might warrant different treatment from those of their peers (women, children, the elderly, disabled, veterans, ex-prisoners, detainees and victims of torture), the suggestion that arrangements be made in respect of refugee groups as a whole was also found to be inappropriate. To conform to the fundamental principles of human rights, safety and dignity may only be applied on a group basis if: this does not violate the rights of individuals; if mechanisms are in place to actively protect those rights; and if the onus is on states and international organisations (including and especially the international supervisory authorities) to ensure that these mechanisms are used (Preston 1995: 8).

In conclusion, the study accepted the case for reviewing international refugee law, given the variance of practice from it, but was unable to propose mechanisms to ensure the effective implementation of the models of reform being proposed. It argued that the proposals seemed to be condoning trends in practice which increasingly reflects the nationalist tendencies of the contemporary recession. If implemented, at times of future affluence, having legitimated the coercive practices currently being used, worldwide, in respect of refuge-seeking groups, they would be difficult to redress.

Case Study 2: Postwar integration in Namibia

Using the model of integration described above, the second case study concerns the situation of war-affected people (WAP) two to three years after Namibia's independence from South Africa, and after a thirty-year war (Preston 1993a). In association with the National Planning Commission and the Ministry of Labour and Manpower Development, this study sought to suggest policy which would further integration and, through it, national reconciliation and reconstruction. Funding for the project came from the Commission of the European Communities. Additional funds were provided by the Overseas Development Administration (ODA), the Africa Educational Trust (AET) and the Swedish International Development Agency (SIDA) for supplementary reports on the labour market integration of former British and Swedish scholarship holders respectively.

The intention of the study was to analyse the situation of women and men seriously affected by the war of independence and the effectiveness of policy, and their own efforts, to facilitate their integration into the newly independent state. The thinking underlying this derived from the frequent indications of unrest among war-affected people in Namibia and complaints that little was being done to help them. These complaints tended to be from articulate groups, in particular former fighters and former teachers in exile schools. Overlooked was the situation of the many ordinary people who continued to suffer the effects of war long after its end. Evidence from other newly independent states in southern Africa suggested that long-term frustration on the part of people seriously affected by the war has been associated with subsequent destabilisation.

To undertake a holistic well-triangulated analysis, the study had many components. They included:

- a review of thinking, policy and action before and after independence concerning assistance to be provided to those still suffering the effects of war;
- a comparative study of postwar experience in Zimbabwe;
- a review of information gathered in Namibia since independence about the situation of people still seriously affected by the war;
- a reanalysis of recent surveys to make full use of information available relating to war-affected people;
- studies of the roles and capacities of international and nongovernment organisations; inclusion in contemporary surveys of questions relating to the labour market situation of returned exiles;
- cross-sectional community studies in rural, peri-urban and urban areas;
- appraisal of assistance directed at the disabled, ex-prisoners, and internally displaced;

- accounts of the demobilisation and rehabilitation of ex-combatants;
- an analysis of labour market integration, including a study of employer attitudes and a complex tracer study of returnee destinations.

A final report combined the different components of the project. It made practical recommendations for ways in which to assist Namibians in general and those in particular who were still suffering adverse effects of the liberation war.

After three years of peace, there were high levels of contentment among the majority black population at the liberation from colonial rule, and at the freedom to move and speak at will. However, the extent to which the constitutional principle of reconciliation masked civil unrest between rival groups in a context of mass unemployment was far from clear. The project found that in spite of efforts by government to remove the instruments of apartheid and create a democratic society, life for most Namibians had changed little. South Africa still dominated the economy and black leaders were often more concerned to emulate white middle class mores than to redress the social and economic injustices of the past. Further analysis was to suggest that those who achieved status on return had come from relatively advantaged social origins prior to departure and in exile (Preston 1994b). Economic hardship meant that the living conditions of ordinary people were worse than previously, with resentment that Namibians had nothing to show for the sacrifice of youth, health and life in the liberation movement. Overall, people with different experiences in the war were adapting well to life together. Those returned from exile with education were finding employment fairly easily, but the majority, exiles and stayers, were without paid work and there was a widespread fear that unemployed ex-combatants would create unrest.

Those encountering problems included ex-combatants of either side and women returned from exile. Most former political prisoners were in difficulty as were those disabled in the war and children returned after years in eastern Europe or Cuba. Schemes to assist the homeless and to train ex-fighters were having limited success in motivating people to become self-sufficient. Everywhere, there was an expressed interest in business schemes, but little knowledge of how to start. On the labour market, returned exiles were finding public sector work, but private employers were suspicious of their qualifications and disparaged their competency. The ratification of qualifications was incurring significant delay in public sector appointments.

Policy proposed related to employment and self-sufficiency, the work of government in the labour market, stress alleviation and a series of measures which targeted the needs of specific groups (women, children, veterans, etc.). Mechanisms were also discussed to improve the support infrastructure in particular through capacity building, in government and NGOs. A proposal was made for the radio network to broadcast a soap opera, to facilitate the shift of unrealistic expectations still held in many quarters, to those that were socially and economically more feasible. Mechanisms to disseminate the findings of the study were also proposed, to raise awareness about the war to peace transition in countries beginning to move towards it.

Case Study 3: Studies of 'Demobilisation and Rehabilitation Programmes'

While the WAP project was in progress, the Africa Technical Section of the World Bank commissioned a study (World Bank 1993) which was to compare 'Demobilisation and Rehabilitation Programmes' (DRPs) in seven countries. They were Angola (1992), Chad (1992), Mozambique (1992), Namibia (1989), Nicaragua (1990), Uganda (1992) and Zimbabwe (1980). The report of the study discusses the different objectives and outcomes of DRPs, in relation to their political and institutional contexts. The study did not claim to be the product of lengthy research and drew its information from policy documents, interviews with those concerned with policy and programme development, and available press reports. Nonetheless, it provides a framework for analysis which can be further developed and against which future studies can be measured.

The report confirmed the mixed record of success with DRPs, and explained this in part at least by the political and economic contexts of their implementation. These included whether there was established and stable peace; the existence of cross-factional power sharing in governments trying to manage the transition from war to peace (Angola, Nicaragua, Zimbabwe); and situations where disarmament and demobilisation had to be negotiated as prerequisites for the elections to take place to establish a democratic peacetime government (Namibia, Mozambique).

The DRPs described appeared to have four purposes – political, security, economic and fiscal – which were not always mutually exclusive. For example, peacetime security can be improved by employing demobilised fighters, but this may be opposed to fiscal objectives. In general, however, the report found that sustained commitment on the part of civilian and military leaders is critical to the reduction of military expenditure and sustained peace. Careful advanced planning of demobilisation and reintegration programmes, together with the participation of all those likely to have some role to play, also seems to be beneficial. Failure to plan reintegration at the same time as demobilisation seems to invite difficulties, as does the frequent failure to include donor and implementing agency representatives in discussions alongside civilian and military leaders. With adequate resources and broad powers, the presence of outside monitors of demobilisation was also found to be beneficial to disarmament, arms controls, demobilisation, legal and electoral reform.

In the case of reintegration programmes, the greatest risks come from institutional weaknesses. These can include weak government, a lack of financial strength, as well as human resources and infrastructural problems. Uncertain stability and lack of information about the kind of assistance wanted inhibit donors. The relative advantage of different types of support is poorly understood, with payments in cash or kind and training or employment schemes being the usual options. Similarly, there is uncertainty about the most appropriate targeting strategy: at the ex-combatants themselves; at their families; at disadvantaged groups which would include ex-combatants and their families.

There is now received wisdom that fighters who come to feel that there is no purpose for their existence in peacetime will be among the first to trigger unrest and renewed hostilities on whatever pretext to give new justification to their lives. Precedents in Angola, Mozambique and Zimbabwe in the immediate neighbourhood of Namibia should discourage any doubts about the seriousness of this. It is important therefore that the process of demilitarisation in Namibia was documented and understood, both for internal planning and so that lessons learned from the experience could be applied elsewhere.

In a follow-up study, a more detailed analysis was undertaken in three countries, Namibia, Ethiopia and Uganda (Colletta et al. 1996b), aiming to identify 'best practice' in war to peace situations concerning the demobilisation and rehabilitation of fighters. Three technical phases in the process were suggested: demobilisation, including disarmament and discharge; reinsertion including resettlement; and reintegration. A fourth phase, reconciliation, was also thought to be critical. In this context, the study addressed institutional and management issues and social dimensions, by undertaking an analysis of the economic impact of the schemes.

The implications of the case studies of repatriation for reconstruction

One of the assumptions underlying each of the three case studies outlined above was that the conditions under which repatriation occurs have implications for the quality of life thereafter. In the case of the proposals to reformulate refugee law, the purpose of the study was to feed into contemporary debate on international refugee legislation and policy. Those who contributed were committed to the belief that the principle of voluntariness of retuin, however vulnerable its contemporary application, should not be forfeited. However, if 'dignity' refers to the availability of the means by which people are to achieve their human potential on return to their country of origin, having freely made the choice to do this, return that is not 'dignified' will incur problems of integration for those returning and for those with whom they associate. This will inhibit the process of both integration and reconstruction, no matter how much programme or project assistance is provided. If implementation were to go ahead, there is a risk that proposed legislation would serve only the interests of asylum states, concerned about high levels of unemployment, and consequent 'threats' to stability and cohesion.

The WAP project assumed that by identifying weaknesses in organic integration processes, it would be able to identify mechanisms for assistance to overcome them and further stabilisation, reconciliation and reconstruction. Based on primary case studies into different aspects of postreturn integration and reconstruction within a single country, the study could itself be seen to be oriented at fostering adaptation and acceptance of the limited scope for this in a context of recession-based reconstruction in a liberalising market. As people talked through their experiences, they reflected on the strengths and weaknesses of their present situation (in terms of family, housing, skills, employment and income, stress, physical and mental health). Often they would provide their own explanations in terms of the availability of work, access to training, national economy and global trends. Sometimes, phrases such as *I've never thought of this way before* would indicate a modification of thinking about their place and capacity in the newly forming state.

The World Bank DRP studies assumed the critical importance of preventing ex-combatant frustration and banditry and ensuing disintegration. They were essentially strategic. Through effectively managed intervention (through DRPs), the researchers argued that states will minimise this risk in ways that can be economically advantageous. Subsumed within the rhetoric of linking relief and development is the assumption that successful fighter integration to civil society will facilitate wider social cohesion. For there to be a peace dividend requires that this will be done cost-effectively in ways which minimise disruptive behaviour.

Outcomes

Despite the assumptions and intentions outlined above, the outcomes of the three case studies were each at some variance with those which might have been expected either in the eyes of the contractor, the researchers and researched, or the public at large. In the study of the social applications of refugee law as they relate to the study of repatriation in safety and dignity, the researchers had found that they were unable to discuss implementation strategy because of what they felt to be non-viable assumptions in the overall policy proposal. As such, because the report did not meet all of its terms of reference, it was not found relevant to the purpose of an international conference at which strategies for implementation of the proposals were to be addressed. This was in spite of the fact that the report contained innovative material and that repatriation in safety and dignity was to have been a pivotal theme at the meeting. Dissemination has occurred through alternative presentations and in writing such as this. Although the investment in the individual case studies on the application of the proposed changes to international refugee law was modest, the political purpose of the overall project was considerable, if it were to be implemented. Overall, it is questionable as to whether it was appropriate for the researchers to have undertaken the work, given their reservations at the outset about its political acceptability.

Both the funding and policy environment of the study of postwar integration in Namibia go some way to explain the limited commitment to post-project implementation of the project proposals that were made. Generous funding for the study came from the European Parliament *Fund for the victims of apartheid.* Its allocation, pre-dating the Namibia government accession to the Lomé Convention, was from short-term discretionary funds available to the initial EU representative for work contributing to postindependence reconstruction. As such, it was not bound by bilateral regulations, which were not yet in place. Although EU staff at the Windhoek delegation and in Brussels gave considerable support to the execution of the work, they were primarily concerned with bi-lateral projects being implemented under the terms of the Lomé agreement. In spite of consistent support from the National Planning Commission and from the Ministry of Labour and Human Resource Development, there was not scope under the agreement for action to be derived from strategy recommended by the report, although efforts were made to frame policy options so that this might occur. Nevertheless, the project gave regular employment and career development to several Namibian researchers and at its peak provided skilled casual work and training (interviewing, data-processing) for up to one hundred others. The enthusiasm for the work demonstrated by the large numbers of people who became involved as informants, advisors, staff or participants at seminars and debriefing meetings, raised new awareness within Namibia about the process of the war-to-peace transition as it was occurring. The distribution of the report in as many places as possible inside and outside the country means that it has been available to those concerned with postwar administration and planning in places which in Africa include Mozambique, South Africa, Sudan, Eritrea, Ethiopia, Somalia and Somaliland. Simultaneously, placed in relevant university libraries of several countries, references to the process of the work and to the implications of its findings for other research are appearing in academic and policy-oriented writing on related issues. If the grant had not been made, the money may well have been retrenched, given that at the time, there were more resources being offered by the international community than there were viable reconstruction schemes in which to invest them.

The impact of the DRP studies to date is of a different order. At the beginning, the motive for the hitherto unexpressed interest of the World Bank in repatriation was questioned inside the Bank, and by those organisations active in DRP development. Also questioned was the strategy for disseminating the reports, through seminars in Paris and Washington drawing international audiences, including representatives of governments, international organisations, NGOs and academic research institutions. However, since then, interest has mushroomed among the members of this constituency so that DRPs are now a major item on the transition-to-peace funding agendas of these organisations (Preston 1997). At the same time, the Bank itself was, by early 1996, already piloting its good practice model in Bosnia and Liberia (although neither was a member of the Bank at the time) and intended institutionalising its involvement.[4] The overarching reasons for this are less obvious, but it seems likely that the modestly initiated DRP research is enabling the Bank to change its strategy for intervention in the economic and social development of postconflict states. Hitherto this was after the establishment of peace and stable democratic government. Now, through the provision of advisory services[5] throughout the war-to-peace transition, in particular through the DRP process, the Bank will ensure practice which it feels will optimally facilitate the process of integration and so of reconstruction. Within this, it is hoped that later, Bank-supported interventions, will be more effectively administered. Given the increasing hegemony of the international financial institutions

4. Interview with Nicholas Gorjestani, 20 March 1996, World Bank, Washington DC.
5. Capital investment will come from bilateral and other funding sources.

in the process of economic stabilisation and adjustment, what is illustrated here may come to be seen as another strand in this process.

Implications

This chapter has argued that, in the twentieth century, voluntary repatriations throughout the world *have* generated policy-oriented, operational and basic studies on repatriation and reconstruction. If originally disparate, the point is now being reached that a comprehensive body of literature is emerging into this final stage of the exile experience. The (until recently) limited visibility of research on repatriation and reconstruction was hypothetically associated with the history of durable solutions, the chronology of war-related migration, the narrowness of the research perspectives being adopted and the lag between writing, publication and other forms of dissemination. Now, this is changed. Research is being commissioned and undertaken by organisations concerned with the implications of repatriation for the reproduction and exacerbation of inequality and instability during the integration process after return. However, as illustrated in the case studies, the extent to which the structures within which the research is embedded allow the direct or indirect transfer of knowledge and resources which is necessary to alleviate disadvantage is likely to be limited. On the contrary, even if research does have an impact, the outcomes may be too disparate for the link to be traced. More likely, whatever its publicised intention, the research process comes to serve other interests, which may further subordinate the subjects of the research endeavour to what are, for them, remote political, economic and cultural institutions. This makes it expedient for researchers and those associated with their work to understand these unavoidable political and institutional purposes, particularly if they believe that they are acting primarily for humanitarian purposes. Only then may they choose how to position themselves as contributors to the normalisation of the discourses within which their work is located. In the case of voluntary repatriation, integration and reconstruction, this means accepting that research serves what are increasingly institutionalised processes in the war-to-peace transition. Future studies of involuntary return will achieve the same ends.

Acknowledgements

This paper was first presented to the 5th IRAP conference, Moi University, Eldoret, Kenya, 9-12 April 1996. It has been slightly modified to include reference to more recent publications.

PART TWO
MASS REPATRIATION OF REFUGEES

3

Revisiting a 'Repatriation Success': The Case of Cambodia

Marita Eastmond and *Joakim Öjendal*

Introduction

Following drawn-out negotiations on the Cambodia Conflict, in October 1991 the Security Council of the United Nations adopted Resolution 718. It was then clear that a massive repatriation operation was about to take place within eighteen months. The peace agreement stated that all 'refugees and displaced persons' were to be repatriated in a 'peaceful and orderly manner' before the national elections which were to be held in May 1993. UNHCR was to assume the operational responsibility for repatriating some 360,000 refugees, most of them from Thai border camps. The operation was clearly a challenging task. Refugees had lived for up to seventeen years in the camps. Cambodia was still in a state of low-intensity civil war and the country was very poor. Many villages from which refugees had fled, no longer existed, neither in many cases were their relatives any longer alive. Moreover, the refugees had already been used as pawns in a political game (cf. Reynell 1989), and their relation to the upcoming elections once again placed them under the imperative of politics.

In this context the repatriation operation has been referred to by UNHCR as one of the largest and most complex operations ever undertaken. The effectiveness of the repatriation operation has been widely recognised and it has been hailed as a model of its kind. The programme certainly was highly successful in moving 362,000 refugees on schedule, in time for the elections, and without any major mishaps.

This chapter takes a closer look at the repatriation of the Cambodian refugees, in the context of the Cambodian peace process and the UN undertakings. An account of conditions in the Battambang province (see Figure 3.1), where the majority of refugees returned, provides a more in-depth view, which will include the experience and perspectives of the returnees themselves on the settlement process. The Cambodian case can at the same time shed light on some of the key issues in repatriation more generally, regarding for example the role of international assistance; long- and short-term perspectives of relief and development, and concerns about repatriation into situations of continuing conflicts.

The research on which this chapter is based took place during an evaluation of Swedish emergency support about two years after the return of the refugees (Bernander et al. 1995). The research investigated how the returnees had fared and identified what factors had promoted or constrained their integration, focusing on the perspectives of the social actors involved. The research included twelve villages in three districts and settlement areas where interviews were conducted with returnees and locals, village leaders and development committees, monks and relevant counterparts and agency staff with experience of the area. To date, there is still very little other empirical data on the reinsertion of returnees in Cambodia, with the notable exceptions of Robinson (1994a; 1994b); Davenport et al. (1995) and a few partly relevant NGO surveys.

The political context of the Cambodian refugee crisis

From its outset, the Cambodian refugee crisis was deeply entrenched in 'high politics'. In the late 1970s, the refugees became a tool in the Cold War; by the early 1990s they were at the centre of the most comprehensive UN operation ever. The refugee crisis as well as its solution was in many ways created and defined by a political context (Chanda 1986; Mysliwiec 1988).

Cambodia's decolonisation was peaceful compared to most other such processes, and throughout the 1950s the country was an oasis compared to, for instance, neighbouring Vietnam. Tensions started to build in the 1960s, however, for both domestic reasons and because of the expanding war in Vietnam. Since 1970, when Sihanouk was overthrown by the right-wing Lon Nol and his supporters, the country has been in a state of civil war, suffering U.S. bombings, Khmer Rouge atrocities, Vietnamese occupation and civil strife.

In 1975, the Khmer Rouge took power and led a radical social experiment that was violent and ultra-nationalistic. Although an estimated 35,000 Cambodians had already managed to flee to Thailand by 1979, the tight control exercised by the Khmer Rouge made any mass exodus impossible.[1] However, by 1979 new political circumstances drastically changed the situation. The Khmer Rouge collapsed in the face of a large-scale Vietnamese invasion. A new regime was installed, dominated by the CPP (Cambodian People's Party).[2] In spite of the fact that Vietnam freed Cambodia from one of this century's most brutal regimes, the invasion was largely interpreted in the 'Western camp', in a typical Cold War analysis, as essentially a communist expansion on behalf of the Soviet Union, and was thus roundly condemned. A resistance movement was supported by the USA, but also by China and Thailand, and resulted in the creation of the Coalition Government of Democratic Kampuchea (CGDK) in 1981.[3] The civil war thus continued in Cambodia and refugees began to flee on a larger scale.

A number of additional factors coincided with the Khmer Rouge atrocities and the Vietnamese invasion to create a refugee exodus from Cambodia. The harvest of 1979-80, coinciding with the occupation, was severely depleted, fuelling fears of an impending famine. A second incentive to move for many was that they had been relocated within Cambodia by the Khmer Rouge. In their search for a place to settle, many eventually arrived at the Thai border. Between 1979 and 1980 over 150,000 Cambodians fled to the Thai border camps. In a second wave between 1984 and 1985, which coincided with an unusually violent dry-season offensive, more than 250,000 additional refugees entered the Thai camps (Banister and Johnson 1993).

The refugee crisis was used throughout the 1980s for a variety of political agendas. It served to legitimise the creation of the CGDK coalition, even though in reality the majority of the refugees were simply peasants looking for a way of surviving, not a politically

1. This chapter deals primarily with international refugees. However it is important to realise that internal displacement has been endemic in Cambodia since the 1960s.
2. CPP is now the Cambodian People's Party. It used to be the People's Revolutionary Party of Kampuchea (PRPK).
3. CGDK consisted of the Khmer Rouge, the Khmer People's National Liberation Front (KPNLF) and the Sihanoukists (FUNCINPEC).

conscious collective (Vickery 1990). The refugee camps were run by resistance factions, and refugees became a source for recruiting guerrilla soldiers, as well as proving to be a considerable magnet for food and medical supplies from the international community. It has been claimed the support from the refugee camps was at one stage crucial in the reconstruction of the Khmer Rouge (Reynell 1989). It has also been suggested that the refugee crisis was created (or reinforced) in order to undermine the Phnom Penh regime, politically and economically, and that the refugees were led to believe that they had good chances of being resettled in a third country (Vickery 1990).

With the Paris agreement in 1991, the repatriation of the refugees (now numbering some 360,000) became a high priority in the 'comprehensive resolution of the Cambodia Conflict' and within the United Nations Transitional Authority in Cambodia (UNTAC).[4] Humanitarian concerns were not, however, of primary importance in determining the agenda and the time schedule for repatriation. The conflict was to be settled through national elections. It was considered important that the refugees were returned and given a chance to vote, both for general democratic reasons and in particular to ensure representation. The refugees were assumed to be politically biased and thus of special importance to certain parties. In addition, repatriation was a central plank in the overall UN operation, being one of its major undertakings and most visible elements. The majority of the refugees were therefore returned during the five months prior to the elections. By May 1993, the repatriation was concluded and widely considered a success. A question that remained was whether reintegration would be equally successful.

The repatriation operation and its immediate aftermath

The three dimensions of the repatriation operation – logistics, direct assistance on arrival and help with reintegration – were planned and implemented as separate elements in the process, but were all conditioned by the principle that repatriation should be voluntary, conducted in safety and dignity and should be to final destinations of the refugees' own choice. The aim determined for UNHCR in the Paris agreements to ensure the 'harmonious reintegration' of the refugees, was intimately linked with a UNDP programme initiative,

4. UNTAC was the UN body administrating the transition process between 1991 and 1993.

CARERE (Cambodian Resettlement and Reintegration), which was to give a development dimension to reintegration, targeting not only refugees but also the many internally displaced, and local communities.

Preparations had already begun in 1989, with a survey of the populations in the border camps and an assessment of the absorptive capacity in Cambodia. Information campaigns were conducted in the camps concerning the situation in Cambodia; all returnees were registered, and their choice of destination recorded. Surveys were also carried out to determine the number of 'extremely vulnerable individuals' (EVIs), whose physical, mental or social condition required special support on arrival. The logistics of repatriation received the strongest emphasis, both in terms of organisation and financing. Services and facilities exceptional for UNHCR, were provided. Large numbers of staff and amounts of relief items were deployed; six reception centres were constructed (Figure 3.1), and repair work was carried out on roads and railways. Direct assistance to the returnees on arrival was also more comprehensive than for similar operations elsewhere, providing food rations not only for the period spent in reception centres but in addition for four hundred days after arrival at the final destination.

Reintegration, despite being the most challenging task, attracted comparatively less attention and resources. Quick Impact Projects (QIPs), planned and implemented very late in the process, were aimed at increasing the capacity of receiving communities to accommodate returnees. Designed to produce rapid, visible and sustainable results, they focused on restoring the infrastructure and basic services within communities, and to a lesser extent on land clearing and agricultural inputs. QIPs also assisted some 10,000 vulnerable families. As sustainable interventions aiming at development, however, they suffered from weak coordination with Cambodian institutions and were not always followed up by more long-term development efforts. Generally reintegration activities were not well synchronised with the repatriation effort. There was clearly a structural impediment in terms of the availability of funding for the reintegration, but also in terms of the long-standing lack of a rational division of labour in part due to different perspectives. While UNHCR focused on the returnees, the CARERE programme wanted to cast its nets wider and tended to marginalise the returnees in the process.

The most important impediment to settling and becoming self-sufficient, and thus to long-term reintegration, was the land issue. UNHCR initially promised the refugees in the camps two hectares of land per family. This promise, however, was based on flawed assumptions about the availability of land for cultivation, made on the

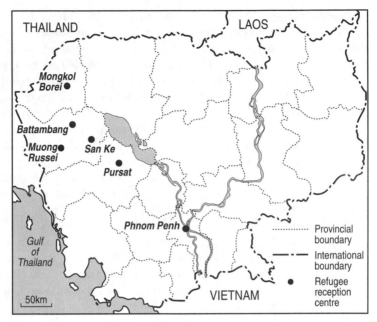

Figure 3.1 *Provincial map of Cambodia*

basis of aerial surveys which included areas affected by war and mines. By the time it became clear that safe and available land was in fact scarce, repatriation had already begun, and UNHCR rapidly changed course and introduced a range of other options instead of land, including cash, housing, employment and family reunion. The cash grant option, amounting to U.S.$50 per adult and U.S.$25 per child, was chosen by the majority of returnees (87 percent). Only three percent of all returnees chose the land option, as this entailed waiting in the camps until land had been identified and many feared they would be the last to leave and end up with the poorest land. The cash option actively encouraged people to return to their native villages, and so these new priorities considerably restricted the originally unqualified freedom of choice of final destination. The large majority of refugees, when initially given a free option of where to go in Cambodia, chose the Province of Battambang (see Figure 3.1).

Return and settlement in Battambang: a question of land

It was reported that in the camps Battambang was idealised by many refugees as 'the land of milk and honey', and many opted to go there when the first survey of destinations was made in the camps. It was believed to be easy to access land and employment in Battambang, and in addition many refugees had previous connections to the province. Its proximity to the Thai border also provided an escape route should the need arise. In fact it was precisely to Battambang that the war returned. Most returnees who went to other parts of the country have been spared the impact of new conflicts. In retrospect it appears that the returnees had inadequate or inaccurate information about Battambang. As early as June 1992 the Khmer Rouge was opting out of the peace process and targeting Western Cambodia for renewed civil war. Eventually, Battambang received 32 percent (117,000) of the returnees, and they amounted to 19 percent of the Province's population at that time.

UNHCR had relied heavily on the local authorities when promising land to the returnees. Recommendations were also sent from the Prime Minister Hun Sen in 1992, asking the local authorities to comply. However, there were never any binding promises for land, and the Vice-Governor of Battambang made clear in a letter to the camps in January 1992 that it would not be possible to supply the land needed (Robinson 1994a). Land scarcity was in fact more acute in Battambang than in the other provinces of the northwest. Although land in Battambang is fertile, the province was severely hit by the civil war and this remained a constraint in terms of settlement and land access. Large areas, in particular in the western part, remained subject to Khmer Rouge destabilisation activities and beyond government control. The threat of violence and displacement of the rural population remained a weapon in the continuing war, as evidenced by recurring peaks of internally displaced people in the period 1993-96. Access to fertile rice land in Battambang is also still sharply curtailed by the presence of mines, especially in certain areas close to the Tonle Sap Lake and towards Pailin and the border with Thailand. Many areas in Battambang province were labelled as no-go areas by UNHCR due to the prevailing insecurity. Returnees nevertheless still ventured to these areas, which were for many their places of origin. The Ratanak Mondul district in the south-western part of Battambang received a large number of returnees despite being one of the most heavily mined areas in the world (Robinson 1994).

Most importantly, the repatriation operation coincided with the process of privatisation of land and land titling. As a result there was and is an ongoing 'scramble for land' in an environment that lacks a proper legal infrastructure and a clear collective consensus on who the right to what land. The privatisation of land has made it a valuable commodity and it is not likely to be very willingly given away. The district, commune and/or village chiefs were often key people in this process, controlling what is labelled as state property. UNHCR and other organisations were involved in land titling for returnees with varying success. The QIPs to prepare local communities for a large influx of returnees were also intended as an incentive for communities to allocate land to the newcomers, but achieved only limited success in this respect. The returnees were asking for an increasingly valuable and limited commodity, the acquisition of which was to a large extent dependent upon bargaining. In this process the returnees were often at a disadvantage, unless they had influential and benevolent relatives in the village.

Preliminary survey data of the situation of returnees at the time the four hundred days of rice rations ended showed that many had not yet begun to farm, and were still waiting for land to be allocated. A survey by World Food Programme (WFP) at the end of 1993 found that 73 percent of returnees were still 'needy' or 'at risk'. In Robinson's survey of four districts in Battambang in 1994 between 30 and 35 percent of the returnees were found living hand-to-mouth (translated from Khmer as 'look one day, eat one day') whereas the figure for locals was 17 percent (Robinson 1994b). In the same year Davenport et al. (1995) described 40 percent of the returnees as 'not managing' to secure basic daily needs. Other surveys in 1994 also found that accessibility to rice land for returnees in Battambang was very low, although there were important geographical variations. In one survey of sampled villages, 15 percent of returnees had no access to rice land compared to 79 percent of the locals (Robinson 1994b). Of these local families, 98 percent owned the land in question, while only 48 percent of the returnees owned the land to which they had access. Davenport et al. (1995) in their study of Battambang found that 99 percent of returnees did not own any land. Although the proportion of landless locals is significantly lower, it is important also to realise that land scarcity is also a problem for many local families. One survival strategy for the landless was day labour. However, we found that the distribution of work was sometimes controlled by the village chief, and returnees were reported to suffer discrimination, receiving work less frequently than locals.

Three settlement contexts

One of the most important variables in the reintegration process identified during our study was the settlement context for returnees.

Important variables in the settlement context included the availability of land; the extent to which land was titled for returnees, and the presence or not of a supportive network of friends and relatives. As the case studies below demonstrate, the different configuration of such variables influenced the extent to which returnees could reintegrate and become self-sufficient, and the relations between the local population and returnees.

Chrouy Ampil is a small village in the Sang Ke district just east of Battambang. Of the 146 resident families, twenty-one are returnee families, all lacking any previous connection to the village. The villagers live essentially from rice growing, gardening and some livestock breeding. Most peasants in the village have less than two hectares of land. A substantial part of the land is 'state property', a dubious category after commercialisation of land in the last few years. After long negotiations with authorities and village monks, the village was selected as a resettlement village. To facilitate reintegration, UNHCR targeted this village with a package of benefits. Together with CARERE they built a school and a road, to serve the entire commune. UNICEF dug wells, and in the adjacent village CARERE built a clinic. The newcomers had chosen the land option when repatriating, and UNHCR actively promoted land preparation in the village, to benefit both returnees and the landless locals. The land was appropriated from unused tracts or from state property. Returnees were given a choice of one hectare close to the village, or two hectares further away. Most of them chose the smaller plot, often because of the security risk associated with the Khmer Rouge outside the village.

There was some resentment amongst the locals that the returnees' land had been titled more quickly than their own. Over time, the returnees were gradually excluded from the good land which they were originally allocated, and given poorer land in exchange. Similarly, those with land close to the village were in some cases forcibly shifted to more distant fields. The returnees had chosen not to complain too bitterly, and on the whole seemed to accept the situation. UNHCR was frustrated by these developments, and it was perceived that the village had violated the contract signed with UNHCR. As law enforcement is weak in Cambodia it has proved difficult for the returnees to retrieve their land.

Prek Prasap is a village some 35 km southeast of the town of Battambang. Of 260 families there, sixteen were returnees, most of them with relatives in the village. The supply of land around the village was restricted by the Khmer Rouge security threat. One girl from the village was said to have been abducted. For locals, the land was properly titled. In contrast the land given to returnees by the village chief was not titled, and furthermore it was remote and so returnees did not feel safe cultivating there. While most of the locals owned their house plots, most returnees did not, renting instead from neighbours or using relatives' land. The village chief talked about returnees as 'temporary' residents for whom the village did not have sufficient land. The village had been selected for a CARERE community development project.

The experiences of one returnee family illustrate some of the common problems encountered by returnees in the settlement context of Prek Prasap. The young couple had met and married in one of the border camps and had two small children. They had decided upon this village after they arrived in Cambodia and the wife had discovered that she had relatives here. The repatriation process itself had been trouble-free, and the four hundred days of food assistance had proved sufficient; however now the couple found it very difficult to survive independently. The couple had chosen the cash option and put some money into building a house and buying livestock. They rented a house plot from a villager and had been given half a hectare of untitled land by the village chief. Some of the cash was also used to bring the husband's mother, with whom they shared their house, and to bring a brother to stay with them. Relations with their family had grown tense as food rations had come to an end..

This household at first appeared to have the key resources of labour, relatives and land. However, their land was remote and had severe security problems due to Khmer Rouge incursions, so they were unable to plant in 1994. Day labour, the common alternative for those without land, had been reduced that year because of flooding. The family did fish and forage, but still had to buy most of their rice, using up the remainder of their savings from the camp. They pinned their hopes on their livestock. They were aware of the development projects in their village but could not make use of them, firstly because they had no rice with which to make the initial deposit required to participate in the rice bank and secondly because the fertiliser bank was of little use to them as they were not cultivating at the time.

Comparing their situation with that of other returnees, especially those with many children, without relatives in the village and with no savings from the camp, this family nevertheless considered themselves fortunate. Local families, at the same time, were consistently perceived as being the best off. As we inquired about whether they received assistance from their kin, the relatives themselves started protesting that they did not have enough even for themselves, let alone for the newcomers. On the whole it seemed that even returnees with kin in the villages to which they returned often relied on assistance from other, unrelated villagers.

In addition to these villages, we also visited two settlement sites dedicated to returnees. The first site visited was located adjacent to a village, and had the same name. Twenty-four returnees and one local family had all been provided with two hectares each of titled land through UNHCR. Everyone had also received seedlings and CARERE provided seeds for vegetable gardens. Nevertheless, the site was characterised by a low morale, and seemed to be on the point of disintegration. The first household visited had dismantled and sold the house provided by UNHCR and now lived in a small poorly-built, thatched hut. The children were ill: one infant had severe burns which had become infected. The family claimed not even to know where the nearest clinic was and said they would in any case have no way of travelling there. The vegetable seeds had not been planted, and seven families reported that they had not even received them. It was confirmed that by CARERE that seeds were in fact delivered to all the families, but it is possible that they were eaten. Four of the seven families interviewed were not growing rice this year, mainly because they did not have their own draught animals and had not been able borrow or pay for the use of oxen locally. The families interviewed seemed to have high expectations of outside assistance which had reduced personal initiative. The overall impression was that the families had no reason to stay, but had not yet found a better alternative. Perhaps the most important explanation was that the site was not a functional part of the adjacent village, nor did it represent an organised social unit in itself.

The second settlement site was remote from other villages in the area. In striking contrast to established villages, it was an open area without trees or bushes, and its 'artificial' character was obvious, manifested through the square house plots arranged in straight rows. At the time of the research the settlement did not have a clear position within the local administrative structure. Of the 130 families settled in this site, thirty were locals, but membership was not fixed, as families seemed to be moving in and out very frequently. Each family had received one hectare of titled rice land and a house plot. Another eighty-five hectares had been promised by the district leadership but was very remote from the site. Resistance by local authorities to allocating more land was strong and UNHCR was involved in a protracted bargaining process. Roads and wells had been provided by UNHCR/CARERE, but pumps installed by an NGO worked poorly. Most families had no relatives in adjacent villages and very few on the site. There was no school in the site and none of the children attended school in the next village, as it was too distant. As in the other settlement site visited, there was a sense that the returnees were becoming dependent on assistance, and that rather than becoming rooted, they were waiting to be offered an alternative 'home'.

The local dynamics of reintegration

The goal of reintegration from the perspective of the organisations working to promote it was the achievement by returnees of an economic status on a par with that of the local population. There were few criteria, however, with which to assess this process and define whether it had been successfully achieved. While this approach reflected a policy of community-focused rather than refugee-specific assistance, difficulties in its operationalisation reflected the complexity of local conditions and the process of insertion. Our case studies from Battambang give an idea of the complex set of factors that affect the local dynamic of reintegration and to which assistance programmes need to respond.

It is important to recognise that returnees do not form an homogeneous population: they represent a range of different social categories, experiences and skills. Economic activity depends in part on access to key resources such as land, labour, working capital and skills. However, the skills required for devising livelihood strategies are as much social as technical. Household economic viability amongst the returnees in Cambodia was also dependent on their position within the local community, including a personal reputation, for example, for reliability. In any rural community of farmers, livelihood strategies are shaped by authority structures, established roles and positions, culturally defined rights and obligations. Even in the context of Cambodian rural villages, where community solidarity has never been strong nor formally structured, there have always been informal patterns of exchange and assistance making up webs of interdependence between households. Such relations had suffered from the disruptions of the last decade so that in many cases returnees had few connections in their village and were immediately disadvantaged.

In our case studies, returnee families who were settled together in one site were rarely related by kinship or associated through ties from the camps. Having lived in the same camp did not seem to have created any special sense of belonging. As an essentially unstructured collection of households, organised from the 'top down' and well provided for, returnee sites resembled the camp situation. Most families interviewed appeared to expect assistance from aid organisations and seemed unmotivated or unable to create a functional interdependence. In the extremely hierarchical nature of Cambodian society, social and economic interaction requires the clear allocation and acceptance of positions of rank. For many returnees it was also unclear where they were located in the local political hierarchy of villages and resource allocation. Our impression was that the dedicated settlement sites were disintegrating. Settlement sites had little potential to become functional social communities on a sustainable basis. They were also extremely costly, both in terms of money and in human resources, although they may have been necessary as a temporary measure for families without other alternatives.

In contrast, in villages such as Chrouy Ampil village, a sense of community did exist, even though there were tensions between locals and returnees. There were a number of institutions with communal activities that promote a sense of belonging, including a wat with ceremonial activities and communal meals and a school with children from both categories. With time, and probably through intermarriage with locals, returnees stood a good chance of becoming accepted and functional members of the community. At the time of our interviews there were indications that relations were already evolving, for example through the exchange of services. Returnees were initially regarded by locals as being favoured by organisations (for example in the form of generous rice rations), and resentment was particularly bitter where there were conflicts over land. These perceptions have been changing (cf. Davenport et al. 1995), returnees are increasingly now perceived as disadvantaged, and sometimes pitied. Many returnees themselves felt that life in the camps had been easier, although nobody seemed to want to return to that life.

The rice rations provided important transitional support. An improvement might have been their delivery on a sliding scale over a longer period: when they ended, many returnees were still not farming, had no access to land and were reliant upon the support of others. For most of the newcomers social networks, with kin or sometimes other locals, proved to be vital support in establishing their new lives. Young returnees without much experience in farming, for example, benefited from local knowledge. However, even through social networks, support was mostly temporary (and sometimes even refused), and returnees had not managed to become self-sufficient. Indeed, they often had to move on in search of new economic opportunities. While relatives could provide connections with leaders who controlled the land, these leaders were at the same time subject to pressure from other locals for access to the scarce land. Land allocated to returnees could be reclaimed (sometimes by relatives) on the basis of it having been 'a temporary loan', or in the ambiguity surrounding land ownership an 'original owner' might sell the land to a third person. Many returnees had expected to suffer political discrimination upon return. Instead, the major obstacle to reconstituting viable lives proved to be the combination of land scarcity, general lawlessness and banditry and their own 'underdog' position.

Repatriation and reconstruction: concluding remarks

The Cambodian experience reflects some of the more general dilemmas arising in large-scale and complex repatriation and reconstruction experiences, including the contrasting priorities of the different involved actors, and the orientation of assistance between long- and short-term assistance and between targeting refugees and more general aims of development. More conceptual questions include the definition of dignified, peaceful and orderly return, and the meaning of terms such as 'reintegration' and 'home'.

In Cambodia the international community and UN were clearly working within the constraints of a political agenda. Political developments in Cambodia, combined with generous financial backing there, provided favourable conditions for return. The repatriation of the refugees was seen by the international community as an integral part of the peace process, and was motivated by the political imperative of having all the refugees back in place in time for the national elections. In this context questions have been raised concerning the voluntary nature of the Cambodian repatriation. Even if a majority of refugees wanted to return to Cambodia, doubts still surround the incentives used and the information provided about conditions in Cambodia. The promise of land was one such an incentive – which transpired to be misleading – that seemed to 'get people on the move'; and initiated a 'race' for the best land. While most returnees returned voluntarily in this modified sense, a limited number did not. In the Khao I Dang camp there were 3,300 'refuseniks' who were reluctant to leave (Robinson 1994a). In the end eight hundred of these refugees were forcibly repatriated by the Thai authorities and given UNHCR support in Cambodia. From their perspective, and perhaps also in retrospect for many of those persuaded to return, repatriation to Cambodia after a decade of waiting represented a defeat.

The Cambodian operation cannot be considered successful simply on the basis of the safe transportation of returnees to their destinations. It was an irony that most refugees were returned to Western Cambodia, a place with continued political unrest, one of the most heavily mined areas in the world and where the infrastructure is in very poor condition. Safety principles and careful planning are important to assist repatriations but do not always fit comfortably with a reality in which the necessary information may not be available and absolute security cannot be guaranteed. While the actual movement of Cambodian returnees may have been a model of management, the postreturn experience points up the difficulties in designing lasting repatriation plans.

The complexity of the Cambodian and most other contemporary return contexts makes the detailed design and implementation of return and reintegration on a large scale an impossible task. In addition, the reintegration process requires local knowledge which planners and organisations rarely have time to acquire. In view of such constraints forms of assistance should empower returnees as the main actors of repatriation, by promoting their own initiatives and ability to devise strategies that fit their specific history and set of current circumstances and that allow them to become participants in the development of economic and political life. Such assistance would also support and empower indigenous institutions and organisations as vital resources in the reconstruction process. Hundreds of thousands of displaced Cambodians repatriated 'spontaneously' from Thailand and Vietnam in the period 1979-84, and there was significant potential for 'spontaneous' return prior to the operation in 1992. Facilitating 'spontaneous' repatriation, rather than vigorously resisting it, and reinforcing self-support measures on arrival in Cambodia, would probably have been more beneficial to the returnees in the long run.

Integration after return is a multifaceted process, that must take into account the roles of actors on many levels, including the local, national and international. In particular local political and social structures in areas of return are a crucial but often neglected aspect in the planning and implementation of reintegration assistance. Our study demonstrates that the local actors in rural Cambodia, including both the resident families and the returnees, constitute a much more socially heterogeneous population than implied by generalised notions of 'refugees' or 'rice farmers' of rural Cambodia. The study also highlights the need to take account of village structures and the traditional independence of Cambodian rural households, where relations of social and economic interdependence between villagers are of an informal nature and evolve over time. Uncertainty and fear are dominant features in rural Cambodia. Strangers are potential threats and few are willing to risk assisting someone who is not well known as a neighbour, friend or relative. Thus, returnees cannot immediately claim a place in local communities, especially because many previous relations have been disrupted over the years of conflict and exile. In addition, the local economic and political structures in Cambodia are in the process of being transformed, creating considerable ambiguity between old and new patterns of ownership, authority and control.

While our data point to the value of food rations as transitional support, and kin as a temporary safety net during the first resettlement phase, they also underline the critical importance of land in terms of the long-term integration and self-sufficiency of households in rural areas. Poverty and vulnerability are pervasive in rural Cambodia, although there can be great local variations. Especially in the context of the weak economic and social structures of rural Cambodia, the 'economy of affection' should not be overemphasised, and kinship should not necessarily be expected to compensate for deficiencies in reintegration support. In this context assistance might better have been aimed at increasing returnees' independence and control in finding their own land or other economic niches, while simultaneously contributing to general development in the communities receiving returnees. Most of the development projects which did target areas of return excluded the landless poor, a category which now includes many returnees. In reaching the same conclusion, Davenport et al. (1995) call for a shift in focus of current development strategies to one based on food security for all: one that is village-specific and based on established trust.

At the same time, the structural constraints to developing self-reliance in the long term in rural Cambodia need to be recognised. Widespread rural poverty and limited access to land and water are major problems that need to be addressed at national and provincial levels. In addition, in Cambodia, as in many other countries to which refugees have returned, memories from the violent conflicts have resulted in a general distrust in villages and among villagers. There is little village solidarity and weak local political leadership, thus there are few welfare structures for returnees who fail to become self-sufficient. Religious institutions such as the sangha (the assembly of Buddhist monks which traditionally assumes the role of community builders in Buddhist societies) will be a vital resource in the consolidation of community in Cambodia, serving the interests of both local development and the reintegration of returnees.

The priority given to 'native village' or 'place of origin' in repatriation strategies reflects the assumptions that planners often make about 'home' and about a link between identity and place. The concept of 'home' is, however, both more complex and dynamic, especially considering the disruptions that countries such as Cambodia have suffered. Is 'home' where one was born, used to live, where one's relatives live (or lived), or anywhere one can make a decent living? While the meaning of 'home' is not culturally universal and not always tied to a single place, the disruptions of war may require new and more pragmatic considerations. For example, when given the choice, many refugees in the camps preferred to return to fertile areas rather than necessarily to their native village.

Terms such as 'reintegration' and 'reconstruction' are equally misleading in the Cambodian context, conveying as they do the impression of people returning to something they once left. In Cambodia, as elsewhere, major social and political transformations in the absence of refugees are vital factors to consider in resettling, securing new livelihoods and defining a new sense of belonging. Traditional conceptions of 'reintegration' may also mask the creative power of returnees to transform a (new) place into 'home' (see Hammond, in this volume). Our case studies in Battambang provide ample evidence of imagination and innovation in the survival strategies of returnees (see also Davenport et al. 1995). Greater attention needs to be paid to 'emplacement' and not only to displacement (Malkki 1995a), that is the social and cultural processes through which a place is invested with particular significance. The settlement sites in our study had little potential to become 'home' and to promote a sense of community and belonging. These sites had not adjusted over time to the local landscape of a place, they did not have a social history (as manifested by a wat), and therefore they did not have an imagined future.

Reintegration as an integral part of the reconstruction effort means tying short-term return assistance into more long-term development efforts that include the local population. In Cambodia, the CARERE project was mandated with responsibility for development, whereby returnees were assisted through a general rural development programme targeted on return areas. The concept was inspired by a similar process in Central America, described by Stein (1997) as a possible model for future operations. The Cambodian experience provides two insights. Firstly, our study reinforces observations about the difficulty of implementing the relief-development model. The poor organisational coordination between agencies with different mandates and styles of operation caused great friction. Partly as a result, QIPs proved not to be sustainable, implemented as they were with great haste. Secondly, our study suggests that development interventions that incorporate the local population tend often to exclude returnees and also the most vulnerable amongst the local population.

In spite of transitional problems, CARERE nevertheless seems to be finding ways of promoting rural development in Cambodia. As a decentralised development effort, it aims at community self-organisation and encourages local participation. It seems that the CARERE formula will be taken up by the Cambodian authorities who, at least at the provincial level, have displayed great enthusiasm for the project. Plans are eventually to duplicate it on a national level. As a participatory effort, CARERE has the potential for ensuring a local perspective and a more in-depth understanding of the complex local dynamics of reintegration and reconstruction. Thus, what began as a centralised repatriation operation is slowly transforming into a more promising and long-term reconstruction effort that integrates local resources and inventiveness.

4

Repatriation and Reconstruction: The Case of Afghanistan

Peter Marsden

Introduction

When Soviet troops invaded Afghanistan in December 1979, they set in motion a major exodus of refugees. By 1983, an estimated three million refugees had fled to Pakistan, increasing to some 3.27 million over the following seven years. A further 2.9 million had taken refuge in Iran by 1991. The refugees in Pakistan were accommodated in camps along the length of the border. They were provided with tents and some household equipment and had free access to food, health centres and schools in the camps. They were also permitted to seek employment within Pakistan, subject to certain restrictions. Most were engaged in daily labouring or pursued trading activities of various kinds. Most of the refugees in Iran, in contrast, were 'integrated' within Iranian society, and permitted to work in designated menial occupations. They were responsible for finding their own housing but had free access to health and education services and were also entitled to food and other subsidies on the same basis as Iranians. One element of the refugee population in Iran constructed their own mud villages close to the Afghan border. These so-called 'spontaneous' settlements were provided with health and education facilities by the Office of the United Nations High Commissioner for Refugees (UNHCR).

When Soviet troops pulled out of Afghanistan in February 1989, it was anticipated that the Soviet-backed government would fall immediately and that the refugees in Pakistan, at least, might return reasonably soon thereafter. The UN Office for the Coordination of Humanitarian and Economic Assistance Programmes Relating to Afghanistan (UNOCA), which was formed in September 1988, was consolidated in preparation for repatriation. Planning at that stage was based on the premise that refugees might travel back in very large numbers, and an additional UN agency, United Nations Logistical and Transport Operations (UNILOG) was formed to oversee the logistics of transporting food, tents and other supplies into Afghanistan. Simultaneously, UNHCR worked alongside NGOs to undertake programmes aimed at rehabilitating the areas from which most refugees originated. In 1990 other United Nations (UN) agencies joined in the reconstruction process and UNHCR reduced its own input. UNOCA continued to facilitate the response of the variety of involved UN agencies, although until only recently it was not mandated to decide on overall policy.

In reality, the Soviet-backed government did not fall until April 1992, and the refugees did not start to return in any substantial numbers until that year. By 1990 the UN had come to the conclusion that a relief approach was no longer appropriate and it opted instead for a policy of providing direct assistance to returnees while, at the same time, continuing to work on the reconstruction of the areas of origin. The breathing space between the commencement of reconstruction programmes and actual return meant that a significant amount of reconstruction had taken place in the areas of refugee origin.

By the end of July 1997, an estimated 2.61 million refugees had returned to Afghanistan from Pakistan and 1.33 million from Iran. This left 1.2 million in Pakistan and 1.4 million in Iran. This chapter provides a critical examination of the repatriation programme to Afghanistan and asks to what extent UN agencies and NGOs have been effective in facilitating reconstruction. It also raises questions about the level of support to residual refugee populations in the countries of asylum. The author is the Information Coordinator for the British Agencies Afghanistan Group, and his responsibilities include the assistance of operational NGOs and donors with their strategic planning in Afghanistan. As such this chapter reflects the collective views of British NGOs working in Afghanistan. It also draws upon individual studies conducted by the author in Afghanistan biannually. In contrast to most other chapters in this volume, the focus is therefore operational.

In the first two sections of the chapter, an operational overview is provided of the repatriation and reconstruction process in

Afghanistan, focusing particularly on protection issues and on the policies adopted for the provision of assistance. The next section provides a contrast to these policy overviews by focusing on the experience of refugees who have returned, drawing upon recent research reports by the author. The final part of the chapter focuses on a number of more systematic issues arising from Afghanistan repatriation, with a particular focus on the contributions by international agencies to strengthening civil society in Afghanistan.

The repatriation process

From the outset, UNHCR made the assessment that the military and political situation in Afghanistan was extremely fluid and that UN agencies and NGOs were not in a position to inform themselves adequately of the situation on the ground in all the areas to which refugees might be returning. UNHCR therefore took the view that returning refugees were themselves in the best position to assess risks, and that it was appropriate to provide limited assistance to those choosing to go back.

At the same time, the conditions in Afghanistan have at no stage been sufficiently stable for UNHCR to consider that repatriation should be encouraged. Rations for the Afghan refugees in Pakistan did end in September 1995, together with the provision of free education, health and water supply services, following a phased reduction over the previous two to three years. The decision to reduce and then withdraw services was not, however, related to the repatriation process. Rather, it resulted from a view taken by the World Food Programme (WFP) and UNHCR, on the basis of annual assessments and specific studies, that most refugees in Pakistan had sufficient access to income-earning opportunities, albeit at a basic level in most cases, to overcome dependence on rations. Indeed, UNHCR has stringently monitored the repatriation process to ensure its voluntary nature.

There have been some accusations of harassment by the authorities in Pakistan and Iran, but the voluntary character of the return has been largely maintained. There have also been instances of the refugees being manipulated to serve the war effort, either being sent into Afghanistan to strengthen particular forces or being forcibly held in the camps because their presence there lends power to the particular rebel groups who control the camps. Nevertheless, it is reported that: 'Despite the discouragement by some Afghan authorities of refugee participation in the repatriation project (and, in some cases, harassment of returnees), the repatriation process has been gradually gathering momentum' (UNOCA 1990).

The relatively slow rate of repatriation to Afghanistan meant that original plans for relief-oriented assistance were abandoned and largely reversed in favour of longer-term reconstruction-oriented assistance (UNOCA 1989). Three main premises to the provision of assistance to returnees evolved. Initially, assistance was targeted on refugees while still in the countries of asylum, in order to avoid an artificial 'pull factor' in Afghanistan. Assistance was then planned to follow the refugees as they returned, and to be distributed inside Afghanistan to also benefit displaced persons and other categories in need. Finally, the extent and level of assistance was to be based on direct assessment of needs area by area, so that it could be adapted to different geographical and social conditions (UNOCA 1988).

In July 1990 a voluntary repatriation pilot project was launched in Pakistan (UNOCA 1992), whereby individual refugee families were given U.S.$150 towards their transport costs and food assistance of 300 kg per family in return for the surrender of their ration passbooks from the camps. Plastic sheeting was later added to the assistance package. The refugees in Iran have used refugee identity documentation rather than ration passbooks to claim a similar repatriation allowance at the border. In determining the size of the assistance package, UNHCR was concerned that it should do no more than provide a temporary cushion while refugees reestablished themselves. There was also concern that returning refugees should not be too advantaged relative to those who had remained in Afghanistan during the period of Soviet occupation.

In addition to rations and basic survival assistance, UNHCR, in conjunction with the government of Afghanistan and other authorities has since 1990 given transport assistance to vulnerable groups of returnees, unregistered refugees and registered refugees whose travel costs have exceeded the travel allowance. Temporary accommodation has also been provided in transit centres in the main urban centres in Afghanistan. Much of this work has been contracted out to the International Organisation for Migration (IOM). IOM has also provided transport for refugees in Iran living in Tehran and other areas distant from the Afghan border to enable them to return to Afghanistan.

The reconstruction process

Most of the reconstruction programmes in Afghanistan have been geared to an improvement in agricultural production, and have included the repair of irrigation systems, flood protection structures, wells, rural roads, bridges and culverts and the provision of improved seeds, fertilisers and pesticides. In addition, health and veterinary care and education programmes have been organised. Of equal importance have been programmes to survey and clear the very large number of mines in Afghanistan and to increase awareness of the risks from mines among the returnees.

Assistance has been provided through UN agencies and NGOs, initially working cross-border from Pakistan and later from within Afghanistan. The decision not to work through the government of Afghanistan was unusual for the UN. The view was taken that during the Najibullah period the government did not have real authority in the rural areas from which most of the refugees originated, which were controlled by various rebel forces through which it was not felt appropriate to channel resources. Although the Mujahidin rebels took over the government in April 1992, the rule of those in power in Kabul was disputed and the government at no point had control of more than a small part of the country. Even when the Taleban took a growing proportion of the country from October 1995 onwards, they were not regarded as being in a position to provide adequately for the population under their control. The practice of humanitarian agencies taking the major responsibility for the survival of the population has, therefore, continued.

It has been easier for both the UN agencies and NGOs to base themselves in Afghanistan since the Mujahidin take-over, working in cooperation with whichever authorities have held power locally. As part of its policy of placing greater priority on the reconstruction process, the UN sought to strengthen indigenous capacity within Afghanistan. It took the view that existing international and Afghan NGOs did not have the capacity or the geographical spread to meet the rehabilitation needs envisaged, and encouraged the formation of a large number of additional Afghan NGOs, most of which worked under contract to the UN. To further facilitate the reconstruction process, UNHCR sought to obtain as much information as possible on the places where most refugees originated so as better to assess needs and target assistance. NGOs under contract to UN agencies were encouraged to work in areas to which it was hoped significant numbers would return, in the hope of facilitating resettlement. To the end of 1992, reconstruction programmes were organised primarily in the provinces of Afghanistan which adjoined the Pakistan border, because of the relative ease of access. UN agencies and NGOs were only able to operate on a reasonable scale in the west and north of the country from the beginning of 1993. UN reports indicate that there has been a clear correlation between assistance activities and refugee return.

A key issue in the provision of rehabilitation assistance is whether it is possible to operate effective programmes while a conflict is ongoing. It can reasonably be argued that, in spite of the enormous difficulties, the provision of carefully thought-out aid can make a significant contribution to the restoration of the economic and social base. However, it has to be recognised that humanitarian operations within conflict situations will normally be relatively expensive.

In seeking to work on reconstruction programmes in a conflict zone, UN agencies and NGOs were taking high risks. It was not always easy to know who held power in any given area. There was a possibility that agencies might be strengthening some leaders relative to others by virtue of the fact that they were delivering aid to the areas under their control. Access to target areas was also difficult at the best of times because of appalling road conditions arising from their deterioration during the war. At certain periods, aid vehicles were also at risk from armed groups and bandits along the road and, in many instances, had to provide assistance or make payments to these groups in order to secure safe passage. This difficulty of access complicated the process of supervising, monitoring and evaluating projects. Agencies have also had to deal with a partial breakdown of societal structures. They have therefore needed to find effective mechanisms for supporting grass-roots and administrative structures. However, in substituting for weakened or absent local authorities, UN agencies and NGOs have, to an extent, absolved the various leaders of their responsibilities towards the populations under their control, thus allowing them to allocate the bulk of their resources towards the military effort.

As they have addressed these constraints, agencies have learnt a number of lessons. Foremost among these has been the importance of establishing effective relationships with beneficiary communities so as to seek agreement on an appropriate way forward. Positive results have been achieved where beneficiaries have agreed to contribute some resources, normally labour, and have also taken responsibility for the shared planning and implementation of projects and for the maintenance of repaired infrastructure. For this approach to be effective, it has been found better to concentrate on a small area and remain there for a reasonable number of years. Agencies have at the same time recognised, through experience, that it is inadvisable to put resources into an area on too large a scale at any one time because of the very real risk that this will promote competition rather than cooperation within beneficiary communities. Generally, it is recognised that time is required, both to gain the necessary information and to establish trust. This approach also necessitates a significant injection of staff resources.

In order to implement a community-based approach, agencies need to acquire an in-depth knowledge of cultural patterns, religious and ideological beliefs, family and community relationships, power structures and relationships, economic survival mechanisms, the wider political and military situation and of the changing dynamic relating to all of these. In addition, agencies need to inform each other of their programmes both to avoid duplication and to ensure a reasonable spread of programmes across the country. Coordination and joint strategic planning are, therefore, vital even though not always easy to achieve.

The reintegration of returning refugees

A continuing difficulty in assessing the exact rate of repatriation has been that many refugee families have opted to return without claiming their repatriation entitlement. For some, this has been a strategy to keep open their options should they need to return in the short term to exile. Certain returnees have indeed resettled in Pakistan and Iran or have, at least, sent some family members back.

It should be emphasised that most of those refugees who repatriated during 1992 and 1993 did not base their decisions primarily on a prior assessment that they could survive financially upon return. The vast majority instead left their countries of exile for Afghanistan in response to the April 1992 fall of the Soviet-backed government. The main basis for the return was that the *jihad* which had led them into exile, necessitated by the presence of a secular force of occupation, had ended with the collapse of that government and the creation of an Islamic government. The pace of repatriation then slowed during 1993, as people realised that the new government was not able to ensure stability and security. Other factors then came into play which influenced the decisions of tribal or village groups or individual families whether or not to return. The fear that others might take their land was a major factor. There were also fears of insecurity, banditry and mines. Many took hard-headed decisions as to the relative benefits of staying in their countries of exile as opposed to embarking on the reconstruction process. Some 'hedged their bets' by retaining a presence at home and abroad, keeping some family members working in Pakistan while others started to rebuild homes and reinvest in the land in Afghanistan.

Some returning refugees kept their families in Pakistan, for example, because of the virtual absence of educational opportunities in Afghanistan, particularly for girls.

Whatever the reasons for the decision to start life again in Afghanistan, it appears from a number of studies and from anecdotal evidence that most refugees have faced a struggle upon their return (Marsden 1997). While some have achieved self-sufficiency, even these have been affected by spiralling inflation and periodic shortages of essential commodities. Many families continue to have some members living in Iran, Pakistan, the Gulf States, Saudi Arabia, Europe and the U.S.A., some of whom send back remittances. There is, therefore, what might be described as a strategy of dispersal. There also appears to be a high degree of mobility within the Afghan population in response to changing personal circumstances and also changing political and military conditions. In addition to the approximately one million who have been displaced within Afghanistan as a direct consequence of conflict, there are many who have moved from village to village, from village to town, or between Afghanistan and neighbouring states in the face of lesser forms of adversity. Within Afghanistan there has been a pronounced urbanisation trend, generated by difficult living conditions in the rural areas and by the return of refugees from an urban environment in Pakistan or Iran without the skills or inclination to reestablish themselves in the agriculture sector.

Discussion

The experiences of UNHCR and other agencies in responding to the Afghan repatriation raises a series of systematic policy issues which relate to repatriation more generally. These include: the balance between relief and reconstruction; defining the adequacy of provision, the challenges of coordination and joint strategic planning, and challenges and potentials of working in conflict areas.

As demonstrated in the preceding discussion, initial planning for the repatriation of Afghan refugees focused on a major relief operation, based on the assumption of a large-scale return in response to the immediate collapse of the Soviet-backed government. In the event both assumptions proved inaccurate. This example raises the very important question of how agencies should evaluate their operating assumptions, particularly those with potentially considerable cost implications. In the case of Afghanistan, the UN drew heavily on thinking in diplomatic circles that the Najibullah government would not survive the departure of Soviet troops and on a very reasonable view that the presence of the Soviet-backed government represented a major impediment to refugee return. It is not clear to what extent they gauged the views of refugees through sample surveys nor is it certain that such surveys would have given an accurate picture of refugee intent in relation to various possible scenarios.

It is also fair to say that it has proved extraordinarily difficult to predict events in Afghanistan. Even seasoned observers have often been taken by surprise. Having said that, it is worth reflecting on whether the UN, even given the scenario that the Najibullah Government would fall quickly, could have adopted a community-based reconstruction approach in support of the repatriation process rather than the very grandiose relief operation which it set in motion. A factor which was apparently not taken into account in the initial stages of the planning process was that Afghans who had remained in Afghanistan, often displaced from their villages, had returned in large numbers as soon as the Soviet troops left and had themselves started the reconstruction process. Neither did the planning process take sufficient account of the fact that refugees in Pakistan were inclined to leave their families behind while they returned to their villages in Afghanistan to rebuild their homes and start work on the land.

It could be argued in defence of the UN that it had to plan for a worst-case scenario, and the possibility of six million refugees returning suddenly to a country devastated by ten years of war did present such a scenario. In particular, the UN did not want to lay itself open to criticism after the event that it had been ill-prepared to avert a humanitarian disaster. It could equally be argued that the UN should have actively discouraged return, knowing that many parts of Afghanistan were mined, and first cleared mines, rather than organising a relief programme.

The UN provided an assistance package to refugees returning under the repatriation programme which was intended to do no more than contribute to transport costs and cover wheat requirements for a few months. It took the view that it was better to put the major part of the resources available into rehabilitation programmes so as to benefit both returnees and those who had stayed behind during the war, who had tended to be poorer than those who had fled. The UN also progressively reduced and eventually ended rations for refugees in the camps in Pakistan. This was based on the assumption that refugees were in a position to be self-sufficient, at least at the level pertaining amongst the poorest members of Pakistan society. The UN was, therefore, aware of and took account of the fact that many refugees were dependent on daily labour and that some were working in brick kilns, mines, prostitution or in bonded labour. At the same time, it introduced a number of safety net programmes aimed at ensuring that the most vulnerable members of the refugee population did not suffer undue hardship. These have proved to be of very limited effectiveness, both in terms of reaching the most disadvantaged families and in providing a significant cushion against destitution.

This raises the importance of ensuring that repatriating refugees or refugees in camps are not significantly better off than the poorest in the country of return or the country of asylum. In a country such as Pakistan where income is very polarised, the very poorest live on the margin of destitution. Similarly, there are many in Afghanistan whose livelihood is highly precarious, particularly in the urban areas and in the mountains of the Hindu Kush. It is questionable as to whether this unfortunate reality justifies refugees or returnees being kept at an equally marginal level of survival.

Another issue raised is whether one can determine a cut-off point in relation to a given repatriation programme, such that those who have not returned by a given date are deemed to have opted to stay and should therefore expect to be self-sufficient. In the case of Afghanistan, there have been a series of incidents inside the country since the repatriation programme began, which have provoked outflows of refugees to Pakistan. There have also been factors which have accentuated the difficulties people have faced in their efforts to survive in Afghanistan, in spite of the reconstruction work undertaken, and which have, therefore, deterred others from returning. The UN has recently had to consider, as a consequence, whether it should reverse the flow of resources from the refugee camps to the reconstruction programme and create new programmes in the camps.

It might be argued that the UN should have been more thorough in assessing livelihood strategies, both in the refugee camps and in the areas of return, than has apparently been the case. Too often, broad assumptions are made based on a handful of interviews with aid officials where interviews with refugees and returnees might produce a very different picture. This has certainly been the case with this author's own studies of coping strategies amongst refugees in Iran and Pakistan and returnees to southern Afghanistan. These have established that refugees are facing far greater difficulties surviving than had been assumed and have challenged the widely-quoted assumption that the extended family system is an important element in ensuring survival. The studies found that members of extended families were often too poor to help each other and that little money was being sent to relatives in Afghanistan from members of their extended families in Iran or Pakistan (Marsden 1996a; Marsden 1996b).

This reality suggests that some kind of safety net system is required which will ensure that vulnerable families do not go under. However, the safety net system established by the UN in the camps has been far from adequate and, in Afghanistan, it has been necessary for WFP and the International Committee for the Red Cross (ICRC) to establish major safety net programmes in both urban and rural areas in spite of the reconstruction programme. Inevitably, many people have slipped though the net and have depended on the charity of others, on the sale of possessions and on what they can borrow, for their survival.

At least to an extent some of the problems in the repatriation programme have been a result of insufficient coordination and joint planning. Action has been taken as a result to agree on standards and to minimise duplication. However, there has been a resistance to both coordination and joint planning arising from competition for funding and other factors. Among the more effective efforts at coordination have been those where donors have enforced coordination and joint planning as a condition of funding. However, proposals to establish self-regulatory mechanisms amongst agencies have not tended to go beyond the drawing board.

Where agencies have found less of a problem is in the sharing of information, both on their programmes and on the complexities of the situations in which they find themselves, although even this has proved difficult at times, particularly during the period of Soviet occupation when secrecy was an issue. There is, nonetheless, growing agreement that it is worth spending a significant amount of time researching the political, economic, social and cultural context of planned operations and engaging in discussions with other agencies to consider the implications of this context.

At a more general level the Afghan repatriation points up some of the particular problems associated with working in conflict areas. A key element in the involvement of agencies in conflict areas is the responsibility they carry to conform to certain reasonable standards in providing services and in relating to the structures which exist. This is particularly important in cases such as that of Afghanistan, where society has largely broken down and where the procedures which would normally apply in a governmental structure do not exist or are in abeyance. Agencies often have to draw up their own procedures which recognise the special challenges of working in conflict zones. Assistance can, for example, inadvertently fuel a conflict by providing resources to one group rather than another. Access is difficult, and information gathering, supervision, monitoring and evaluation are all more complex than they would be in a nonconflict situation.

There is, at the same time, the potential for agencies to contribute towards the management or even resolution of conflict. In Afghanistan this has arguably been achieved with a degree of success through the strengthening of civil society. During the early years in Afghanistan, agencies tended to work through local military commanders but, once the security situation eased, sought increasingly to engage in discussion with traditional structures at the village level as a basis for programming. This was seen to be beneficial not only as a means of achieving a more effective use of resources but also as a mechanism for strengthening what remained of civil society in order to cement the fabric that existed and create the conditions for people to come together to work on reconstruction as an alternative to fighting.

In the rural areas, this has led to clear progress in the process of restoring the agricultural base after years of neglect resulting from the period of population displacement. Returning refugees and displaced people have inevitably taken the major responsibility for reconstruction but there is clear evidence that NGO and UN programmes have strengthened the recovery process.

In the cities, progress has been less easy to define. Many of the UN and NGO programmes there have maintained a relief focus or have sought to secure minimum standards. To the extent that they have worked with neighbourhood structures to implement these programmes, it is true to say that the consequent strengthening of civil society constitutes progress. However, with a worsening economic situation in many of the cities, agencies are, at best, stemming the process of decline. Their efforts have, for example, been significantly undermined by the departure of professionals in the administration in response to the successive changes in authority.

The encouragement given by the UN to the creation of Afghan NGOs was aimed to establish further structures which could assist in the rebuilding of civil society. However, the UN found that it was not sufficiently resourced to support their development or adequately to monitor the programmes which they managed under contract to it. As a partial result of this, a majority of the NGOs have not yet moved beyond the stage of being, in effect, engineering or building contractors with minimal, if any, links with community-based structures.

Conclusions

Over the eight years of its involvement in Afghanistan the UN has moved from being involved mainly in a supply operation to a level of involvement which has increasingly sought to work with and strengthen indigenous structures and coping strategies. It has struggled with various options as to how best to support civil society in a situation where the governmental administration has effectively ceased to function. The process of exploring these options is still ongoing.

From the experience of UN agencies and NGOs working in Afghanistan, it can be argued that a policy of strengthening civil society within a situation of conflict is an effective mechanism for facilitating a repatriation and reconstruction process. However, agencies could substantially improve their effectiveness in implementing such a policy by giving even greater priority to the process of discussion with beneficiaries, to informing themselves on the context in which they are working and to coordination amongst the various agencies. This necessarily implies changes in both staffing and funding policies so that staff are engaged on reasonably long-term contracts and funds are provided to ensure that these staff can remain in post.

Whatever the success of the reconstruction process, the economy in Afghanistan has not yet grown to the point where it can provide for the remaining refugees in Pakistan and Iran, who are existing at a very marginal level and without any guarantees of continued hospitality on the part of the host countries. In supporting a repatriation and reconstruction process, it is therefore important that the international community continues to take responsibility for those left in exile until such time as they can be reabsorbed within their home economy, and that it provides such support at a level which ensures survival. Notions of comparability with the poorest in the host society and the society of origin should not be taken to an extreme where many face destitution.

Looking to the future, UN agencies and NGOs will continue to support the reconstruction process, with perhaps greater targeting in response to specific requests from refugee groups in Pakistan particularly. The objective in relation to the refugees still in Iran is to further strengthen the economy of the western provinces so that the mostly young people who have returned back to Iran since the repatriation in search of casual labouring work can be increasingly provided for within the rural economy. However, any further repatriation of families is subject to political constraints arising from the Taleban presence in western Afghanistan.

Acknowledgements

This paper was prepared with financial assistance from the Commission of the European Communities. The views expressed herein are those of the Information Officer at the British Refugee Council, and do not represent any official view of the Commission.

5

Contradictions and Control in Repatriation:
NEGOTIATIONS FOR THE RETURN OF 500,000 ERITREAN REFUGEES

Lucia Ann McSpadden

Introduction

During the longest standing armed conflict in Africa – the Eritrean struggle for liberation from Ethiopia – over one-quarter of Eritrea's population became refugees. The majority, as many as 500,000 people, sought asylum in Sudan, where some have now been for up to thirty years (Kibreab 1996a, Kibreab 1996b). In May 1991, after thirty years of trench warfare, Eritrea achieved liberation from Ethiopia. Although there is acknowledgement of food and humanitarian aid supplied during the war to nongovernment-controlled areas through the Sudan-based Cross-Border Operation, there is a clear and pervasive sense within Eritrea that Eritrea had to and did win its independence alone, without help from any nation or international body. In April 1993 an official referendum was held with over 99 percent of eligible Eritreans affirming their wish for Eritrea to be an independent nation. Until the referendum the Eritrean People's Liberation Front (EPLF) was the Provisional Government of Eritrea (PGE). The issue of the return of the refugees from Sudan to Eritrea quickly became a salient issue for PGE, for the United Nations High Commissioner for Refugees (UNHCR), and for international donors.

The first aim of this chapter is to explore the negotiations for the organised repatriation of the Eritrean refugees in Sudan prior to their actual return. These negotiations, starting formally in 1991 and informally even earlier, have been particularly prolonged and difficult.[1] In the context of these negotiations, the second aim is to analyse the international and national complexities of repatriation and the current and evolving modes of organising such large-scale movements.

The primary basis for the study on which this chapter is based were personal interviews, conducted between November 1994 and October 1995 with the following sets of respondents: government officials from Canada, Eritrea, Finland, Germany, the Netherlands, Norway, Sweden, Switzerland and the U.S.A.; staff from UNHCR in Geneva and Eritrea, the UN Department of Humanitarian Affairs (DHA), the United Nations Development Programme (UNDP) and international nongovernmental organisations (NGO); various participants in the Cross-Border Operations, and former fighters. These interviews were supplemented by participant observation at the Donor Workshop (Asmara, Eritrea; 19-20 May, 1995). This workshop was convened by the government of Eritrea to present the Plan of Operations for Phase One of the repatriation programme, *'Programme for Refugee Reintegration and Rehabilitation of Resettlement Areas in Eritrea'* (PROFERI). This research was carried out as part of a larger study by the Life and Peace Institute, Uppsala, Sweden, analysing prior conditions affecting the possible repatriation of Eritrean refugees in Sudan.

Repatriation: reintegration, power and peace

Repatriation is a peace issue, and peace must be seen as a *process*, not an event. The work of the complex array of intergovernmental agencies, nongovernmental organisations and national governments in repatriation sets conditions which encourage peace or conflict to develop. Repatriation negotiations provide a context in which the intertwined issues of national sovereignty and institutional mandates are played out. Understandings of the linkages between relief, development, disaster preparedness, mitigation and capacity building are tested. The resolution of these conflicts of interest and understandings is difficult, especially in a contested process such as the Eritrean refugee repatriation. Yet it is critical, as it affects the present and future well-being of communities and the individuals

1. The focus and time period of the study upon which this chapter is based was the negotiation process during the time between the liberation of Eritrea (May 1991) and the end of the pilot phase of the organised repatriation programme (May 1995).

within them as well as the ongoing relationships between powerful international actors:

> The overriding objectives of any government overseeing the transition from war to peace are threefold: to consolidate the peace, provide emergency relief and establish the country on a path of sustainable development. These objectives are closely interdependent, and . . . have to be pursued simultaneously: if any one fails, neither of the others can be achieved (UNRISD 1995: 116)

The gap between relief and development in the UN system is well known (Rogers and Copeland, 1993; Duffield and Prendergast 1994; Stein 1994). The necessity, as well as the difficulties, of expanding relief and humanitarian assistance to include attention to capacity building and sustainable development has been increasingly debated within the UN system. In UNHCR specifically, the concern in this context during the 1970s was how to link refugee aid and development, while in the 1990s the focus has shifted more to linking returnee aid and development. The paradox facing UNHCR is that even though repatriation 'marks the beginning of the end of UNHCR's involvement with an uprooted population' (UNHCR 1994a: 8), UNHCR is at the same time mandated for responsibility for refugees until a durable solution is found. There is now an understanding that 'UNHCR has a responsibility to assist with the reintegration of refugees, not simply to organise their repatriation' (UNHCR 1995b: 176).

The assumptions and principles of returnee aid and development which have informed the current approach emphasise that longer-term programmes are needed for political, economic and social reconstruction and reconciliation. These programmes also need to be development-oriented from the outset; need to bridge the relief and rehabilitation gap; need to target entire communities, and need to be incorporated into national reconstruction and development efforts. In order to accomplish this aim the contribution of the many agencies along the relief to development continuum needs to be clarified, integrated and coordinated.

UNHCR has responded with short-term, locally focused, Quick Impact Projects (QIPs), which are low cost, one- to two-year projects with the immediate goal of enhancing returnee integration and a secondary goal of being *a bridge to long-term sustainable development.* QIPs were originally implemented in Central America, and have now been used in many other countries. They have attracted donor support and have achieved some significant and positive results (UNHCR 1995a). The responsibility for medium- and longer-term development lies with UNDP and other partners. The long-term success of QIPs therefore depends upon effective linkages with these agencies. Although there has been progress in cooperation between UNHCR and UNDP (UNHCR/UNDP 1995), their different mandates, operational styles, and fund-raising capacities continue to make cooperation difficult (UNHCR 1997a). In this context, an evaluation report prepared for UNHCR argues that more attention should be given to 'the potential role of indigenous actors, particularly local authorities, "non-recognised entities", NGOs and … the beneficiary communities themselves' (UNHCR 1994b: 11). The same report suggests that UNHCR changes its terminology from 'returnee aid and development' to 'returnee aid and rehabilitation' to reflect a more realistic expectation upon UNHCR.

It is clear that power is central to effective repatriation and reconstruction. Power is enacted through the many different agents of repatriation – local, national and international – and underlies the negotiations for return. Gasarasi argues in his review of development, resettlement and repatriation for a 'polity primacy approach' in refugee studies (Gasarasi, 1997), that is, for a focus upon the condition of the state and upon the very present power issues including both the nature of the state to which the refugees are returning and the shifting political interests of rich donor states. In this chapter, the focus is specifically on the roles of the state of origin – Eritrea – and UNHCR and its donors, in the repatriation process. Clearly host states are also important venues for power conflicts during repatriation, and Sudan has certainly played an important role in the negotiations over the return of Eritreans; however its relationship to the process is beyond the immediate scope of this chapter.

Eritrea and the repatriation context

The challenges faced by the government of Eritrea are enormous. After thirty years of trench warfare and scorched earth tactics by the Ethiopian forces, Eritrea is devastated. The physical infrastructure has been almost totally destroyed (UNRISD 1996). The natural resource base is fragile and degraded (FAO 1995; Gebremedhin 1995). Providing adequate food for the current population of about three million persons is problematic: nearly 80 percent of the population is dependent upon food aid (Fahlen 1995). In this context the capacity to absorb 500,000 refugees from Sudan is doubtful.

The population of Eritrea – approximately 50 percent Muslim and 50 percent Christian – also includes indigenous African religions. There is a goal of including all groups in the nation-building process in order to avoid political conflict based on ethnic rivalries. However, the fact that the majority of refugees in Sudan are Muslims, many with a previous relationship to the Eritrean Liberation Front (ELF) which opposed the EPLF during the liberation struggle, presents a challenge to this goal of nation building based on ethnic and religious inclusion (Kibreab 1996b).

Nevertheless, from the perspectives of several UNHCR officials interviewed, Eritrea represented the one ray of hope in the Horn of Africa. The government, currently operating on the principle of the one-party state, has widespread, although not unanimous, support. It has broad ethnic and religious representation at the higher levels. There continues to be a strong sense of internal loyalty and a military-style commitment to the cause of Eritrea. The government of Eritrea, furthermore, has proven itself, according to UN personnel, Western government and NGO sources, to be honest and 'clean' in their governing. Confidence in the integrity of the leadership is widespread. This confidence is strengthened by the fact that since liberation thousands of former fighters have, until recently, been working in the government without salary, including at the highest level.[2] Most importantly, the country is at peace. As a representative of the Swedish government put it:

> We were eager to get going with the repatriation. We had supported the Eritrean people, and now this was an excellent situation in which to really do repatriation quickly and well. But it didn't happen. It got all bogged down in misunderstandings. (Interview with a representative of the Swedish Government)

As the above quotation illustrates, despite the hopes of UNHCR and the international community, repatriation to Eritrea has proved a protracted and complex process. One UNHCR official stated that the Eritrean repatriation negotiations had become the most highly politicised that he had ever experienced. The former head of the Commission for Eritrean Refugee Affairs (CERA), described the negotiation experience as a 'fierce battle of four years'.

From the negotiations for repatriation to Eritrea emerge a number of systematic themes which have implications for repatriation experiences more generally. These include issues of inter-governmental agencies' mandates and disjunctures between them, and differences in philosophies of what constitutes adequate or

---

2. In a recent process of government reorganisation approximately 10,000 civil servants were released. Those remaining now receive salaries.

responsible repatriation. Another theme with a particular salience in the case of Eritrea is the relationship between the recipient country and donor countries, a relationship embedded in the context of indigenous control and local capacities.

The historical context affecting negotiations

Following the opening by UNHCR of a permanent office in Asmara in November 1991, considerable difficulties around the repatriation negotiations emerged. Some of these were embedded in an historical distrust of the UN by the Eritrean government based on the fact that the UN had done nothing to prevent its annexation by Ethiopia in 1962 (Habte Selassie 1989). More recently, the refusal by the UN and UNHCR officially to recognise the international legitimacy of the Provisional Government of Eritrea (PGE) prior to the referendum was especially bitter. A request to the UN by the UNHCR Chief of Mission in Asmara for the presence of representatives of PGE at a UNHCR Executive Committee meeting in Geneva was turned down on this basis. The request came to represent a failed attempt to establish trust in the seriousness of UNHCR's efforts to negotiate for repatriation. A former CERA commissioner, reflecting on the failure to establish trust, analysed the situation as indicating the lack of importance which UNHCR placed upon Eritrean repatriation:

> There was a long debate going on [internationally] ... No one [would] involve themselves in repatriation before the referendum ...For UNHCR ... Eritrea ... was not on a priority list. They were not serious; they were reluctant to cooperate in simple things .... We see it from the logical point of view that people want to go back. It is a peaceful country. There is no reason for UNHCR to be reluctant to cooperate in repatriation.

In addition to a lack of trust by PGE in the UN system, the fact that many governments assisted Ethiopia during the years of Eritrea's struggle is a vivid memory. For example, the Eritrean liberation struggle, as an organised movement, never received the kind of international support that the African National Congress in South Africa enjoyed (Cliffe and Davidson, 1988). Such lack of international support lends credence to the Eritreans' perception that they won their liberation struggle by themselves.

Recognising that there are historic reasons for the Eritrean government to distrust the UN system should not, however, lead one to oversimplify the Eritrean government's position in regard to self-reliance and independence expressed, among other ways, in the Government's tight controls on external aid interventions. The Government's positions, a product of thirty years of the liberation struggle, are authentic to its self-understanding and probably would not have disappeared even had UN played a more positive role in the past. The Eritrean government as a liberation movement had little exposure to international agencies or their mandates, established methods, expectations and limitations. There was an assumption that 'UNHCR ... is almighty ... has a lot of money (and) ... does what it wants'.

In this context, basic disagreements, misunderstandings and contradictions rapidly emerged. Most significantly, there were differences in understandings of what repatriation as a total process should entail; of how funding should be determined, obtained and dispersed, and of how the repatriation process would be monitored and evaluated. The outcome was that after nine months of negotiations, UNHCR and the provisional government of Eritrea were unable to reach an agreement regarding an organised repatriation programme for the refugees in Sudan. The UNHCR office in Asmara was effectively no longer operational. Only in March 1994 was a UNHCR Chief of Mission once again stationed in Asmara. Relationships turned around positively, and concrete plans for a pilot phase of repatriation were developed.

A brief chronology of events

In autumn 1991 PGE presented a budget of U.S.$600 million for a comprehensive programme of return and reinsertion, apparently with the understanding that UNHCR had responsibility for *all aspects* of the refugees' return including its extension into national development. This proposal was later reduced to U.S.$200 million for the initial repatriation of 250,000 refugees.[3] UNHCR and PGE were, however, divided over basic issues. A 'difference of principles' was the phrase often used in interviews. PGE insisted on placing repatriation within a total development approach for the entire country. Osman Saleh, head of CERA at that time, stated in correspondence that:

> Repatriation and Reintegration programmes should be linked to the
> overall development programme of the country – Eritrea – to help [the

3. By way of comparison the repatriation and reintegration programme of 1.7 million Mozambican returnees cost some U.S.$145 million to implement. That repatriation was one of the largest ever undertaken by UNHCR.

refugees] become self reliant and prevent their possible back flow. Guaranteeing them a solid future was one of my chief aims. UN agencies and resources had to be mobilised.

UNHCR, however, stated that donors would not fund development activities by UNHCR. It was '... a matter of degree and what donors would fund ...'; for example, UNHCR would not replace the water system in Massawa, but would dig a small number of tube wells. Another specific example recounted by the former UNHCR Chief of Mission concerned shelter. PGE proposed a plan for concrete block houses with an estimated price of U.S.$900 – U.S.$1,200. UNHCR, in contrast, stressed a community-based approach, perceiving that the donors would question such a high amount of funding for shelter and would ask why the returnees needed concrete block houses when rural Eritrean people lived in huts. The UNHCR proposal to include the Eritrean repatriation programme within the Special Emergency Programme for the Horn of Africa (SEPHA) was similarly unsatisfactory to PGE which argued that SEPHA had a short time-frame, and that the limited absorptive capacity in Eritrea meant that repatriation there needed to extend over a long period of time (CERA/PGE (EPLF) 1992).

In December 1991 the first international appeal for Eritrea was posted. UNHCR estimated an initial requirement for U.S.$50 million,[4] stressing that they did not expect to receive the full amount immediately. Particular projects therefore required targeting, both in response to limited funds but also to raise further funding through a demonstration of success. The importance of this 'demonstration effect' was confirmed during interviews with several donor representatives. However, PGE insisted that only plans for the *total repatriation programme* for the 500,000 refugees should be developed and funded. PGE refused to allow UNHCR to begin discrete, preliminary projects. Similarly, although UNHCR and PGE both supported a community development focus in repatriation, PGE refused an area-by-area approach insisting that as the whole country had suffered in the liberation struggle, it would be unfair to target assistance on specific areas. The government stated that it could not 'bear the consequences ... (which might) sow the seeds of future turmoil and instability ...' (CERA/PGE (EPLF) 1992:2).

4. Throughout the interviews and in PGE documents estimates of the specific amounts vary. For example, reference is made to U.S.$24 million, U.S.$50 million and U.S.$68 million. In the final analysis, what was most salient was not the actual amount, but that on any of these estimates it was a much smaller amount that estimated to be required by PGE.

Throughout the increasingly polarised negotiation, the issue of how to determine an adequate level of funding was always present. PGE, citing the very high costs per head for repatriation exercises such as those in South Africa and Namibia, perceived that UNHCR was discriminating against Eritrea. UNHCR insisted that repatriation costing is not on a cost per head basis, but on the basis of need. Nevertheless, it was a tension that could not be resolved. In the fall of 1992 direct negotiations between PGE and UNHCR came to a halt. The UNHCR office was reduced to one administrative staff member. After the April 1993 referendum the UN Department of Humanitarian Affairs (DHA) took over the intergovernmental efforts. A repatriation plan was developed in close consultation between UN, PGE, NGOs and donor governments. DHA presented the 'Joint Government of Eritrea and United Nations Appeal for Eritrea' (PROFERI) to more than 120 government and aid organisations at a donors' conference.

Under this plan all of the refugees in Sudan (estimated at over 400,000) would be enabled to return and be reintegrated in Eritrea. The total cost was estimated at U.S.$262 million. However, the pledges in response to this appeal amounted to U.S.$32.4 million of which only U.S.$11 million was new money. The remainder was food aid through the World Food Programme and would have been available in any case. In response to questions about why the donor response was so unenthusiastic, a number of issues were raised. A recurrent theme was the donors' assessment that PROFERI was not a 'pure' repatriation; that it was rural development plus repatriation which would demand a long-term commitment. In addition, the government of Eritrea had declared its intention to rely exclusively on national project management and execution, thus limiting the involvement of NGOs to monitoring and evaluation. Donors were uncomfortable with this approach both because of an uncertainty about the capacity of the Eritrean administration to manage a vast set of activities, and because donors were largely channelling their money through NGOs. Finally, and importantly in the post-Cold War context, Eritrea was of little political significance to donors.

With the failure of the PROFERI appeal of July 1993, the government of Eritrea, UNDP, DHA and UNHCR reconvened to plan on the basis of the limited funds available. The government allocated 45 million Birr (approximately U.S.$7.5 million) for a Pilot Phase to repatriate approximately 4,500 households from Sudan. According to some observers, the Pilot Project would not have started unless the Eritreans had taken the initiative without waiting for pledged moneys. The first organised returns from Sudan to

Eritrea took place on 14 November 1994. The Pilot Phase continued until May 1995, and approximately 20,000 persons were repatriated under its auspices and received initial reintegration support. The Pilot Phase served as a basis for Phase One of PROFERI which aimed to repatriate some 135,000 Eritreans beginning in September 1995. As of the writing of this chapter, Phase One had not yet begun.

Challenges for community-building and peace

In reflection upon the stalemate which was reached over the negotiations for repatriation to Eritrea, the government of Eritrea presented five main reasons why UNHCR's proposals had been unacceptable:

1. UNHCR was perceived as discriminating against Eritrea by proposing a lower cost per head for the Eritrean repatriation than for the South African and Namibian repatriations.
2. UNHCR was refusing to include reintegration and development in repatriation.
3. UNHCR was perceived as *unwilling* rather than *unable* to commit the necessary funds to Eritrea.
4. UNHCR was offering 'piecemeal' assistance only. From the perspective of the government of Eritrea, to begin repatriation without full, guaranteed funding was too risky.
5. UNHCR, it was felt, was 'killing time' by proposing reviews of project proposals.

In an almost mirror opposite view, the basic reasons for the UNHCR not being able to accept the Eritrean government's proposals were as follows:

1. The level of funding requested was unrealistically high.
2. What the government was proposing was not repatriation but the development of the entire country.
3. Although UNHCR recognised the need for development linked to repatriation, UNHCR's mandate is for repatriation. The donors were unwilling to fund UNHCR in development activities.
4. Donors would not fund the total repatriation project 'up front'. UNHCR and the government of Eritrea needed to start with small pilot projects and use their success to promote increased and further funding.
5. The donors and the UNHCR could not accept a 'just trust us and give us the money' approach. Project plans need to be agreed

upon. UNHCR must be able to present programmes and requirements authoritatively to donors.

Beyond these specifics, the negotiations for the repatriation point to some important challenges within the international refugee system, especially as it relates to repatriation (McSpadden 1997).

The 'principled issue' of incorporating national development into the process of repatriation was the 'up front' issue. Although the Eritrean government stressed the difference of perspectives compared with UNHCR, it would seem that there were not basic differences in principles. UNHCR clearly supports a community- rather than group-focus for reintegration programmes, and has put considerable effort into finding ways to link repatriation to reintegration with development – QIPs being the most striking effort.

There were, however, different expectations of how the process would function, concerning, for example, which agencies were responsible; what time-frame was appropriate; how much funding could be secured and what sort of 'development' could be operationalised by UNHCR umbrella. As one high-ranking UNHCR official stated in an interview, the conflict revolved around the fact that UNHCR could not deliver what the government of Eritrea judged was needed, but neither could it deliver what the Government of Eritrea assumed UNHCR had responsibility for. The 'mandate dilemma' is not new, but it certainly exacerbated the difficulties in Eritrea. The Eritrean government clearly expected UNHCR to fund and to assume responsibility for major community development as part of its repatriation activities. This was an unrealistic expectation. The development of effective linkages to facilitate evolution from short-term rehabilitation and reintegration projects into longer-term development efforts poses a major contemporary challenge for UNHCR in all repatriation contexts.

Instrumental to resolving the mandate dilemma is the establishment of field-level coordination. In the Eritrean situation it seems that it was difficult for UNHCR to develop effective local working relations, particularly with UNDP. One reason was the changing of personnel and sometimes the lack of UNDP staff in Asmara. This changing of UN personnel also affected relationships with the Eritrean government. One NGO staff member, a long-time worker in the Horn of Africa, reflected:

> One of the major problems of the whole negotiation process was that the UN agencies kept on changing personnel. I don't know how many new

faces the Eritreans had to deal with – that was why the NGOs … were useful agents at the time. We were known by the officials of CERA. Each time a new (person) from the UN turned up, a different ideology and methodology was brought to bear. Some were deeply sceptical of the Eritreans, some obsessed with their own technocratic expertise. Few hung around long enough to see through the process.

The difficulty of linkage is not, however, limited to the mandate gap. It recurs in the funding for repatriation and development activities. The contradiction is that *economically* the funding is separate, that is emergency humanitarian aid funding is administered separately from development aid. However, at a *policy* level, there is an assumption of a continuum between humanitarian aid and development funding (Voutira 1996). A Swedish Foreign Ministry staff summed up the typical donors' perspective:

> Donors and governments understand repatriation as moving refugees from 'here' to 'there', not development. For donors, repatriation equals census in camps, transportation, way stations, some sort of reception, some beginning basics the refugees will need to get started, like seeds …. What UNHCR can offer is pure repatriation; development is not within their mandate. Schools and clinics, for example, are the responsibility of another UN agency.

UNHCR clearly understood the donors' position and operated within the negotiations from this perspective. The donors have apparently been reluctant to fund PROFERI whereas they have funded development-linked programmes as part of repatriation through CIREFCA and PRODERE in Central America (Cuny et al. 1992); through the Joint Support Unit in Cambodia; and in Mozambique where, by June 1996, approximately 1,500 QIP projects had been initiated with a typical budget of less than U.S.$40,000 each (UNHCR 1997a). It might be suggested that the donors were willing to fund short-term, low-budget projects but not PROFERI which was perceived as a long-term development programme and which seemed to provide the returnees with a higher standard of living than other rural Eritreans. As UNHCR noted in the report of the Mozambican repatriation, the donors '… were perhaps somewhat more interested in UNHCR's capacity to deliver quick impact than its ability to promote sustainable development' (UNHCR 1997: 48). This comment is supported by the observations of other analysts who lament '… the growing aversion of donor governments to support long term rehabilitation and reconstruction programmes' (Duffield and Prendergast 1994: 172).

The Eritrean government's negotiating stance, experienced as unrealistic, difficult, stubborn, and often confusing by UNHCR, many international donors, and more removed observers is, on the one hand particular to Eritrea. On the other hand, it points to some more general issues of the role and nature of the state in repatriation. The posture adopted grew out of thirty years of a liberation struggle which was almost unique in the African experience. The provision of public welfare (e.g., health care, education, food) was linked with mass political mobilisation. This approach to relief management in the midst of incredible war-related suffering was in stark contrast to the more typical 'predatory approach' (Duffield and Prendergast 1994) found between combatant and noncombatant within internal war situations, such as in Ethiopia, Rwanda, Cambodia or Afghanistan. Self-reliance during the struggle was a basic philosophy and operational approach drawing upon voluntary efforts and political support. These achievements within the liberation struggle relate to the insistence upon independence and self-reliance which underpin the government's commitment to national control in development and repatriation. This approach necessarily limits the role of indigenous and international NGOs to that of funding, monitoring and evaluation.

However, the issue of the capacities of the government to be able to move from a wartime struggle to engaging the complex challenges of reconstructing a war-torn society with its devastated economy, continuing food insecurity, and lack of material resources remains. It is a daunting task. Certainly donors questioned CERA's organisational and management skills. The military style of decision making, necessary and effective during the liberation struggle, is still the predominate approach taken by the Eritrean government according to many who have been negotiating or planning with government officials. This was described as decisions having to be made 'at the top', resulting in a tightly controlled and insular process which made it difficult to know if a decision had, in fact, been reached. A number of illustrations were offered by UNHCR staff indicating their assumption that a particular decision or action had been agreed upon in face-to-face discussion with government officials, only to learn that the government did not, in fact, concur.

In addition to the nature of the relationship between the donors and the recipient state, several other issues of broader relevance became apparent during the course of this study. It is clear, for example, that inadequate funding and a delay in the delivery of funds hampered the implementation of the Pilot Project. The UNHCR Chief of Mission highlighted a 'Catch 22' situation:

... clearly, donors will not continue to support relief to Eritrean Refugees in the Sudan forever. Yet, limited support for reintegration has contributed to the inability to fully implement the comprehensive pilot phase, thus making it difficult to meet donor expectations as to quality and adequacy of preparation in settlement sites. In addition, due to delays between pledges and the actual time of payment, CERA has been expected to meet requirements with insufficient funds.

In discussing the issue of funding with donor representatives, several key priorities surfaced, which clearly affected the Eritrean negotiations but which are typically also present in the broader international context. One was the political agenda of donor countries in the post-Cold War context (Ferris 1993). A second was the linking of aid with the utilisation of services from the donor country. A third issue was the linking of continued aid to careful reporting which meets international accounting procedures and standards as a measure of government accountability and transparency.

The lack of the involvement of refugees and the refugee communities in these priorities and indeed in the total process is glaring and disturbing (McSpadden 1996). Refugees need to be conceived not just as 'problems' in need of assistance, but as resources for the rebuilding of Eritrea. Refugees as individuals and refugees within communities bring with them the individual strengths of risk-taking and decision making – the hallmarks of refugees worldwide. They also bring years of experience in rebuilding communities with new survival skills learned in exile. A study by the Life and Peace Institute investigated the factors which have influenced the decision by Eritrean refugees whether to return home. Based on interviews with over seven hundred household heads in Sudan the study concluded that:

> Most of the factors that are discouraging Eritrean refugees from returning home are directly linked to the lack of social, physical ... and economic capacity of absorption in their country of origin. The evidence shows that there is a strong relationship between the refugees' possibility to return home (under the existing conditions of security and political stability) and national reconstruction (Kibreab 1996b: 197).

This finding would suggest that the government of Eritrea's emphasis upon funding for national development is not misplaced. It also suggests that the fact that Eritrea is a politically peaceful and stable country, unlike many countries to which refugees are being repatriated, is an essential condition for economic issues to take precedence.

Conclusion: control, cooperation and challenges

One of the most pervasive reasons for the conflict over the negotiations for repatriation to Eritrea was the issue of control. UNHCR guarded against a creeping expansion of its mandate, insisting that its role is to motivate, to advocate, to encourage, and to solicit the contribution of funds from international donors. The government of Eritrea, sensitive to the dangers of outside control and of losing what so many have struggled for and sacrificed so much to achieve, refused to allow others to dictate conditions which have significant effects upon the nation. The donors, the main actors in the international refugee system, face multiple and increasing demands, and are caught between political, economic and ethical demands.

According to long-time observers, the Eritrean government's approach is being watched carefully by some other African nations as a possible new way of dealing with NGOs, donors and the 'international system'. Although it is premature to come to any conclusions, it is possible that we are seeing the development of a new model of North-South relationships even in the context of extreme economic need. In fact, the Eritrean government's reliance upon national execution could provide the approach whereby the various UN agencies, bilateral aid agencies and international NGOs could work together to achieve the basic goal of bringing the refugees back. By working with the government of Eritrea, steps could be taken towards ensuring the involvement of the returnees and the local communities in planning, implementing and controlling their own community development.

Eritrea, as the 'one ray of hope in the Horn' could, with donor support, provide an opportunity to handle repatriation in new ways, testing the efficacy of a new model of North-South cooperation. Political stability coupled with clear economic and environmental needs could make the consequences of various approaches quite clear. This would be a contribution to improving repatriation in other contexts. Most importantly, the refugees would be repatriated. In the absence of some such cooperation the Eritrean government may, in the end, 'go it alone' with less than minimally adequate resources. Even worse is the possibility that the refugees may not be able or willing to return. It will, as usual, be the returnees and their communities which suffer and peace and stability which are compromised.

That the refugees remain in Sudan six years after Eritrea's liberation is an internationally and ethically unacceptable situation. The early window of opportunity – the moment to be seized – was missed due to the negotiation conflicts. Now the refugees are caught between the political hostilities of Sudan and Eritrea which have effectively halted organised repatriation and seem to have contributed to the recent expulsion of UNHCR international staff from Eritrea. Everyone – UNHCR, donors, the government of Sudan, and the government of Eritrea – says that repatriating the refugees is of the highest priority. What is needed is goodwill and cooperation to make such statements truth rather than rhetoric.

6

Repatriation from South Africa to Mozambique – Undermining Durable Solutions?

Chris Dolan

Explanations for the promotion of 'voluntary repatriation' as the preferred solution to the refugee cycle in the 1980s and 1990s tend to be sought in the field of international relations. Is it a reactive solution to problems within the international organisations? Harrell-Bond (1989) argues that it may be cheaper than long-term protection in the host countries. Allen and Turton (1996) view it as a 'pragmatic' response by the international community to avoid giving serious consideration to the other two 'durable' solutions and to reduce the likelihood of manipulation by host governments hungry for international assistance. They also imply that it goes hand in glove with the 'new realism' of 'militarised humanitarianism' (Allen and Turton 1996: 3). The increasing salience of national identities in the vacuum left by the end of the Cold War and its concomitant 'western'/'communist' ideologies is no doubt a further component. It is perhaps in this latter sense that the current High Commissioner for Refugees herself believes that 'properly planned and funded repatriation can help bring national and regional stability' (UNHCR 1994d). There is little room in these explanations to examine the motivations and practices of the refugees themselves, despite the gesture towards refugee agency implicit in the use of the qualifier 'voluntary'. Nor is much attention paid to the impact of the local socioeconomic and political context on the actual implementation of this policy. In this chapter I examine the Voluntary Repatriation Programme of Mozambicans from South Africa, a remarkably unsuccessful component of an operation which a UNHCR publication proudly described as 'the largest such program ever undertaken by UNHCR in Africa' (Dixon-Fyle 1994: 24).

Planning for the Mozambique Repatriation Operation began in earnest following the signing of the Mozambican General Peace Accord between Frelimo and Renamo in Rome on 4 October 1992. It was a flagship for the 'decade of voluntary repatriation' declared by Mrs Ogata in the same year, but built on a range of previous 'voluntary repatriation' exercises, including repatriation from Djibouti to Ethiopia (Crisp 1984), from Pakistan to Afghanistan (ICVA 1988), Thailand to Laos, and from various countries to Namibia and South Africa. The task in hand was considerable. Reflecting a dramatic intensification of the Renamo–Frelimo conflict from 1984 onwards (Hoile 1994; Vines 1995), the population of Mozambican refugees found in neighbouring Tanzania, Malawi, Zambia, Zimbabwe, South Africa and Swaziland had grown from 44,000 in 1984 to an estimated 1.7 million, or more than 10 percent of the Mozambican population in 1992. Malawi received the largest number, followed by South Africa. A further four million were estimated to be internally displaced (USCR 1993).

Writing in 1994, the UNHCR set a two-year timetable for the repatriation of the refugees: 'By 1996, UNHCR's $203 million repatriation and reintegration program is aiming to empty camps and settlements in neighbouring countries, and to set 1.5 million returning Mozambicans on the road to self-sufficiency' (Dixon-Fyle 1994: 24). In the final analysis the total cost of the programme was U.S.$108 million, of which only 20 percent was used on transport and repatriation, while 80 percent was used for the reintegration programme in Mozambique, particularly in the form of 'Quick Impact Projects' in districts with large numbers of returnees (UNHCR 1996a). Some 1.7 million refugees returned, though only 378,000, or 22 percent, used transport provided by the UNHCR (UNHCR 1995c: 6). While initially impressive, these aggregate figures mask the fact that in the case of South Africa, only 31,589, or just under 13 percent of the originally planned-for 240,000, returned to Mozambique with UNHCR assistance.[1] The settlements in South Africa were not emptied.

---

1. Even these figures are likely to be optimistic, given that many people used the transport several times under different names until the UNHCR tried to clamp down on this practice.

The UNHCR Voluntary Repatriation Programme from South Africa

The first steps towards a Voluntary Repatriation Programme were the signing of a 'Basic Agreement' between the UNHCR and the South African Government, on 6 September 1993, followed by a tripartite agreement between the UNHCR and the governments of South Africa and Mozambique on 15 September. Under this agreement, nearly ten years after the major in-flows began, group refugee status was finally granted to Mozambicans who had arrived between January 1985 and December 1992, or had arrived as contractual labourers in the early 1980s and become refugees *sur place* due to the prevailing security situation in Mozambique (UNHCR 1993b).[2] The Basic Agreement adopted the refugee definitions given in the 1951 UN Convention and the 1969 OAU Convention (see Article III), though carefully circumscribed:

(c) The presence of a refugee shall thereafter be regularised provided that the continued presence alone of such a person shall not establish any claim to permanent residence or any similar right in South Africa.

(d) Refugees shall enjoy full legal protection, but shall not have automatic entitlement to social, economic and welfare rights, provided that they shall not be treated any less favourably than aliens generally in the same circumstances. (Article IV, Section 11['Treatment'])

In practice this post hoc legalisation of the refugees' situation served principally to allow the implementation of a Voluntary Repatriation Programme (VRP), which began in March 1994, shortly before South Africa's first democratic elections. In the run-up to this, Masungulo, an NGO linked with the Catholic Church, conducted a survey to establish people's willingness to return, and subsequently ran an information programme about the repatriation and conditions in Mozambique. Food relief, which since the mid 1980s had been organised by the Catholic Church, was phased out. The initial plan was to end distributions in December 1993, but they were extended until early 1994 as the UNHCR did not wish to be seen to be inducing repatriation. Médecins sans Frontières-France (MSF-F) was contracted to set up and administer five transit camps in South Africa (Mhinga, Homu, Majeje, Rolle, Mangweni), where returnees

2. Throughout the intervening period there was no domestic legislation, with the South African police and Department of Affairs working on the basis of the Aliens Control Act (Act 96 of 1991). This act is primarily concerned with whether or not a person entered the country legally rather than with their reasons for entry.

received a medical check-up and any necessary vaccinations, before being transported by International Organisation for Migration (IOM) trucks to one of eight transit centres in Mozambique. From there the *Nucleo de Apoio para os Refugiados* (NAR – the Mozambican government department responsible for refugees) took people to homes within 20 km of the transit centres, while IOM was responsible for more distant final destinations.

The South African transit camps were intended to process five hundred returnees per week each. This would give a total of 2,500 per week, or 10,000 per month, adding up to 240,000 over the planned-for two-year period (UNICEF 1994). This turned out to be vastly overoptimistic, and even in the best week of the entire UNHCR programme, only 1,316 people, or just over 50 percent of the originally planned-for 2,500 per week, were transported.[3] A decision was therefore taken in late August 1994 to reduce the planned total to 120,000 instead of 240,000. The number of transit facilities in Mozambique was reduced from eight to three (Chokwe, Mapai and Moamba), the closing date for registration was set at 31 December 1994, and for the operation as a whole at 31 March 1995, a year earlier than initially intended. The members of the tripartite commission were asked to consider application of the Cessation Clause.[4]

By the closing date of 31 December 'UNHCR South Africa succeeded in registering approximately 63,000 refugees of which 31,589 returned by 5 April 1995' (UNHCR 1995d). A further 35,471 had returned 'spontaneously' from South Africa by December 1995, making a total of 67,060 (UNHCR 1996b). Figures for total returnees, both organised and spontaneous, show insignificant numbers in most districts in 1993, a peak in 1994, and a surge in the final month of the repatriation, March 1995. Apart from Chicualacuala in the north, the only district bordering South Africa which showed significant returnee numbers was Massingir (4,956). Magude district, area of origin for most refugees in Mhala district in South Africa, showed very low total numbers for the three-year period (627 according to UNHCR 1995d), though the Masungulo survey had suggested it was the most popular destination of all three southern provinces and the UNICEF survey placed it second after Maputo, with an estimated 15 percent of households interviewed intending to return there, compared with only 2 percent intending to go to Chicualacuala (Masungulo 1993).

3. The transit centre with the lowest overall turnout was Mangweni in KaNgwane.
4. Third Meeting of Technical Committee of the Tripartite Commission between the Government of Mozambique, South Africa and the UNHCR, 19 August 1994, Hotel Polana, Maputo.

Given the link made by UNHCR between levels of repatriation and levels of reintegration support, there were clear repercussions on many districts bordering South Africa. In its literature the UNHCR (1995a: 2) wrote that 'The task does not end with the repatriation phase. The main challenge now lies in making repatriation a durable solution by supporting the sustained reintegration of returnees in their areas of settlement'. This was reflected in their 1994 budget in which U.S.$51 million (64.5 percent) of a total of U.S.$79 million was spent inside Mozambique. In 1994, major UNHCR coordinated reintegration activities in the three southern provinces of Gaza, Maputo and Inhambane concentrated on food distribution (more than 6,000 tonnes over the period April-December 1994) and the distribution of more than 35,000 seed and tool kits (UNHCR 1995d). In 1995 greater emphasis was put on Quick Impact Projects (QIPs) in the health, education, water and roads sectors. The criteria for implementation of QIPs were 'number of returnees, previous UNHCR involvement, other rehabilitation activities, and percentage of population who are returnees' (UNHCR 1995d). The priority districts in southern Mozambique in 1995 were Chicualacuala, Massangena and Mabalane (all in Gaza province), and Mabote district in Inhambane province. Chicualacuala and Massangena were the two receiving districts with the largest numbers of returnees over the three-year period 1993-95 (17,122 and 11,769 respectively). These figures included 8,020 repatriated by UNHCR from Tongogara and Chambuta camps in Zimbabwe in the period July – December 1994.

An examination of the Voluntary Repatriation Programme shows that its failure to meet its *stated* objectives (to repatriate 240,000 Mozambican refugees) can be attributed partly to flaws in the conceptualisation and implementation of the programme itself, and partly to a range of external factors over which UNHCR had no direct control, but which it failed to accommodate. It thus suggests a number of ways in which the model adopted was at odds with the notion of a 'durable solution'.

Flaws in the UNHCR programme

It is possible to identify a number of major flaws in the design and implementation of the UNHCR programme, which undoubtedly impacted negatively on its overall success. The major weakness in the planning process was that it was based on a faulty assumption about how many people were interested in returning at that point in time. From March to August 1993, Masungulo, an agency of the South African Catholic Bishops Conference (SACBC), conducted a UNHCR-commissioned survey of 6,348 refugee households in the three main hosting areas, Gazankulu, KaNgwane and Winterveld. The emphasis on rural homeland areas reflected the areas in which the church and other NGOs had operated and excluded those who had migrated to urban areas. These biases were compounded by the questionnaire used, and the actual data collection method.[5] The finding of most interest to UNHCR, namely that 83.7 percent of those interviewed intended to return to Mozambique, was based on a simple, closed 'Yes/No' question, 'Do you intend to return to Mozambique?' Those who answered 'yes' were asked where they wished to return to, but not 'when?' or 'under what circumstances?' Neither were they asked who in the household would take the decision to repatriate, nor whether the household would repatriate together or in stages. UNHCR felt that 'the Catholic Bishops Conference has undertaken what appears to be a thorough survey of the Mozambicans', and continued planning for the repatriation of 250,000 over a period of two years. This figure was based on food distribution lists for the major refugee hosting areas (UNHCR 1994e).

Contrary to the Masungulo survey, a further survey conducted in early 1994 by UNICEF 'to identify categories of vulnerables and their wish and ability to return home in safety and dignity', found that in southern Gazankulu (i.e., Mhala district) 'the great majority of both women and men heads of households were *not* willing to repatriate', while in KaNgwane 'the vast majority of both female headed households and male headed households are willing to repatriate' (UNICEF 1994). This more nuanced view of the wish to return corroborated the UNHCR's own fact-finding mission, which had, in the space of two weeks in late 1993, discovered that 'a considerable number of Mozambicans with families in the homelands are working on farms and the mines' and that many others were integrated and had no wish to return (UNHCR 1993c: 2).

Despite the fact that UNHCR (1993c: 2) described five different settlement patterns in its reports ('Camps, Settlements, Mixed Settlements, Villas/Villages, 'Home, City and Underground Dwellings'), the information campaigns suffered the same rural bias as the Masungulo survey, and were targeted primarily at the rural homeland border areas. UNHCR felt that, 'Although large numbers of Mozambicans are known to reside within the PWV (Pretoria-Witwatersrand-Vaal) area, security considerations may militate

---

5. Rodgers, G, (1996: 5-6) describes how mass meetings were called at which refugee men were lined up in a row and interviewed.

against any overt and systematic status determination exercise' UNHCR 1993c: 3). They thus did not accommodate the dispersed nature of refugee households, and the fact that absent male migrant workers retain major decision-making powers, even though not physically present (UNICEF 1994: 17). Most Mozambican refugee migrant respondents in Johannesburg, claimed never to have heard of UNHCR, or at best only in the final days of the repatriation.[6] Even in the rural areas information campaigns appear to have been targeted primarily at the known 'refugee' settlements. In one informal settlement, in which over 80 percent of the inhabitants are of Mozambican origin, respondents either denied all knowledge of UNHCR, or stated they did not go to information meetings because they were for 'refugee settlements only'.[7] The fear which the information campaigns prompted is indicated by a South African respondent who knew about the repatriation, but had never asked anybody any questions about it for fear that he might be suspected of being a Mozambican himself.[8]

Where UNHCR did have contact with the refugees, they failed to take their advice. In southern Gazankulu (Mhala district), the local refugee relief committee, Phalalani, was consulted about the siting of the transit camp. The committee disapproved the proposed site, which was almost exactly in the centre of the district and not easily accessible for the two major concentrations of refugees at either end of the district. They suggested that it would make more sense to have two smaller transit centres at the sites of the reception centres during the 1980s, one in the north of the district, the other in the south.[9] MSF-F went ahead with their proposed site without informing the relief committee of the final decision until after work had already begun on building the camp. When asked the motivation for this, the UNHCR protection officer argued that the chosen site had a much better water supply and that furthermore, *the fact that people would have to make their way to the camp independently would be a demonstration of the voluntary nature of their return.*[10] In the event, numbers presenting at some transit camps were so low that a radical change in policy was adopted.[11] IOM

6. Interview with Mozambican refugee (SM), Protea North, 2 April 1995. Interview with Mozambican refugee (RM) staying at Alexandra township, Protea North, 2 April 1995.
7. Interviews in Lillydale B, July 1995.
8. Interview with local, Lillydale B, 10 July 1995.
9. Notes on emergency meeting of the Phalalani relief committee with UNHCR and MSF representatives, Tintswalo Hospital, Acornhoek, 18 March 1994.
10. Idem.
11. The largest number of returnees from Rolle (Mhala district) was 114, and this in the final week of the operation.

trucks were sent out to known refugee settlements to encourage people to come, and no limit was set on what could be transported.[12] One returnee who had come back before the Voluntary Repatriation commented that the VRP 'was a good thing. It was excellent. If you had a dog, a cat, a chicken, even the stone you use to scrub your feet, they would take everything for you! It was splendid!... I regret I didn't wait for repatriation, I would have saved so much money'.[13]

For the refugees there was only one serious problem with the actual transport arrangements, namely that after discovering that some people had travelled on the repatriation wagons two or more times, UNHCR refused to take any individuals, particularly young men, insisting that they would only transport family groups. This effectively made it more difficult for a household to repatriate strategically in the sense of leaving some household members in the host country to maintain whatever structural advantage was to be derived from exile while at the same time sending other members to the place of origin to reestablish a base there.

The confusion of rates of return and absolute numbers

The rural bias of the programme, which made it difficult for urban members of dispersed refugee households to participate in the process, was compounded by the timetable. The decision to reduce the target planning figure from 240,000 in 24 months to 120,000 in 12 months, failed to recognise that the problem was at least partly one of rate (refugees were not repatriating at a rate of 2,500 per month), rather than of absolute numbers. Had they explored reasons for low rate of return they might have considered repatriating 120,000 over a period of 24 months or even longer, in other words the same target figure but at a much reduced rate. The very narrow window of opportunity was problematic in at least two ways. It ignored the fact that decision makers were often not present for much of the year. It also did not allow time for information to trickle back from those who had returned to Mozambique and resettled successfully. As one returnee, asked how she felt about the repatriation, put it: 'As we see it, the repatriation wasn't bad. The problem was the deadlines. The majority of the people didn't believe the war was over. Many, when they realised they could go back, had

---

12. Personal observation and discussion, Rolle Transit camp, June 1994.
13. Interview with elderly male returnee (75+), Muine, Magude district, 3 March 1996.

already missed the operation'.[14] The time for registration wa_
shorter, with registration closing at the end of December 1994,
though families presenting themselves at the transit centre after that
date were also taken.[15]

The logic of the law and
'There is no place like home'

The failure to plan for a different rate of return is symptomatic of the
rigidities of the conceptual framework of the international refugee
system, which reduces complex processes to simple, linear and
reversible sequences of cause and effect. Richmond (1994: 71) has
pointed out 'the inadequacy of any definition of 'refugee' that singles
out one element in the causal chain, such as having a 'genuine fear
of persecution', because such fear is often only one factor in a much
more complicated relation between predisposing factors, structural
constraints, precipitating events, and enabling circumstances'. Yet
under Article 1.C (5) of the 1951 Convention, refugee status ceases to
apply if a refugee 'can no longer, because the circumstances in
connection with which he has been recognised as a refugee have
ceased to exist, continue to refuse to avail himself of the protection
of the country of his nationality'. Thus, just as in algebra if $x + y = z$
then $x = z - y$, so in international refugee law, if *Individual citizen +
War = Refugee*, then *Refugee - War = Individual citizen*. In this system,
the key factor is 'war', and its removal is indicated by the signing of
peace accords. Thus, the very first paragraph of the Tripartite
agreement which forms the basis for the repatriation programme
recalls that 'the General Peace Accord of 4 October 1992 between
the Mozambican Government and RENAMO has laid the
foundation for peace, stability, democracy and social and economic
development in Mozambique' and therefore the signatories agree on
the establishment of a Tripartite Commission for the Repatriation of
Mozambican Refugees from South Africa.[16]

This model of wholly reversible cause and effect, in which the
individual's movements are essentially determined by macro-level
events (e.g., the signing of a peace accord), has little room for the
complexities of micro-level decision making. It thus conflicts with

---

14. Interview with returnee (AC), Simbe, Magude district, Mozambique, 16 March
    1996.
15. Third Meeting of the Technical Committee of the Tripartite Commission, 19
    August 1994.
16. UNHCR, Tripartite Agreement, 6 September 1993, p2.

the notion that return should be 'voluntary', or in other words involve some element of individual agency on the part of the refugee. This is both a conceptual hurdle, and, as the South African case shows, a serious programmatic issue for the UNHCR. Allen and Turton (1996: 17) have argued that 'the case for return is often made on the grounds that it is the best solution for displaced people themselves'. It is important to point out that UNHCR was itself ambiguous about this: in its publicity about the repatriation it suggested that there was no tension between the objectives of the programme and individual choices, by implying that return to place of origin was synonymous with return 'home' and that the desire to return there (i.e., 'home') was beyond question (Coles 1985). The Coordinator of the Mozambique Repatriation Operation observed 'that people have this strong, compelling urge to go home. Their yearning to return is not reduced by the time they spend away' (Dixon-Fyle 1994: 24). The use of language such as 'compelling urge' and 'yearning to return', suggest that return 'home' satisfies such a primary instinct that it does not require independent justification, and overrides the impact 'the time they spend away' may have had on the refugees' relationship with their place of origin (Warner 1994). The critical choices which they faced in deciding whether to return or not, are conveniently sidelined. This rather simplistic view was captured in the title of the United States Committee for Refugees' December 1993 report, 'No Place Like Home: Mozambican Refugees Begin Africa's Largest Repatriation' (USCR 1993), also used by *Time* Magazine in an article describing the beginning of the VRP under the title 'There's no Place Like Home'.[17] Counter to this belief was the explicit linkage made UNHCR between repatriation and reintegration: 'The task does not end with the repatriation phase. The main challenge now lies in making repatriation a durable solution by supporting the sustained reintegration of returnees in their areas of settlement' (UNHCR 1995c: 2).

UNHCR South Africa fell between the two stools. On the side of refugees as rational decision makers they argued that:

these Mozambicans are becoming more and more convinced that their principal concerns . . . are being seriously addressed. For example, their rabid fear of land-mines is subsiding as they have become certain of the sincerity of the massive effort being exerted by their Government and the international community, especially UNHCR, to clear the land of these dangerous remnants of war ... the vast majority ... in this country where most see themselves as unwanted persons, are convinced that, as rural

17. *Time* Magazine (South Africa), 4 April 1994.

folk, feel and are convinced that they will be a lot better off returning home to their own land from where agricultural self-employment opportunities beckon to them ...

But they concluded, on the side of basic instinct that: '. . . love of country – the power of the adage that "there is no place like home" – is seen to underline the growing desire on the part of the Mozambicans in South Africa to go back to their own country' (UNHCR 1993d). Thus the acknowledgement of rational decision making is conflated with basic instincts: 'love of country' emerges as a conflation of rational decisions based on information about low levels of risk (a pull factor?) with psychological feelings of rejection by the host country (a push factor?), rather than a primary instinct detached from externalities.

The wider context: 'push', 'pull' and 'hold' factors or 'predisposing' factors, 'structural constraints', 'precipitating events', and 'enabling circumstances'?

While the factors identified by UNHCR as of concern to the refugees are critical ones, they are by no means exhaustive. Is it possible to identify factors 'pushing' from Mozambique and 'pulling' towards South Africa? For example, it has been argued that 'in trying to understand when and why repatriation occurs, it is important to examine both factors related to refugees' living conditions in the country of asylum as well as those which pertain to the improvement of conditions in the country of origin' (Basok 1990: 283). Or should we be thinking in terms of 'structural constraints, precipitating events and enabling circumstances'? A more thorough identification of the possible factors influencing the refugee's decision to go or to stay may help us to gain a sense of whether the internal flaws of the UNHCR Voluntary Repatriation Programme were critical in the (non) repatriation of Mozambicans from South Africa. There are a priori grounds to think not: the majority of refugees who returned from the other countries to Mozambique did so without UNHCR assistance, a strong indication that the assistance, while welcome, is unlikely to be the decisive factor. Rather, it is only one among the many 'predisposing factors, structural constraints, precipitating events, and enabling circumstances' which frame an individual's decision to move (Richmond 1994: 71).

One might assume that degree of integration in the host country would 'predispose' the individual in a positive or negative sense towards repatriation. Yet it emerges as a very problematic indicator, both in terms of how we measure integration (both in terms of content and unit of analysis), and because, to the extent that we are able to measure it, there does not appear to be a direct correlation between levels of integration and likelihood of return. Contrary to the stereotypical image of an undifferentiated mass of people who fled at a moment's notice and remained in a state of immutable dependency until further notice (almost essential if the model of reversible cause and effect required by refugee law is to work), patterns of flight from southern Mozambique were strongly influenced by the history of labour migration to South Africa. The individual's preflight position within this pattern of migration (differentiated by age, gender, migration history and household composition) resulted in complex and differentiated patterns of flight, and also meant that people were very differently equipped to deal with adapting to life in the host society. Some had friends and relatives already in the country who were prepared to host them and could guide them to employment opportunities. Others, notably single mothers who had lost their husbands, were far less likely to have access to such resources.

Fieldwork findings suggest that levels of social and economic integration were relatively low after ten years. While linkages did ease the way for some newly arrived refugees, their integration was not simply a continuation on a larger scale of historic patterns of migration and integration. The loss of Mozambique as an option and the need to defer to South Africans for all basic needs of food, shelter and employment, involved a fundamental shift in the power-relationships between Mozambican and South African, and marked a radical departure from prewar migrant–host relationships. Although UNHCR's vision of the refugees as a mass of undifferentiated 'rural folk' who sought 'agricultural self-employment opportunities' was somewhat anachronistic, most refugees in South Africa were unable to reestablish the balance between subsistence agriculture and a cash income derived from migrant labour which had characterised their household economy in southern Mozambique.

A more important determinant of individual integration appeared to be age at time of arrival. Younger generations were able to access the homeland schooling system, which both socialised them and afforded opportunities to acquire the status of South African citizens if their headmasters were prepared to sponsor them. This has resulted in many cases where the high level of an individual's 'integration' is at odds with the continuing marginal position of his or her wider household, adding another layer of complexity to the decision about whether to go or stay: should the older generation forfeit the opportunity to return to their land or should the young generation forfeit the educational and economic opportunities of South Africa? Should the household split or stay together?

These dilemmas were particularly difficult to answer as the timing of the voluntary repatriation programme coincided with dramatic changes in South Africa. The first democratic elections came just one month after the programme began and ushered in a government which promised to be radically different to the previous regime. There is no doubt that some refugees returned to Mozambique to avoid the fighting they feared would follow the elections. However, the opportunity to obtain South African identity documents, and the hope that if they voted for Mandela they would be allowed to stay in South Africa, acted to 'hold' many refugees in South Africa (Masungulo 1994a). One respondent in KaNgwane estimated that:

> about half the adults in this area now have IDs, most of them purchased just before the elections last year. Men are more likely to have purchased than women. In many households just one person has one, as a kind of protection for the whole household. The central government allowed various political parties to go around from village to village getting details and information for the issuing of IDs. All you had to do was join the queue. Mozambicans had to have R100. The ANC really pushed this process. People who were late were only issued with temporary cards.[18]

The weeks immediately preceding the April elections saw a surge in the number of repatriates on the UNHCR programme (2,495 compared with 1,040 in March), with numbers dropping again in May (1,499). Writing in late July, Masungulo, the organisation responsible for the information campaign, argued that, 'It was predicted that there would be blood shed after the elections in April this year and this contributed to their "wish to return". However, the peaceful state of the country and job opportunities at the moment changed the situation' (Masungulo 1994a). The next major surge in numbers came in September (2,255) immediately preceding the Mozambican elections in October, and was maintained up to December, after which numbers dropped drastically (Table 6.1).

Some Mozambicans wanted to see the outcome of the Mozambican elections and see if the peace held, before venturing to return (Masungulo 1994b). It thus appears that for the majority of people the opportunity to participate in the South African elections and the associated hope that their situation would improve under a

18. Interview, Shongwe Mission, 3 November 1995.

Table 6.1. *Numbers returning from South Africa to Mozambique by month, March 1994 to January 1995*

Month	Number repatriating
March	1040
April	2495
May	1499
June	1802
July	1542
August	1739
September	2255
October	2408
November	2429
December	2532
January	1237

Source: IOM Repatriation Statistics (unpublished statistics, Nelspruit Office, South Africa).

black government, coupled with a 'wait and see' attitude to the Mozambican elections, served neither to 'push' nor 'pull' them back to Mozambique. A more accurate description would be to say that the election processes and uncertainty about their outcomes served to 'hold' people in South Africa. In terms of a model of decision making one could argue that people simply had insufficient information on the basis of which to make a 'rational' decision.

In practice, the post-election experience has been both negative and positive for refugees still in South Africa. The South African Department of Home Affairs' policy towards 'illegals', has hardened. The South African Police have established Internal Tracing Units (ITUs), in fourteen major centres (In Nelspruit, Johannesburg and Welkom these are known as 'the Maputo Squad'), and two 'Aliens Investigation Units' have also been established at a national level (Minaar and Hough 1995). There have been reports that the police will reward members of the public who to assist them with information leading to the arrest and deportation of 'illegals'.[19] Deportations have increased rapidly and border patrols have been stepped up. By contrast with the very low VRP figures, some 80,926 Mozambicans were forcibly deported by the South African National Defence Force and the South African Police in 1993 alone,[20] followed by 71,279 in 1994.[21] This despite the Government's official position

19. Interview, Orlando West (Soweto), 17 August 1996; *Weekly Mail & Guardian*, 21 July 1994; *Citizen*, 29 June 1995.
20. *Financial Mail*, 9 September 1994, 'Illegal Migrants: No turn of the tide'.
21. *Business Day*, 8 March 1995, 'Fewer Illegals Repatriated'.

that '(t)he voluntary character of the repatriation operation would be adhered to until the Cessation Clause was invoked, after which the residual caseload would be dealt with in terms of the Aliens Control Act'.[22] In the event, the cessation clause was finally invoked in December 1996, by which point several hundred thousand further deportations had taken place. A total of 157,425 deportations were reported for 1996 alone (Department of Home Affairs 1996). Obviously not all of those deported fall within the definition adopted in the Basic Agreement, but refugees enjoyed no de facto protection, despite the UNHCR's basic agreement with the South African government, and were inevitably among those deported. In a tit-for-tat exchange with the Mozambique government, the South African government has now introduced exorbitant visa charges for Mozambicans entering the country legally.

The potential for deportation to 'hold' people back from repatriating properly should be considered. All accounts of deportation agree that the deportees are given no opportunity to collect their money or belongings, nor are they permitted to contact their families.[23] Those who have been deported explain that they are obliged to come back; they have to collect their money and goods, and they generally have family in South Africa who are dependent on them for support, or family in Mozambique who are dependent on them as a cash source. A particularly telling case was that of fifty Mozambican women working on a sugar plantation. Catholic priests had to intervene to prevent their deportation, as many of them had young children at home (in KaNgwane), some of whom they were breast feeding.[24] Logically, the more difficult the South African government makes it to come into the country, the less likely those already in it are to risk leaving. Knowing the costs and dangers they will be confronted with if they come back acts as a deterrent to repatriation.[25] Again, this can neither be described as a push nor a pull factor, more aptly as a 'hold' factor.

Despite these negative developments, a number of policy initiatives in South African in 1996 partially justified a 'wait and see' approach; the population at large benefited from the introduction of

22. Third Meeting of Technical Committee of the Tripartite Commission between the Government of Mozambique, South Africa and the UNHCR, 19 August 1994, Hotel Polana, Maputo.
23. For example, interview with street vendor, Protea North (Soweto), September 1996.
24. Interview with Catholic priests, Shongwe, 2 November 1995.
25. One interviewee in Protea North (Soweto) chose not to use the UNHCR VRP because he did not want his name to be recorded, as he feared this might make it 'more difficult for me to come to South Africa', 2 April 1995.

free health care, to which refugees, at least in the rural areas, have de facto access.[26] In addition to signing the 1951 UN Convention and the 1967 OAU Convention, the Government introduced a three-month amnesty for SADC citizens who could prove that they had been resident in the country and in gainful employment for five years or more. Under this amnesty such individuals would obtain permanent residence rights. This amnesty was due to run for three months from the beginning of July to the end of September. The response rate was poor, with only about 200 000 applicants by the end of the three-month period, and many refugees reporting difficulty accessing the process. Interviews carried out with refugee households in northern Mhala in October 1996 found that while many people had heard of the amnesty and would qualify at least in terms of length of stay, they did not have the money to make the journey to the nearest Department of Home Affairs offices in Thulamahashe, some thirty kilometres away.[27] Furthermore there was no guarantee that those who were turned down would not be deported immediately. The lack of response to this first amnesty prompted a further one specifically targeted at Mozambicans, which is currently under way.

If it is correct that both the elections and the amnesties served to 'hold' the majority of refugees because they were reluctant to make a choice on the basis of insufficient information this reinforces also the point made while discussing the short time-frame of the VRP; namely that it did not allow time for information of a reassuring nature about the situation in Mozambique to filter back to South Africa.

The situation in Mozambique and UNHCR's reintegration strategy

Scepticism about conditions in Mozambique was justified. Even the UNHCR, reporting on a mission to Gaza province prior to the VRP, reported that '(r)eturnees will be travelling to all the districts of what is a very large province, with a weak economic base, poorly supported infrastructures, very little opportunity (but massive potential), and an uncertain future' (UNHCR 1993e). A later field visit carried out by MSF-F concluded that:

[t]he situation in the regions bordering South Africa is not very good in terms of food security, access to health care, education and drinking

---

26. Interviews with seven refugee women in New Forest and Hluvukani, 27 & 28 July 1996.
27. Interviews with refugee women, Hluvukani, 5 November 1996.

water … The problems facing Mozambique are long term in character and perhaps do not justify the stopping of the repatriation process. However, it is vitally important that returnees are aware of the situation in Mozambique in order to ensure a truly voluntary repatriation. More should be done to facilitate cross-border inspection visits by community representatives before they commit themselves to return (MSF-F 1994a).

The teams working for the Masungulo Information Campaign reported that refugees requested to go and see conditions in Mozambique, and also that 'They want assurance from the Mozambican Government regarding social infrastructures (clinics, shops, transport, water pipes and schools!)' (Masungulo 1994b). Certainly schooling and health facilities were problematic or non-existent in many areas, obliging some returnees to leave their children in South Africa or in urban areas. The scale of the deficit was evident:

I have been here since 1987. The school system began to suffer in 1983. Then there were 83 schools in the district. By 1992 the number was reduced to only 13 around Magude. We had 204 teachers, but they became unhappy with the situation and left, some for South Africa, some came here and some went to Maputo. By 1992 there were only 89 teachers left. Rehabilitation is beginning. We opened two schools last year. This year we will open four and two more in 1997. There is a lack of human resources and building materials. We must work according to our means: very slowly.[28]

Schools were reconstructed with assistance from the NGO community, and the UNHCR reintegration strategy was a component of this. However, such assistance was limited by the policy of allocating reintegration funds on the basis of numbers already returned. As such, QIPs rewarded those who had returned (provided there were enough of them), rather than providing an incentive to return. In other words, they were unlikely to 'pull' people back to Mozambique, particularly not to Magude district, with its sorry figure of 627 returnees. As the District Director of Agriculture there pointed out, when asked how returnees survived: 'They wanted to take the risk and so returned to their places of origin. Only then did the organisations take the risk of rebuilding infrastructures and distributing food'.[29] One local person suggested that more money should have been spent on reintegration and less on repatriation:

28. Interview with substitute District Director of Education, Magude, 1 March 1996.
29. Interview with District Director of Agriculture and Emergencies, Magude, 7 March 1996.

They will come back if there are minimal conditions – schools, hospitals ... the Government should lend money to business people to rehabilitate the shops. They must make investments. There is nothing in the villages. IOM just left people in the bush. Of course they went back. It was a waste of money. They could have used it to rehabilitate areas and then the people would have come back on their own.[30]

Inevitably the QIPs could not address some of the most serious problems. Reports suggest that even in Chicualacuala, a UNHCR priority district, the situation in 1994 was dire:

In Lathlala (a village near Chicualacuala) they planted maize, sorghum, millet, groundnuts, cowbeans and pumpkins. They harvested nothing save a few pumpkins the seeds of which the women grind down to make a watery soup. The harvest was destroyed by a combination of drought and rats. The rats even dug some of the seed out of the ground before it germinated. Stocks are very low and also threatened by the rats ... The people survive on roots, nuts and fruits from the forest. (MSF-F 1994b).

An *nduna* (village headman) who was taken by UNHCR on a visit to Chicualacuala to allow him to inform his 'people' in South Africa about the situation in Mozambique, asked what advice he would give them, said:

I'm going to tell them the truth ... I cannot tell them that there's food there or that they will have water to quench their thirst, cook and clean themselves. Or that their animals will be able to drink water – because if I do that I will be lying ... They cannot work either – and even if they had money they couldn't buy any food because there are no shops for more than 60 kilometres.[31]

The loss of a cattle-based economy

By 1996, after heavy rains and good harvests, the picture was considerably better. Most returnees interviewed in Magude and Mapulanguene were in their middle ages or older, and many were female. Apart from the young men interviewed, who had generally been deported from South Africa, respondents were pleased with their return to Mozambique because it allowed them to get back to

30. Interview with General Manager of Manica Mineworkers Supplies, Magude, 29 February 1996.
31. *City Press*, 21 August 1994, 'It's not good to be home': 19.

a more independent way of living.[32] There were no complaints about the repatriation process, although many people interviewed had in fact made their own way back, supporting UNHCR's claim that while they assisted just over 30,000 to return, a further 30,000 returned independently. Though there were numerous reports of very sporadic official assistance once back in Mozambique, with very few exceptions, those interviewed appeared to have attained subsistence levels, though standards of living were far lower than before the war. The following is a typical response to the question 'how would you compare the situation here with South Africa?':

> Life here is easy, it is easy because we don't need to buy wood, we don't buy water, food also we don't have to buy – as you can see, we have a lot of maize in the field and our granary is also full, we also have other crops on their way in the fields. The main reason we like our own country is that we can do something to survive. Life in South Africa isn't bad, the problem is that they don't give any space to cultivate, saying that 'you are people from outside.[33]

The main difficulty was the lack of cattle. Before the war Magude was the 'richest cattle-breeding district nation-wide, with nearly 200,000 head of cattle between commercial farmers and the family sector, according to the District Authorities. Only some 2,000 cattle survived the conflict' (Lauriciano and Waterhouse 1994:15). Many returnees had had herds of thirty or more head of cattle, and now have none.[34] Asked how people survived before the war, the District Director of Agriculture pointed out that:

> When the machamba (crops) failed, they relied on their cattle. Men worked in South Africa and sent the money to buy cattle. There were plenty available right here in Magude. It was difficult to find someone who bought anything besides cattle.

Q: Will this ever be restored?

> People need to adapt. It's a shame. They can't work anymore, even water they collect on foot. Cattle weren't just for meat. They were for transport, for agriculture and for exchange.[35]

---

32. A gap in the methodology was that we did not interview families which returned with the repatriation and subsequently returned to South Africa.
33. Interview, returnee from KaNgwane, Panjane, July 1996.
34. Interview, returnee from KaNgwane, Panjane, July 1996.
35. Interview with District Director of Agriculture and Emergencies, Magude, 7 March 1996.

Although there is a scheme for rebuilding cattle herds, this apparently is not benefiting the poor:

> Look, Chissano was here personally and told us that he would bring cattle ... but what happens is that our leaders who were appointed to do the distribution gave the cattle to themselves, to each other – they gave it to the party secretaries and other chiefs, so even though that guy from the government, Chissano, had said that there would be no discrimination in the distribution, we are not given anything.[36]

The only way of rebuilding a herd of cattle is therefore through access to cash, and that has to come from South Africa as there are few sources in Mozambique.

Q: Do you believe that the war has ended?

> Yes I do but it is not a good time for me to go home because there is no job and some of the people who were returned by the UNHCR in Ximbhutse [Magude] have started starving. Some of them came to Johannesburg now. Currently I would like to work in South Africa to provide for my family in Mozambique. I will only go back if there is a place to work in and with enough money that one can make a living out of it.

The remittance of goods and finance to returned family members in Mozambique, could in principle permit an informal reconstruction process. This possibility is considerably reduced by current policies in South Africa, notably that of deportation. In numerous interviews with returnees they pointed out sons who had been deported, often for the third or fourth time, always returning because of belongings left in South Africa.[37] Although some returnees were receiving support from those still in South Africa, this appeared to be for survival purposes rather than visible reconstruction. The manager of Manica, a transport company dealing primarily with goods remitted by contract workers, noted a marked shift in the content of goods sent back by those working in South Africa, away from capital goods and towards foodstuffs:

> Seventy to eighty percent of the families here have relatives working there. There is no employment in the countryside ... Our main business now is in food and construction materials, in that order. A miner's order will be between 300 and 1,000 Rand. Because of the hunger here we get orders for R1000 in food alone.[38]

36. Idem.
37. Idem.
38. General Manager of Manica Mineworkers supplies, Magude, 29 February 1996.

The District Director of Agriculture and Emergencies also observed that 'Before the men working in South Africa only brought money to buy cattle. Now they only buy food. Even the miners only send food through Manica. Families used to pick up household goods, now it's only food'.[39]

In the light of the discussion of the elections as a 'holding' factor, it is interesting to note one explanation given for South Africa's increasingly hard line:

Q: Whom did you vote for?

We all voted for Mandela, its just that later we threw away those documents (they were given a 'small white card'), we were all afraid of reprisals.

Q: You mean you knew who you were voting for?

Yes, even now if you show me a photos I can point him out to you.

Q: What happened after the elections?

I can't answer that, its a bit difficult.

Q: I'm referring to the promises they made during the elections.

What happened was that after the elections there were a lot of imprisonments and deportations, they said that we had to be captured and deported because we had raised the number of votes for Mandela, so we Shangaans had to be expelled because we gave Mandela the victory, and Buthelezi no longer wants us in South Africa.[40]

Discussion and conclusions

In the introduction I suggested that the need to examine the extent to which the motivations of those promoting voluntary repatriation converge with individual, household or group motivations. I also suggested that the voluntary repatriation model itself appears to pay little attention to the influence of the specific socioeconomic and political context surrounding individual repatriation operations. That there may be considerable divergence between the macro objectives of the international actors (in this case UNHCR's

39. Interview, Magude, 7 March 1996.
40. Interview with woman returnee, Matongomane, June 1996.

objectives of 'national and regional' stability) and the micro-objectives of the supposed beneficiaries is clear from this case study. I have argued that elements of the UNHCR's programme widened this gap: UNHCR was selective in its use of information about the refugees' situation, it chose to ignore their advice (siting of transit camps), it sought to prevent multiple cross-border trips, it would not accommodate a slower rate of return than that originally planned. Yet these were all relatively minor problems which could be easily remedied. Rather than being the main cause of the refugees' reluctance to return, the flaws in the repatriation programme served to throw into sharp relief and to exacerbate a number of deeper sociopolitical dynamics which were beyond the immediate control of the UNHCR.

In seeking to identify more significant factors which would influence the individual and household decision whether to return to Mozambique, I have suggested that in addition to 'push' and 'pull' factors, there were both what Richmond calls 'predisposing factors', and what I have called 'hold' factors,. Whereas 'push' and 'pull' suggest immediate forces in the here and now, 'predisposing' factors refer to events in the past, while 'hold' factors are issues/situations about which the future is unclear. Some or all of these are taken into consideration by individuals in making the decision to go or to stay. In discussing whether or not the experience of refuge predisposed people to return, I concluded that although levels of social and economic integration of refugees as a group were relatively low, this did not predispose them to return to Mozambique at the first opportunity. Firstly, patterns of integration of some individuals (e.g., younger generation through schooling) cross-cut group ones and serve to hold entire households *in situ*. Secondly, and somewhat counter-intuitively, it is precisely the lack of integration which serves to 'hold' Mozambicans in South Africa. An important impediment to 'integration' is their lack of legal status, which produces profound economic and social vulnerability rather than helpless 'dependence'. While the inputs of those who remained in South Africa into reconstruction of their home areas in Mozambique cannot be quantified, the potential to remit goods and finance to areas of origin in Mozambique and thus begin a process of informal reconstruction, is weakened by low levels of economic integration. This already low potential is further weakened by an ensemble of increasingly restrictive policy measures towards 'illegals', most significant being forcible deportation, whereby employment, the means to an end, is disrupted and whatever goods and money have been accumulated are lost. The paradoxical effect is that Mozambicans who might otherwise have chosen to return to Mozambique with their accumulated possessions, are obliged to stay longer in South Africa to achieve the same objectives. Under these circumstances repatriation becomes a higher and higher risk choice for the individual or household.

Uncertainty about how these policies would change in the wake of a change in government in South Africa and elections in Mozambique, was sufficient grounds to hold some people in South Africa. The elections provided some with an opportunity to 'legalise' their status, and others with motivation to 'wait and see' what the outcome would be, whether negative (return/descent into war), or positive (a more friendly government in South Africa). The low level of reconstruction in Mozambique, a function of low levels of return and poor harvests in 1994, the year of the VRP, are also shown to have weakened the 'pull' of Mozambique, at least until those who did return could signal that their return had been successful.

To include 'predisposing' and 'hold' factors in the calculation of likelihood of return, is to acknowledge that decision making takes ongoing and unfinished processes into account, and therefore that repatriation is a fundamentally iterative process, in which an ongoing calculation is being made about how the socioeconomic and political conditions in both host country and country of origin affect the prospects of different individuals within the household. While the information can never be complete, there are good grounds for designing programmatic interventions for voluntary repatriation in a way which allows iterative processes to occur. At the level of status determination, recognising that the original causes of flight are overlaid by adaptive processes in the country of asylum, which are powerfully determined by the host, both at a local and at a policy level, also involves recognising that they are not automatically reversible upon the signing of a peace accord. The internationally-used categories of refugee as either political or economic do not adequately capture these adaptive and iterative processes. The two units of analysis in refugee law, i.e., individuals or entire population groups, cannot adequately accommodate interdependence of individuals, households and entire populations and the way these shift over time.

UNHCR shows no signs of taking these complexities into account. As suggested above, the relationship of vulnerability at the heart of the nonreturn of Mozambicans is powerfully determined by the policy of the host government. Indeed the host government appears to be the dominant actor, supported by a powerful chorus, the host society. In this scenario, UNHCR played an interesting support role.

Having repatriated as many as would go 'voluntarily' within the VRP framework, and reduced the planning figure from 240,000 to 120,000, UNHCR automatically redefined those who remained as illegal immigrants, thereby 'facilitating/legalising' their deportation and perpetuating the relationship of vulnerability between Mozambican and host. By abandoning its protection responsibilities and doing nothing to reassure Mozambican refugees that they would enjoy freedom to cross the border again in a legal fashion, UNHCR effectively further undermined the possibility of repatriation being a durable solution. A discussion of who benefits from maintaining a large body of illegals who provide cheap labour and pay regular protection money is beyond the scope of this chapter.

If the real objective of voluntary repatriation is to facilitate return, it needs to accommodate iterative processes. Policy planned around what governments/agencies think *should* happen is unlikely to succeed if it fails to take into account what does happen. Knowledge of population requires a variety of levels of aggregation: individual, household, areas within country of origin, nationalities, with age and gender as key variables in planning. The interdependence of the different categories also needs to be taken into account. Voluntary repatriation programmes also need to actively address factors which 'hold' people in a country. In the South African context, the ease with which supposed 'push' factors such as deportation actually become 'hold' factors needs to be noted. The major tool which is used to create a push, the deligitimisation of the individual, in fact raises the risk of returning to the country of origin and thereby creates a 'hold' factor. In the context of reconstruction and development in a region where international aid has probably already peaked (e.g. closure of programmes in Mozambique), informal strategies of reconstruction and development and their relationship to labour migration need to be seriously considered, if the country of origin is to have any 'pull'. As Allen and Turton (1996: 17) have argued in a different context, 'the area within which people are able to make decisions for themselves' needs to be maximised. Perhaps most importantly, repatriation should only be considered truly 'voluntary' if people go, even though they know that they could stay in conditions of dignity rather than ongoing vulnerability.

PART THREE
THE COMPLEXITY OF REPATRIATION

7

Repatriation from the European Union to Bosnia-Herzegovina: the Role of Information

Martha Walsh, Richard Black
and *Khalid Koser*

In December 1996, the UN High Commissioner for Refugees, Sadako Ogata, announced that requisite conditions had been satisfied to end the 'temporary protection' of Bosnian refugees, setting the stage for 1997 to be the year of repatriation from the European Union. According to UNHCR, at the end of 1996 there were 835,000 Bosnian refugees in twenty-five host countries in Europe without a 'durable solution', of whom it was projected that around 200,000 would return in 1997 (UN 1996). Half of these returnees were expected to come from Germany alone (UNHCR 1997b). While the vast majority of returns to Bosnia-Herzegovina were expected to be spontaneous, 1997 saw an increased effort amongst most EU member states, and by UNHCR itself, to initiate assisted return programmes and to facilitate and/or encourage Bosnian repatriation.

The particular nature of return and projected return from the EU to Bosnia has its origin in the unusual status granted to many Bosnians on their arrival in Europe, and indeed in the special circumstances of the war which forced them to flee. One initial point is that the war in Bosnia, bound up in the wider conflict in the former Yugoslavia, did not create conditions in which there was a 'simple' exodus of war-affected refugees to third countries. Instead, the pattern of displacement was complex. In addition to up to a million people displaced at one stage outside Bosnia, there were also over a million people displaced within the country itself. Of those who were displaced 'externally', around half went to Croatia, Slovenia, or the rump of Federal Yugoslavia, and thus in one sense were 'internally' displaced. More importantly, this pattern of forced migration arguably formed part of the strategy of war, such that 'ethnic cleansing' and its associated displacement could be seen as the whole purpose of the war itself (Minear et al. 1994). In such circumstances, limiting displacement and facilitating return as quickly as possible became one conceivable strategy to oppose the war, or at least its worst excesses (Cunliffe and Pugh 1997).

Whatever their view on the war, it is certainly clear that EU states perceived themselves as being faced with unacceptably large numbers of refugees from the former Yugoslavia, that were seeking, or might seek asylum in Western Europe. Most EU states shied away from granting full refugee status to those fleeing the war, offering instead a form of 'temporary protection' until such time as the war should end. This was a political compromise. For receiving states 'temporary protection' addressed a number of issues. It represented a mechanism for circumventing or suspending established asylum procedures, to avoid overload of the asylum system, as well as granting fewer rights to those allowed to stay. Perhaps as importantly, it reinforced signals that those displaced would be better to remain within the region, where they would be close to their 'homes', and potentially part of a wider solution to the conflict. For the UNHCR 'temporary protection' represented the only way that states not directly affected by the Bosnian influx in Europe might be persuaded to share the 'burden', and provide at least some refuge to people whose 'homes', and often lives, had been destroyed. This 'burden-sharing' was also important for some governments, notably Germany and Austria, although in practice it occurred on only a very limited scale in most EU countries.

With the signing of the Dayton Peace Accords, there was an initial flow of optimism amongst both governments and some refugees that the process of repatriation to Bosnia from Western Europe could begin, as peace returned to the country. However, this is a process that has been fraught with difficulty. Although the military provisions of the Dayton Accords were implemented, two further conditions for lifting temporary protection in Western Europe – the proclamation of an amnesty and the establishment of functioning mechanisms for the protection of human rights – were fragile at best. Constraints to return remained numerous, with even one of the more optimistic reports on the progress of UN operations in 1997 noting 'continued political obstruction and restrictions on movement, lack of confidence, the destruction of homes coupled with the slow pace of reconstruction, and the lack of employment' (UN 1997). Meanwhile, most EU countries had already conferred what was effectively permanent status on the majority of Bosnian refugees they hosted (Black et al. 1997). As a result, the extent of return by mid-1997 was way below the target for the year, although UNHCR remained hopeful (UNHCR 1997b).

Despite this shaky start, however, pressure for repatriation, and funding for it from UNHCR and a variety of donors has remained strong. Unilaterally lifting 'temporary protection' altogether, Germany stood out within the EU as advocating the accelerated (and if necessary, forced) return of all Bosnians under their protection. In addition to the refugees in Germany, there were also significant numbers of candidates for return in other countries who did not meet criteria for transfer to a more permanent status and thus remained vulnerable to forced or induced return. A range of European countries have pushed ahead with encouraging voluntary return, both as a response to public pressure, and because this was seen as the only route to a lasting 'durable solution' for these refugees.

This chapter examines the return process for Bosnian refugees living in European countries, focusing on a major strand of policy that has been designed to facilitate return – namely, the provision of information on conditions for return. The chapter focuses on initiatives in European Union countries, although it is important to note that there have been significant developments in Bosnian repatriation from other non-EU countries, notably Switzerland, Norway, Slovenia and Croatia. The chapter is based on research carried out in twelve EU countries during 1996-97, as well as extensive fieldwork within the Republic of Bosnia and -Herzegovina. In the EU fieldwork was not conducted in Spain, Portugal and the Republic of Ireland, where the number of Bosnians was too small to justify field visits.

Within the EU, in-depth interviews were conducted with officials of ministries of the interior and foreign affairs, nongovernmental organisations (NGOs) working with refugees, as well as Bosnian associations. Within Bosnia, semi-structured interviews were conducted with governmental officials at the municipal, cantonal and national levels, embassy personnel, representatives from international and nongovernmental organisations and returnees from five EU member states who had participated in various return programmes.[1] In addition to Sarajevo, visits were made to Mostar, Kljuc, Bihac, Bosanska Krupa and Sanski Most. Emphasis was given to the Una Sana Canton as it was expected to receive the largest influx of returnees from Europe.[2] These interviews sought to explore the different layers of the information flow between Bosnia and the host countries which impact on repatriation policy and programmes.

The role of information in the return process

Analytical frameworks concerned to explain when repatriation occurs have typically focused on the question of conflict resolution (Suhrke and Zolberg 1989) or the motivations of the international community (Harrell-Bond 1989). However, a host of recent empirical studies have highlighted the importance of refugee decision making in the repatriation process (Bascom 1994), and have demonstrated that the parameters used by refugees to determine when it is appropriate to return often differ from those used by involved agencies.

There is ample evidence in migration studies that information about a prospective destination is critical in the migration decision-making process (De Jong and Gardner 1981), including in the case of return migration (King 1978). Early studies focused on the differential availability of information in explaining why prospective migrants behaved in different ways. Later approaches showed that just as important as information availability are the more qualitative features of information flows, such as their frequency and accuracy. A number of empirical studies have suggested that how refugees perceive conditions in potential destinations can similarly be crucial in their decision whether to move (Koser 1996b). Drawing upon evidence from Latin America, Larkin et al. (1992) assert that refugees will often only move to another country when they are reasonably certain that they will be able to exercise power and control over their own fates there. Meanwhile Crisp (1984) demonstrates how the experience of witnessing other refugees forcibly repatriated from Djibouti back to Ethiopia prevented further refugee migration there.

Other empirical studies suggest that the significance of information in the decision-making process similarly applies to repatriation (Christensen 1985; Akol 1987; Basok 1990). In a study of the repatriation of Mozambican refugees from Malawi, Koser (1997a) shows that the differential receipt, evaluation and use of

1. In-depth interviews were conducted with two returnee households from Denmark, three from the U.K., six from Germany, one from the Netherlands, and two from Sweden.
2. Due to the political/military situation during the field research, a planned visit to the Republika Srpska was aborted. However, according to UNHCR, returns to the RS constituted only 3 percent of all returns up to mid-1997.

information by refugees was an essential element in explaining their return decisions. He demonstrates how refugees evaluated information on the basis of three main characteristics, namely: its reliability, accuracy and content. In this context, the supply of accurate and objective information is one way that the international community might be able to facilitate repatriation. However, one of the ways that the perceived reliability of information is determined is its source, and refugees in Malawi were found to place far more trust in personal as opposed to institutional information sources.

Not only is information a critical variable for refugees and returnees, it is also an important issue for policy-makers. Thus as Pottier (1996a) observed for the Rwanda emergency, agencies' lack of information about (and understanding of) cultural, economic and political aspects of the region reduced the confidence of humanitarian workers and placed limitations on their ability to respond to specific needs. More importantly, as Harrell-Bond et al. (1992) have pointed out in their attack on the pitfalls of 'counting refugees', information, and especially accurate statistical data, can be used as a powerful tool to direct agency accountability towards donor governments rather than towards the refugees they are supposed to assist.

For the purposes of this study, three categories of information on return were identified: information for refugees, information for host governments, and misinformation, a problem found to be particularly relevant to Germany. What is striking is the gap between both the types of information, and the preferred media for collecting and disseminating information chosen by refugees and governments respectively. Thus whilst information can clearly be seen as important, the accuracy and relevance of information varies widely from one source to another, influencing its usefulness as a basis for decision making by the various parties. Where there has been effective dissemination of accurate and relevant information in the Bosnian case, this can be seen to have both stimulated, and deterred repatriation. Whilst such a varied outcome may not be seen as a 'success' by some governments and agencies, for whom the total number of returns is critical, this does provide a basis for return to proceed in safety and in dignity, and to genuinely contribute to the reconstruction process, rather than representing a continuation of the cycle of forced migration.

Information for refugees

In so far as return to Bosnia since 1996 has been voluntary, the provision of information to refugees about conditions for return, or alternatively their acquisition of such information, can be seen as a critical factor in influencing the decision-making process. This explains the emphasis that has been placed on providing information by both European governments and assistance agencies, and their frequent enthusiasm for proposals for return assistance which prioritise information gathering and dissemination. Information centres, information reports, and public information campaigns have all become part of the standard package to encourage return, both within host countries and in Bosnia-Herzegovina itself. The extent to which these initiatives have had a major influence on refugees themselves, however, is questionable.

Perhaps the earliest form of information provision directed at those with 'temporary protection' in EU countries was the initiation of public information campaigns, to inform refugees both about imminent changes in legislation within the host country which might affect their security of residence, and about the possibilities for return after the signing of the Dayton Accords. For example, in France, a government circular was disseminated through the main social assistance agencies working with refugees in both French and Bosnian, alerting those holding an *authorisation provisoire de séjour* of the fact that such 'temporary protection' was ending, and providing information about voluntary assisted return schemes.

One of the ironies of such campaigns was the speed with which they were set up by European governments. Thus although there was clearly a need to inform those holding 'temporary protection' permits of policy changes that would affect their legal status, the chorus of encouragement to return effectively came before very much in the way of concrete information about conditions in the former Yugoslavia were available to those governments. In general, states relied on UNHCR as a source of information, such that the new optimistic tone of the High Commissioner in late 1996 justified their own optimism. In turn, the information that was disseminated about return tended to be dominated by details of schemes of assistance to return, rather than details of conditions on the ground once people had returned.

Mechanisms for disseminating the information that was available also varied in their nature, and, as a result, their effectiveness. Most returnees interviewed inside Bosnia-Herzegovina stated that they received information on assisted return programmes through contact with social workers in host countries. Usually, this was as a result of a refugee discussing the desire to return to Bosnia with their case worker. Even where formal information on particular schemes was not readily available from government sources, those who were eager to return had generally sought out information themselves. Thus, of those interviewed, it appeared that the participants in assisted return schemes had either been well connected to a Bosnian network or were familiar with the social support services and systems in the host country. However, some spontaneous returnees from Germany who might be classified as vulnerable (elderly, infirm) reported that they had not received information on assisted return programmes. This suggests that those most in need of assistance may not have the links or communication skills to access this information. Moreover, the fear of deportation for the most vulnerable may compel them to depart hastily, without seeking further information.

For information on Bosnia itself, though, quite different channels appear to have been used. Thus, with a view toward assisting refugees to make an informed decision about voluntary return, international organisations and some Bosnian NGOs have established information networks on conditions in Bosnia and the availability of assistance in repatriation and reintegration. Some NGOs and international organisations have established the capacity to respond directly to questions from refugees abroad. Caritas Sweden initiated such a programme early in 1997 in an effort to combat what they perceived to be too positive a picture emerging in the media about conditions in Bosnia. In general, however, refugees in Europe appear not to have turned to official channels, whether governmental or nongovernmental, as a source of information on conditions in Bosnia. For example, the International Federation of the Red Cross established such a service in late 1996, but by mid-1997 this remained undersubscribed. One of the few exceptions is Job 22, a Bosnian NGO which was founded in 1994 to provide information to refugees on legal concerns. Based in Sarajevo, they reported receiving 210 requests per month in mid-1997, mostly from Germany and Republika Srpska, though recently there has been an increase in queries from Austria.

Rather than relying on such official channels, all of the returnees and refugees in Europe interviewed during this research reported their main source of information to be friends and relatives who remained in Bosnia. Telephone bills were reported to have been a serious drain on income received in host states, detracting from the amount saved. Bosnian television and radio programmes were also an important source, though they were perceived as being dominated by the nationalist media. None of the Bosnians interviewed upon return or in Europe reported seeing the 'Repatriation Information Reports' published by UNHCR (see below), or any other information published by international organisations.

Meanwhile, most returnees interviewed reported that they did not know where to go for assistance for different problems once they had returned to Bosnia. In general, they had not been advised of the existence of different organisations prior to departure and/or were overwhelmed by the number of agencies and institutions on the ground. The result was considerable confusion, as returnees (mostly spontaneous) usually turned to UNHCR for assistance in any number of areas. The municipalities are officially the focal point for assistance to returnees, but the efficacy and willingness of the authorities to deal with returnee issues varies from municipality to municipality. By mid-1997, UNHCR had undertaken to establish a network of nineteen information centres throughout Bosnia. During August, one month after being established, the five centres in Una Sana Canton received 434 clients, 84 percent of whom were returning refugees. Not surprisingly the bulk of the visits concerned questions relating to shelter and property. Interestingly, however, the second most common query did not concern employment, but rather information on other NGO activities. This would seem to attest to the confusion and absence of information elsewhere.

Information for host countries

In addition to information provided to, and acquired by, refugees and returnees themselves, the other side of the coin of information gathering concerns information that is available to host country governments. In practice, governments within the EU rely on a number of sources for information about conditions in Bosnia, each of which can be used to inform repatriation policy and programme development. These include international and nongovernmental organisations, military sources, embassy personnel, and, in theory at least, returnees themselves. However, a conclusion worth highlighting is how little, by mid-1997, European governments had developed systems and mechanisms to learn from the practical experience of returnees, in comparison to the wealth of information from other sources. This paradox is examined in the section below.

One of the earliest public sources of information for governments planning return schemes was that of the 'Repatriation Information Reports' (RIRs) published in English and Bosnian by UNHCR in Sarajevo. These reports, based on data gathered from their field offices around the country, as well as from other international organisations (reflecting UNHCR's role as 'lead agency' for humanitarian assistance to the former Yugoslavia), were not aimed solely at governments although, as was noted above, their direct use by returnees themselves appears to have been either limited or nonexistent. However, they came to represent a major source of information for governments, as well as being widely available to nongovernmental and international organisations, particularly once they were placed on the internet. Some governments, notably Germany, Austria, Sweden and Denmark, have established their own independent capacity for information gathering of relevance to return. Thus the Swedish and Danish embassies established a repatriation post to channel information between Bosnia and Scandinavia and serve as a facilitator for return efforts, whilst the Netherlands was proposing to do the same in mid-1997. Germany and Austria set up coordination offices in Sarajevo for this purpose. Nonetheless, for the remaining EU countries, and even for these five states, RIRs remained influential.

However, given the role played by information gathered and disseminated through RIRs in host countries' decision making, and especially in certain cases in the determination of refugee status, one somewhat disturbing trend in 1997 was the handing over of information gathering for these reports to the military. After being taken on by SFOR (the NATO-led international Stabilisation Force), the first issues were apparently so inaccurate and misleading that UNHCR requested the name of the reports be changed to 'Draft RIRs'. For example, the Draft RIR for Mostar produced in May 1997 stated that '... approximately 35 evictions of Bosniaks from Western Mostar had been reported to the EU Administration since the Dayton Accords'. However, the Office of the High Representative (OHR) Weekly Bulletin No. 28, 9 December, 1996 reported that sixty-nine such evictions had taken place in 1996 alone. The OHR Weekly Bulletin of 10 February reported on the eviction of twenty-eight Bosniaks from West Mostar in one day. Moreover, the mandate of the EU Administration in Mostar expired on 31 December 1996. In addition to the inaccuracies, the main critique of the Draft RIRs was that the picture which emerged from the reports was much rosier than reality. This is perhaps understandable, given the tendency for the military to concentrate on areas in which it has competency, such as assessing infrastructure and enumerating incidents in which military intervention was necessary, rather than political or social tensions, or other complex issues (e.g., discrimination on the basis of age, disability, gender or other traits) that may have serious consequences for individual returnees. Nonetheless, it is of great concern, particularly given that the German Courts had previously based decisions to refuse asylum on the RIRs. The December 1996 issue of the UNHCR RIR specifically stated that it should not be used to determine a refugee's asylum claim.

Of course, one would expect European countries whose troops are present in Bosnia to be involved in military intelligence gathering, and there is little doubt that they were at the time of writing. However, even outside the context of military intelligence and RIRs, there was increasing concern amongst NGO field staff by mid-1997 over the militarisation of information-gathering. For example, in June 1997, Germany despatched a special military unit to SFOR to gather information which would be sent directly to the Federal Ministry of Interior. The establishment of a 'Repatriation Information Centre' (RIC) in the suburbs of Sarajevo in July 1997 was a joint initiative of UNHCR, an Austrian NGO, and SFOR. As with the RIRs, the RIC was established to provide information – including information on the internet – to a wide range of possible 'clients'. Other forms of information gathering of relevance to the safety of return – notably human rights monitoring conducted by the European Community Monitoring Mission (ECMM) were also dominated by ex-military personnel, not least because many of those responsible for monitoring troop movements and military actions during the war had remained in post.

At the time of writing in late 1997, Sarajevo's Repatriation Information Centre represented the largest effort to date to gather and disseminate information on conditions for return to Bosnia-Herzegovina. The Centre, aimed at 'centralising all information relating to returns and making it available to all involved' (UN 1997: 7), was established essentially as a database, whose intended users were decision makers, defined as host country governments, the national and entity governments of Bosnia, international organisations, Dayton institutions, NGOs and individual refugees and displaced persons. The categories of information covered include data on host government policy, policy of the Bosnian government(s), procedures for return, re-integration and reconstruction projects, and information on organisations involved in these projects. However, a number of teething problems emerged in its early months, and many of the intended users (staff of embassies, NGOs, and international organisations) expressed frustration with the RIC. For example, the Centre was criticised for not translating (or intending to translate) any of the information into the Bosnian language, whilst there was a perception that the quantity of material collected had not been matched by an efficient and user-friendly method of retrieving it. Additionally, the RIC is dependent on organisations to provide it with relevant data and information, and while it does not analyse the material, there is a process of selection. Once again, concern was expressed that there was an emphasis on over-accentuating the positive on the part of RIC staff.

In the midst of all this information-gathering activity, it is perhaps surprising that information on the practical experiences of refugees who have returned is much more sparse and, to a large extent, anecdotal. Thus as of late 1997, only three agencies were systematically monitoring the situation of returnees who had come back from European Union countries through their programmes, whilst one had also provided an undertaking to UNHCR to monitor the situation of deportees from Germany arriving in the Tuzla region. The International Organisation for Migration (IOM) was planning to implement a mechanism to monitor the experience of returnees on the German Assisted Return Programme (GARP) but had not done so by September 1997. The Swedish repatriation liaison officer was also planning to undertake in October 1997 a random sample survey of returnees from Sweden. It should be noted that obtaining information on the experience of returnees is not a straightforward task, given that once back in Bosnia, people may relocate a number of times before settling if they are not returning to their area of origin. However, as one embassy spokesperson candidly admitted, the real priorities of host governments also do not lie in finding out such information, since the 'success' of return programmes is not related to experience after return, but rather the total numbers who have been able to reach Bosnia. In this context, research is an add-on, not a means for evaluation.

As noted above, there are some exceptions to this lack of systematic knowledge about return experiences. Whilst those NGOs engaged in monitoring activities reported plans to use the results of surveys of 'their' returnees to inform future programme decisions, a rather different example was provided by the repatriation programme from Switzerland. In this programme, returnees are asked to fill out a questionnaire on arrival in Bosnia-Herzegovina, and then again six months later, in which they could report on their experiences. This is facilitated by the fact that relocation grants paid by the Swiss government are made in two instalments, one week, and six months after return. Whilst being able to cope with information on much larger numbers of returnees, this system does not however allow the Swiss government to respond rapidly to the problems of individual returnees.

Problems on return: misinformation and mistrust

Given Germany's policy toward repatriation, and the number of Bosnians living in Germany without secure residence status, the flow of accurate information about the situation in Bosnia is perhaps more important there than in any other host country. Yet, ironically, it is in Germany where there appeared to be the greatest lack of information and dissemination of misinformation. Routinely, Bosnian government officials, agency field staff, and returnees commented on the fact that returnees from Germany were the most ill-informed returnees from any host country. This is despite the fact that some 800 information centres were established throughout Germany by NGOs to assist in disseminating information on repatriation, and the existence of the Sarajevo-based German Advisory Office for Rehabilitation and Reintegration. Yet not only did it appear that the refugees in Germany were ill informed, but also there is evidence that staff in supporting organisations had not been adequately briefed. For example, one refugee received a letter from an agency in Bonn responding to queries about their return programme, which directed him to Job 22 for help in accommodation and income support, even though Job 22 only responds to information requests concerning legal matters. Also, a staff member at another international organisation expressed concern that counterparts in Germany were not sensitised to the complexities and problems associated with repatriating Bosniaks to Republika Srpska.

The dissemination of false or misleading information appears to be particularly problematic when the only contact refugees have had is with the police, though this varied from *Land* to *Land* (and is also likely to be dependent on the individual point of contact). For example, people whose visas were about to expire reported being told by authorities that return to Bosnia would be unproblematic and upon arrival, their housing, employment and other social needs would be addressed by the municipal authorities or an international agency, usually UNHCR. In one case, a man reported seeing a German official on television who said returnees could go to the Bureau of Employment and collect DM 180 per month. While this information may have been taken out of context and misunderstood, the fact remains that these are the perceptions people have and upon which they may base their decision to return spontaneously, rather than seeking additional information on assisted return programmes. And significantly, returnees from Germany reported that the situation was worse than expected whereas those from other countries said it was better.

Of course, the charge of 'misinformation' on the part of government and agency officials is a serious one, and it is not the intention of this chapter to suggest that all, or even the majority of those advising potential returnees in Germany were handing out incorrect information, nor that they were doing so deliberately. However, there are powerful reasons why information flows to Germany in particular should at the very least seek to 'accentuate the positive', given the commitment on the part of the German government (and increasingly other governments, notably Austria) to respond to the concerns of that part of public opinion which wants to see refugees returned as soon as possible. UNHCR is not immune to such pressure either, given that 50 percent of its 1997 budget for the former Yugoslavia was allocated to return of refugees from abroad, but that only half of that budget had actually been committed by donors. In this context, it is unsurprising to see it claiming at the end of June 1997 that 'the number of returnees from western Europe have been higher than expected', and predicting a 'dramatic increase in the number of people, particularly families, who will choose to recommence their lives in Bosnia and Herzegovina' (UNHCR 1997b: 1), even though a careful assessment of the data which followed this assertion showed returns below what appears to have been predicted for western Europe by the month of June, and the rate of return remaining relatively constant from March to June 1997, despite predictions that it would increase by over three times.

Given a climate in which information is open to manipulation – whether consciously or unconsciously – by agencies and governments whose interest it is to talk up return, it is perhaps unsurprising that official channels for repatriation information are viewed at best with a degree of mistrust by potential returnees. However, the fact that returnees do not rely on information provided through official channels is not simply a question of mistrust; in addition, there are very real constraints on the ability of 'official' organisations to provide the type of information that is most needed by potential returnees. Such information is often very personalised – not, for example, whether conditions in general in an area are safe to allow return, but whether a returnee's own house is still habitable (and uninhabited), and if so, whether his or her neighbours will allow return, or chase the prospective returnee away. This point highlights the question of the extent to which return to Bosnia can at present be viewed as a return 'home'. The nature of initial displacement described in the introduction to this chapter has, for example, produced a situation in which many of those displaced internally are living in the houses – the 'homes' – of those who fled abroad.

Whilst return organised through assisted schemes by the IOM and UNHCR does take such housing problems into account, insisting on a verification process to confirm that the returnee will have somewhere to live on return, the same is not true for many returns from Germany, where ultimate responsibility for providing housing is seen by the host government to lie with the local authorities. Such a position – which means that necessary detailed information may not be available to the prospective returnee – reflects the fact that Germany alone was expecting in 1997 to return over ten times more refugees than any other western European country. The result is that for some returnees at least, return has not signalled the end of displacement at all, with external refugees simply becoming 'internally displaced'. Alternatively, return of a refugee to his or her original house can result in the displacement of those who were occupying that person's house in their absence. Seldom has this involved the return 'home' of these internally displaced people, with violence and intimidation being used by nationalist groups in several high profile cases, to prevent the reversal of 'ethnic cleansing'. Moreover, where return has been to the refugees' original house, there has often been resentment amongst those who stayed, at investment in the repair of the homes of those who left during the war.

Together, these problems indicate the need for very detailed information on the part of prospective returnees. However, faced with this desire for personalised information, there is one type of official or semi-official scheme that has been relatively well received by Bosnian refugees in several countries, namely the opportunity to organise 'look and see' visits to Bosnia-Herzegovina, in order to collect information about the conditions for return at first hand. These visits have been organised in some cases by government (Sweden and Denmark), and in other cases by NGOs – including some Bosnian refugee associations. Thus in France, the *Association de Bosniaques en France* organised buses to take refugees back to Bosnia in both 1996 and 1997, obtaining an agreement from the French government that they would be allowed to return to France without losing their current legal status (mostly 'temporary protection', but also some recognised 'refugees') on return. In this particular case, the French government also assisted by negotiating safe transit for the buses through Croatian territory, which had initially been refused due to the fact that Croatia did not recognise the 'returnees' identity documents.

For those who have participated, such 'look and see' visits appear to have factored significantly in the decision-making process, though it may well be that the majority have decided against returning in the short term after the visits. For those who were positively disposed to returning to Bosnia, such trips allowed refugees not only to assess the situation first-hand, but also to make preliminary preparations for their return. Additionally, some who initially returned on a 'look and see' visit decided to stay on. Sweden is now exploring the possibility of extending the assistance available for return to those who decided to stay permanently whilst on a 'look and see' visit. It was suggested by returnees and by Bosnian government officials that such programmes be expanded and subsidised by host governments,[3] although it is worth noting that in Denmark, government officials were concerned that the state would be criticised in the media for 'paying for the holidays' of refugees in Bosnia.[4]

Conclusion

This chapter has discussed the role played by information in promoting or retarding the process of return of Bosnians who were granted 'temporary protection' in western European countries after the war in the former Yugoslavia. Given the continued volatility of the situation in Bosnia, the difficulties faced by returnees, but also the potential role that they and the international community could play in the reconstruction of the region, it is clear that the flow of information both to refugees themselves, and to governments developing policy towards return and reconstruction, is of critical importance. It is perhaps ironic then that this very uncertainty has weakened the reliability of some, at least, of the information that has emanated from the region; since as agencies and governments find it difficult to meet targets for return and reconstruction, the incentive is there to paint a rosy picture of conditions on the ground.

In general, the evidence of this chapter is in line with evidence on the production and use of information on the conditions for return elsewhere in the world, namely that the information which potential returnees actually trust is that which is generated by themselves or by people they know well, and which is oriented directly towards their own personal concerns. Such information is likely to vary widely: for those refugees with children, a common if not overwhelming concern is with the availability of education; for those who are sick (including those evacuated from Bosnia on 'medivac' programmes), availability of appropriate healthcare may be the key.

3. A returnee from Denmark who had participated in a 'look and see' tour stated that the Danish authorities deduct social assistance from those who are selected to participate in the programme which she said was a deterrent for potential participants.
4. An alternative to state funding was found in France, where tickets on buses were sold to Bosnians in employment in France, who had secure status, but who wanted to visit relatives in Bosnia, at a price that helped to subsidise those using the trip for 'look and see' purposes.

For all except the very old and the young, employment situations are likely to be a key variable, although this in turn will vary depending on whether potential returnees have found gainful employment in their host country. Meanwhile, for all returnees, shelter is a key short-term variable, a factor recognised by most European countries, and reflected in the priorities (if not necessarily the actual funding) of agency programmes within Bosnia-Herzegovina.

To respond to such individual demands for knowledge is difficult, but not impossible. On a small scale, and with a high ratio of information gatherers and providers to receivers, such information can be made available to prospective returnees. On a rather larger scale, the Swiss return scheme represents a good example of efficient data gathering, reflecting how the way a programme is set up can influence the collection of information and consequent monitoring of the programme. However, it is important to note that at the time of writing, the results of these questionnaires had not yet been published. Meanwhile, to draw a link between the efficiency of data collection and the 'success' of the Swiss programme more generally would be erroneous. Such an error has its roots in the assumption that 'success' can be measured by the number of people or families that have been encouraged to return. However, this high level of participation in the Swiss scheme seems to have less to do with the availability of good quality information, and much more to do with the fact that many Bosnians in Switzerland were given little choice but to return.

Ultimately, then, information represents only one part of a broader set of factors that influence individual decisions to return, and indeed government and agency policy towards return. Collection and dissemination of information for returnees has clearly been prioritised in the case of Bosnia-Herzegovina, and an increasing volume of material is available to refugees, agencies and, indeed, to researchers. However, whatever the quantity of information, severe limitations remain on its usefulness in the absence of a climate in which the decision to return is freely made.

Acknowledgements

This chapter is based on research on the 'Conditions for the return of displaced persons from the European Union' funded by the European Commission, Secretariat-General, Justice and Home Affairs Task Force, to whom we are grateful for support. The opinions expressed are those of the authors, and do not necessarily reflect those of the Commission.

8

The Point of No Return: The Politics of the Swiss Tamil Repatriation Agreement

Christopher McDowell

This chapter is about Tamil asylum migration during the years of the Sri Lankan conflict between 1983 and 1995, and attempts by the Swiss authorities to return failed asylum seekers to Sri Lanka. The focus is on the country of asylum, rather than on the country of return and aims to do three things. First, to explain why the Swiss authorities went through the arduous exercise of negotiating a return scheme aimed solely at failed Sri Lankan asylum seekers. Second, to describe the political and social consequences of the return scheme for the Swiss Sri Lankan population. And lastly, to explore alternative approaches to return which could have the potential to promote voluntariness, fairness and sustainability.

Part of the rationale for a chapter of this kind is based on an assessment that in order to understand fully the implications of a return scheme it is as important to examine the situation in the country of asylum, from where people are going to be repatriated, as it is important to examine the conditions to which they are going to be returned. Repatriation is enormously complex, raising issues about reintegration and development, international law and human rights, security and justice, developed world-developing world relations and much more besides. This discussion touches on that complexity by arguing that examinations of return should scrutinise closely the reasons that lie behind governments' decisions to pursue return schemes, and analyse with care the effects and implications of return arrangements on the entire asylum population – not just those targeted for return but also those exempted.

This chapter is based on three years of research in Switzerland between 1991 and 1994, during which time the author spent four months in the Swiss Federal Office for Refugees reviewing and retrieving data from dossiers containing papers relating to claims to asylum submitted by Sri Lankan citizens to the Swiss government. Provided with important socioeconomic and political base-line data which painted a rich picture of Tamil asylum seeking between 1983 and 1994 and the patterns of flight from Sri Lanka and entry into Europe, the author sat in on cantonal police asylum interviews, and conducted extensive interviewing with Sri Lankan asylum seekers and longer-term residents in Eastern German-speaking Switzerland, Germany, France and Britain. During the course of research, and in subsequent presentations, it became clear that the accumulation and analysis of such data is essential if we are to achieve a fuller understanding of asylum migration and the dynamics and political and social consequences of repatriation.

The Tripartite Agreement

The three-way Agreement between the government of Switzerland, the government of Sri Lanka and the UNHCR in Geneva to facilitate the 'voluntary' return of failed Sri Lankan asylum seekers to 'safe areas' of the island was signed in February 1994. The Agreement was the culmination of negotiations between the parties over more than a decade and contained within it three particularly important components concerning Europe's handling of the asylum issue.

In the first place, asylum seekers whose application for asylum had been rejected would be returned to a country in which a civil war continued and showed no signs of resolution. For this to happen, the parties to the Agreement reached a consensus in their analysis that within Sri Lanka, the south of the country was deemed to be an area of relative peace and stability to which returnees could return in safety and dignity. Second, the UNHCR took an active role in negotiations leading up to the Agreement and confirmed that it would be involved in the limited protection of returnees under something called 'passive monitoring'. UNHCR involvement in this way effectively endorsed the Agreement and was seen by other European governments with growing Sri Lankan asylum populations as a positive development. Lastly, the Swiss Federal

Office for Refugees came to a gentleman's agreement with the Liberation Tigers for Tamil Eelam (LTTE), the leading Tamil rebel group opposing the Sri Lankan government, that the LTTE would not interfere with or scupper the return scheme.

The repatriation scheme was devised on the basis of last-in-first-out and exempted those individuals who could not be returned for obvious security reasons, and would apply in the first instance only to those with established links (family, employment, residence) in the south of Sri Lanka. Swiss and international NGOs opposed the return scheme for a range of reasons.

Firstly, independent reports of the course of the conflict in Sri Lanka showed clearly that in spite of increased levels of contact between an apparently more flexible government and opposition groups, island-wide insecurity remained chronic and there was little hope of an end to the fighting. NGOs argued therefore that the south of Sri Lanka did not constitute an internal safe flight alternative, and that without active and long-term monitoring – as opposed to passive and short-term monitoring – the security of returnees could not be assured. This assessment was based in part on evidence that earlier returnees from Europe had been deliberately targeted by either, or both, the Sri Lankan security forces (who suspected returnees as being rebel activists) or one of the Tamil rebel groups (see Amnesty International 1987). Furthermore, for those returnees who could not establish themselves in the south, alternatives were strictly limited and it was likely that returnees would be obliged to join the hundreds of thousands of Tamils who were unable to return to their homes in the north and east of the country and were forced instead to seek shelter and protection in camps for the internally displaced situated in either LTTE- or Government-held areas. Such camps could not promise returnees safety and dignity.

Secondly, opponents of the return Agreement argued that the voluntariness of the scheme was questionable and in fact failed asylum seekers had no choice in the matter because, as is common to other repatriation schemes, either those targeted were returned through the scheme, or they were forcibly repatriated after a failure to comply (see also Stein 1986). More broadly, the Swiss-Sri Lanka-UNHCR Agreement was criticised for sending a green light to recipient governments around the world that return to Sri Lanka of potentially up to 300,000 people who had sought refuge in the West was now viable and could be conducted under the auspices of the UNHCR, on a modest budget, and with only a limited duty to protect.

Finally, the author's own discussions with Sri Lankan government officials and UNHCR desk officers suggested that both were reluctant parties to the Agreement. During the early 1990s the process of liberalising and modernising the Sri Lankan economy demanded the strengthening of external trade links, and it was through Switzerland that Sri Lanka planned to insert a wedge to open-up such opportunities. The Sri Lankans hoped that government-to-government collaboration over the return issue would open the way to a 'constructive' working relationship between Colombo and Bern leading to collaboration in other areas. Within the UNHCR also there was concern that pressure was being applied from Bern for the organisation to involve themselves in a scheme which was, strictly speaking, beyond the UNHCR's mandate – as returnees were failed asylum seekers and no longer 'people of concern' to the organisation. Corridor gossip hinted that UNHCR cooperation was in some way linked to the continuation of privileges accorded to the organisation by their hosts, the Swiss government. Officially, however, UNHCR Sri Lankan desk officers argued that they had no choice but to participate in the scheme because at least they could offer a little protection to returnees, and some protection was better than none (which would have been the situation if they had declined to become party to the Agreement).

It should come as no surprise that a bilateral Agreement of this kind had unequal partners, but the implications of such inequality for decisions about return can be far-reaching and require further research. Certainly the Swiss government held the strongest hand of cards, but the return scheme was not without danger for them. Although Switzerland has a human rights record of which it is proud and wishes to maintain intact, details of the Agreement became public at a time of great sensitivity due to mounting criticism about Switzerland's treatment during the Second World War of Jewish refugees and their assets. The highly visible deportation of Sri Lankan 'refugees' to a war-ravaged country could only further damage the country's claim to be the cradle of humanitarianism. Though wary of this danger, pressure from within the country for *something to be done* about the asylum issue did not relent.

Recession, Foreigners and Return

The main objective of the return scheme was to limit the potential of high immigration in the future. To those observing the negotiations leading up to the signing of the Agreement it was apparent that the scheme was designed more to act as a deterrent to further asylum seeking from Sri Lanka (and elsewhere), than to reduce the numbers of asylum seekers already in the country. Since the early 1980s, the Swiss government has pursued the whole range of asylum management options open to recipient governments but with little apparent effect. Measures such as capping social assistance provisions for immigrants, restricting the right to work, closing down opportunities for family reunion, levying special refugee taxes, scrutinising more closely claims to asylum, beefing up border controls, adopting the so-called 'white list' and truncating some determination procedures sent signals, but did not significantly affect the rates of entry or the rates of acceptance. Swiss politicians hoped that the threat of repatriation would not only send a stronger signal but would strengthen the government's management capabilities.

Support for the return Agreement therefore came from political parties and lobby groups (particularly on the right) and from within the country's administration which had long been calling for a more determined approach to the asylum issue. It was felt that schemes to promote the repatriation of asylum seekers could shore up a fairly threadbare asylum policy which had failed to keep apace with the demands which increasing rates of asylum migration presented. For much of the 1980s Swiss asylum policy had produced few bold initiatives, in large part because policy making was bogged down in the day-to-day tasks of handling asylum claims and the ongoing efforts to reduce both the backlog and the time it took to determine a case.

Paradoxically, however, from within the political right and particularly among employers' lobby groups in the hotel and catering sector, there was also resistance to changing the status quo. The evolution of Switzerland's asylum policy was characteristically *laissez-faire* and led to the creation of a sort of free market in asylum where asylum seekers were permitted to remain in the country on a string of uncertain temporary residence status's whilst their cases were being considered. The period of consideration – or more accurately, inactivity – which was lengthened by the backlog, was quite literally a testing time during which asylum seekers had an opportunity to prove that they could secure for themselves – and perhaps their family – a livelihood in Switzerland without being dependent on the state. It became a sifting process, and those asylum migrants who were in employment, were economically free-standing and had children in education could climb the legal status ladder, while those who fell by the way remained on a more insecure status. Hoteliers and restaurateurs liked this policy because it provided a steady supply of low-cost waiters, food preparers, dishwashers and room cleaners who realised the sense in diligence, hard work and cooperation. Employers were naturally resistant to any change that threatened a subsidised labour force.

Asylum seekers, and indeed some refugee campaign groups in Switzerland, recognised that on balance such a *laissez-faire* approach was in fact quite beneficial to Sri Lankan asylum seekers. With some 32,000 Sri Lankans, Switzerland in the early 1990s had the largest relative Tamil refugee population in Europe. Most were in employment and those who were not received social assistance that was generous when compared to other European countries; they lived in a country which was scenically beautiful and offered more opportunity (in health, education and income) than risk. The approach to policy, however, was not sustainable and as the Sri Lankan Tamil asylum population in Switzerland grew and asylum seekers began arriving from other countries, most notably Bosnia and elsewhere in the former Yugoslavia, so a more interventionist approach was adopted. The new approach, underpinned by repatriation, was not as responsive to demands for labour but was arguably more responsive to public opinion.

The mood of the Swiss public at the time of the announcement of the return Agreement meant that it was received favourably. It was a mood shaped by four interrelated areas of concern: the economy, crime and drugs, Europe and foreigners.

The pessimism of the Swiss in the early to mid-1990s had its roots in a long but shallow recession which began in the autumn of 1990 and resulted in rates of unemployment not seen since the 1930s; manufacturing and banking business migrated overseas, inflation increased, domestic investment declined, and the national budget deficit climbed steeply. For many Swiss the certainty had gone out of the job market and the realisation set in that the country could no longer afford to maintain traditionally high levels of expenditure on health, pensions, social security and education. Something had to give, and as happened elsewhere in Europe, concern about the increasing burden on limited state resources was at its sharpest when assistance to Switzerland's foreign population was raised.

The proportion of foreigners in Switzerland has risen steadily since the 1950s. According to official Swiss statistics, at the end of 1992 there were 1,213,463 foreigners resident in Switzerland, and a further 475,000 nonresident foreigners (asylum seekers, cross-border commuters, seasonal workers etc.), constituting 23 percent of people in Switzerland. Just under 900,000 of the 1.2 million resident foreigners were employed, as were a majority of nonresident foreigners. This meant that in 1992, foreigners constituted a third of Switzerland's total working population of around 3.6 million at a time in which Swiss citizens were struggling to find employment. The connection between the foreign population, state expenditure and Swiss unemployment was by no means clear and causal, but the very nature of the Swiss political culture and its devolved taxation system meant that individuals – who pay the largest portion of earned income at the local level rather than to the state – felt keenly that *their* tax money should only be directed to where it is needed, and in a way that is justified by genuine need.

During the recession, many Swiss felt that there was insufficient justification for an increased payment of the country's declining wealth to a growing foreign population. From the debate at the time there was an impression that the majority of this increasing population were *foreign* foreigners, i.e., non-Europeans and distant asylum seekers, who were dependent on the state. In fact, this was not the case, as 92.2 percent of resident foreigners were European or citizens of EFTA countries, and the majority were in employment. However, the issue of concern was the relatively small though sharply increasing population of asylum seekers and illegal immigrants. Switzerland is a multicultural society comprising many overlapping communities and Swiss citizens are prepared to live side-by-side with non-Swiss where basic cultural demands are reciprocated. One set of basic demands is that non-Swiss respect the Swiss way of doing things, do their job of work diligently, pay their taxes, make few demands on others and support their families. In the early-1990s it was felt, particularly in the eastern, more industrialised part of Switzerland, that elements of the foreign population were failing to reciprocate those basic demands.

Evidence of this failure could be seen on the streets and was reported widely in the press (see McDowell 1996: 55-59; Mathis 1997: xxv). In the first half of the 1990s Switzerland shared disproportionately the 'burden' of the war in the former Yugoslavia by accepting some 300,000 refugees. Meanwhile, its Turkish Kurdish population had grown to 80,000, and both communities figured prominently in Swiss criminal statistics. Regular press reports stated that 70 percent of all crime and 57 percent of violent crime in Switzerland was committed by foreigners, a third of the prison population was Yugoslav and 60 percent of drugs-dealing was said to be in the hands of non-Swiss – and the major share of this had been captured by Albanian Yugoslavs from Kosovo. The Swiss reacted strongly to such reports. It was felt unacceptable that people fleeing a conflict and who were received in good faith and given protection and means of a livelihood, should abuse that good faith by committing crimes and pushing drugs to their host's children. The drugs and crime issue was a significant factor in reducing public sympathy towards foreigners and asylum seekers and increased support for the repatriation of failed asylum seekers[1] and the expulsion of 'criminal refugees'.[2]

These issues came to a head in December 1992 in a referendum to decide whether or not the country should ratify the European Economic Area (EEA) Agreement and take the first step down the road to European Union (EU) membership. The substance of the debate leading to the EEA vote should have been focused on Europe-wide economic matters, but predictably the debate narrowed to 'domestic' concerns about the Swiss way of life, national identity, unemployment, and political and economic self-determination: the often acerbic European debate bundled together the issues of concern touched on above, and brought the debate about asylum to the heart of political debate, rather than at its periphery.

The 6 December referendum returned a 'No' verdict by an extremely narrow margin, 0.3 percent of the people. The most significant feature of the vote, however, was the sharp internal differences expressed in the regional and the canton-by-canton results; the treaty was soundly defeated in the cantonal count, but there was a stark contrast between its acceptance in the western French-speaking cantons, and the massive rejection it received in the more populous German-speaking parts of the country. The debate fed directly into the public's concern about immigration and asylum, and repatriation as a part solution was widely welcomed.

Having set the general 'Swiss' context within which the return Agreement was negotiated and received, this chapter now describes the political and social consequences of the return scheme for the Swiss Sri Lankan population.

The Return agreement: community formation and division

In order to understand the social and political implications of the return Agreement for the Swiss Tamil population it is necessary to examine the composition of the population and the ways in which repatriation and the threat of repatriation polarised Tamil opinion, increased the social distance between Tamil groups and radicalised Tamil political activity in Switzerland.

1. *Der Bund*, 23 April 1993.
2. *Blick*, 17 May 1993.

The anti-Tamil riots in Colombo, Sri Lanka's capital city, in July 1983 triggered the first wave of Sri Lankan asylum migration to southern India, Southeast Asia, Europe, Australia and North America. Since 1977 low-level anticipatory migration had taken place largely by professionals to Europe, America and Australia, and there was increased rebel traffic between the Northern and Eastern Provinces of Sri Lanka and southern India. It was in the period immediately after the riots, however, that Tamils began entering Switzerland and asked for political asylum. As Table 8.1 shows, 24,781 Sri Lankan citizens sought asylum in Switzerland during this period, making Sri Lanka the second largest source country for asylum seekers in Switzerland behind Turkey. By the time negotiations about the return Agreement reached the final stages and the intent was public, discernible groups within the Swiss Tamil asylum population were forming.

Information retrieved from the Swiss government's archives revealed general patterns of Tamil asylum entry since 1983. The overwhelming majority of Sri Lankan asylum seekers in Switzerland were Tamils (98 percent), of whom 93 percent originated from the Jaffna Peninsula or the Vanni region to the south of the Peninsula. Of the remaining seven percent, three percent originated (that is, had their home, place of education and/or place of work) in the East and four percent from Colombo. Two-thirds of all arrivals originated from rural areas, and one-fifth of those originating from the Jaffna Peninsula came from islands off the northwest Peninsula coast. Three-quarters of asylum seekers were male, though by 1993 equal numbers of men and women were arriving and claiming asylum. On average both men and women asylum seekers were aged in their mid-twenties, and a majority were either married on arrival in Switzerland or subsequently married another Tamil asylum seeker

Table 8.1 *Asylum Application Submitted by Six Major Source Countries to the Swiss Federal Authorities Between 1983 and 1991*

Country	Year								
	1983	*1984*	*1985*	*1986*	*1987*	*1988*	*1989*	*1990*	*1991*
Turkey	1,972	2,639	3,844	4,066	5,817	9,673	9,395	7,262	4,324
Sri Lanka	845	1,236	2,764	593	895	1,516	4,809	4,774	7,349
ex-Yugoslavia	74	102	138	119	131	818	1,365	5,645	14,205
Lebanon	19	49	107	144	375	529	2,477	5,533	1,352
Zaire	1,005	756	442	214	191	136	419	758	1,426
Pakistan	121	364	286	392	581	659	1,027	1,213	1,330

Source: McDowell (1996: 117); Federal Office for Refugees, Bern

within three years after arrival. Only six percent of asylum migrants were heads of households, almost a half of all arrivals were eldest male children, and more than half of women were eldest unmarried daughters. This pattern of migration would suggest firstly, that marriage was part of the migration strategy adopted by Tamil families, and secondly, that young men were noticeably mobile and particularly vulnerable to rebel recruitment and government security force actions.

An analysis of the caste composition of Tamil asylum seekers who arrived in Switzerland between 1983 and 1991 showed that 63 percent of the population were *Vellala* (traditionally cultivators) and 13 percent *Karaiyar* (traditionally sea traders and fishermen) from the western side of the Jaffna Peninsula. Both are 'touchable' castes and *Vellala* and *Karaiyar* form the bulk of the Jaffna Tamil middle-class landowners; in recent years, political and economic power has moved between these two castes. Over time, however, the caste profile of the population did not remain constant and by the mid-1990s the indication was towards a greater mix of castes, a decline in the proportion of *Vellala* (from 71 percent of the total in 1985 to 48 percent of the total population in 1993) and an increase in the proportion of *Karaiyar* and subordinate castes.

The education profile of the Swiss Tamil population showed that, on average, asylum seekers had better education qualifications and had spent longer in education when compared to national statistics for Tamils in Sri Lanka. However, data gathered during fieldwork gave a clear indication that after 1987 both levels of educational attainment and actual time spent in school decreased quite markedly, and by 1993 asylum entrants' education record was on par with estimates of the national situation in Sri Lanka. In terms of employment, it could be seen that more than 50 percent of arrivals were engaged in artisan, trading or other commercial activities during the twelve months before their departure, and most of that economic activity was non-farm. By the early-1990s, however, an increasing proportion of asylum entrants were unemployed, or had resorted to working on family land, work which in the past had not been preferred.

The data retrieved from the Swiss Federal archives paints with a broad brush a profile of the Swiss Tamil population at the time the Agreement was being considered. A period of more intensive fieldwork, including survey work and interviews, revealed in more detail some of the group dynamics and exposed the ways in which the return Agreement altered those dynamics. Of particular significance was the emergence of two groups of Sri Lankan Tamils in Switzerland. Within each of these groups there were subgroups (for example, mainland Peninsula and island Vellala, Muslims, and certain lower castes), but an important cleavage existed. On the one hand, there were those Tamils (termed here *immigrants*) who arrived between 1983 and 1989 and who had become successfully integrated into the economy; this group of Tamils were no longer dependent on the state, and had officially given up their bid for asylum in exchange for a form of renewable residence. On the other hand there were those Tamils (termed here *asylum seekers*) who had arrived in Switzerland after 1989, who had, for various reasons, been unable to integrate into the economy, and continued to hold the status of asylum seeker (in other words their application for asylum remained pending).

The immigrant Tamil community was identified as being heterogeneous, largely comprising lower-middle class *Vellala* united through associational migration into households based on core or extended families, with distinct, but overlapping and cohesive, subgroups. The population of asylum seekers – reflecting shifts in the course of the conflict throughout the 1980s and into the 1990s and recruitment practices by rebels, improved *schlepper* networks, and greater mobility among lower-caste and lower-class Tamils – was also identified as heterogeneous, largely non-*Vellala*, rural rather than urban, and comprising single men (rather than family-based households) with looser and less cohesive subgroups. In essence, the divisions between immigrants and asylum seekers were based on class, urban/rural, and experiences of conflict in Sri Lanka, and a further clear divide in terms of their status and level of security and integration in Switzerland.

The community divisions described here arose, in part, out of the patterns of flight from Sri Lanka and the patterns of entry into Switzerland. Both of these were in turn shaped by the nature and course of the conflict in Sri Lanka, the 'professionalisation' of asylum migration, and by the actions of the Sri Lankan state and the rebel groups, in particular the LTTE. However, these preexisting and processual divisions became hardened and significant in Switzerland firstly because of changing attitudes towards foreigners and asylum seekers on the part of the Swiss Government and Swiss citizens as hosts (those changes, as described previously came out of concerns about the economy, Europe, crime and drugs); secondly, because of the asylum and immigration policies pursued by the Swiss authorities; and lastly because of the policy of return.

Together, these attitudinal and policy changes impacted differently on the two groups. For example, the recession, which reduced employment opportunities for 'refugees' from all of the major source countries in Switzerland, hit the population of Tamil asylum seekers harder than it did Tamil immigrants. Immigrants were, as already described, more settled, better established in work and families, and therefore somewhat protected against the effects of recession. Asylum seekers on the other hand spent longer and longer periods out of work, became more dependent on the state and were subsequently increasingly visible to the Swiss tax payer as 'nondeserving' foreigners failing to reciprocate the basic cultural demands discussed earlier.

The hosts' perception of Tamils as nondeserving had a dual effect. On the one hand, it served to bolster popular support for the return scheme. On the other hand, it led immigrant Tamils to distance themselves even further from Tamil asylum seekers because it was, they believed, the presence and activities of asylum seekers (idling in railway stations and on street corners) that threatened their continued stay in Switzerland. While immigrant Tamils, who were no longer legally classified as asylum seekers, enjoyed the status of temporary resident, the permits they had worked to acquire and the privileges that came with those permits, could be withdrawn at any time. Aware of this, immigrant Tamils resented the presence of recently arrived asylum seekers and came to share a common cause with the Swiss in supporting last-in-first-out Tamil repatriation.

This polarisation between Tamil groups affected both social and economic interaction between the better established immigrants and the more recently arrived asylum seekers. But equally significantly, the isolating of asylum seekers and the insecurity of their status through the threat of repatriation changed the political dynamic of the Swiss Tamil population.

Throughout most of the 1980s, Tamil political activity in Switzerland had been fairly low-key. Research uncovered that the overwhelming majority of pre-1990 asylum seekers were politically inactive, describing themselves as being more the victims of the struggle rather than its perpetrators. Their support for Eelam was lukewarm and they were concerned that the new Tamil political leadership sought not only an independent Tamil state, but one in which the traditional power of the *Vellala* was removed.

In the 1990s, however, the situation changed. The new arrivals – who as we have seen, had spent longer in Sri Lanka struggling to survive the conflict, had suffered disrupted education, came from a lower class and lower caste background than the 1980s Swiss-bound Tamils – were more radical than their immigrant counterparts. By 1991 the LTTE had succeeded in establishing an efficient and far-reaching network of helpers and organisations in Switzerland by drawing on this pool of support. The LTTE leadership understood perfectly well the dynamics of the exile community. The fear of repatriation felt by asylum seekers, particularly single young men who were out of work and did not have the social or moral protection of a family network, forced them to turn to the LTTE. In the past, the Tiger organisation in Switzerland had been largely concerned with fund raising. Pressure from asylum seekers, however, obliged the LTTE to address Swiss Tamils' very real concerns about repatriation and protection, obliging the exile organisation to take a more active role.

In the final section of this chapter I consider alternative approaches to return which could have the potential to promote voluntariness, fairness and sustainability.

Reconsidering Return

It has been argued in this chapter that the Swiss–Sri Lanka–UNHCR return Agreement resulted in a series of negative consequences for the Tamil asylum population, the Swiss as hosts, Swiss-Sri Lanka relations and perhaps also negative consequences for the course of the conflict in Sri Lanka. Three main effects of the Agreement were identified: first, it exacerbated divisions within the Tamil population; second, it helped to harden the Swiss public's attitude towards asylum seekers and foreigners; and, finally, the Agreement changed the nature of and intensified exile Tamil political activity in Switzerland. It has further been argued that extraneous issues to do with Europe, trade, crime and foreigners shaped disproportionately the repatriation debate in Switzerland and blocked out the more pertinent issues relating to protection, dignity and human rights. And finally, the decision of the UNHCR to become involved in the return scheme has been criticised. In becoming a party to the Agreement the UNHCR provided a stamp of respectability but there is little evidence to suggest that the organisation's involvement added either quality or integrity to the overall repatriation process.

But how could things have been done differently? The permanent reintegration of failed Tamil asylum seekers in Switzerland was not an option acceptable to either the Swiss public or the government. The possibility of delaying execution of the Agreement until the war in Sri Lanka was over was rejected first, because the conflict was regarded not as one that was politically engineered, but rather as one of the many typically intractable Third World 'ethnic confrontations'; and second, because even if there were a cessation in fighting, the NGO lobby would argue that continuing poverty, human rights abuses etcetera would mean that conditions for return would never be acceptable because Tamils would be returned to a situation in which the Sri Lankan state could not or would not ensure the rights to which a returnee is entitled. Return was therefore inevitable, but the conduct of return could have been different.

From the Swiss experience it can be argued that a repatriation which is fairer, more durable and less destabilising could only be achieved with a radical restructuring of the relationship between host governments and their refugee populations. At present, contact between asylum populations and governments is mediated largely through authorities that pass down judgements on individuals' legal claims or assess access to social support; in this way, refugees and asylum seekers are burdensome. The majority of asylum seekers wish to see an end to the conditions which precipitated their flight and exile. Certainly there are some for whom the continuation of conflict is advantageous and they will expend energy to prolong and intensify a conflict rather than work to bring about a resolution. For those asylum seekers, domestic laws in the country of exile should ensure that illegal and nondemocratic exile political organisations are not given the freedom to operate. However, the overwhelming majority of asylum seekers do not involve themselves in such activities, and it is with this silent majority that host governments and the UNHCR should develop strong relationships of trust.

Such relationships, mediated through representative organisations, would promote the dissemination of accurate information about host government policy and future thinking, as well as about the situation in the country of origin. Such contact would break down mistrust and demystify the asylum determination regime. The exile voice, previously dominated by well organised and well funded political parties or political wings of military organisations, would come to reflect a wider range of opinion and would have the potential to open up new opportunities for conflict resolution through international mediation.

In relation to return, the opening up of channels of communication between asylum-seeking groups and host governments could lead to discussions and practical suggestions about the ways in which durable return could be achieved. The linking of repatriation with opportunity for reintegration should begin in the country of exile where refugees themselves participate in negotiations about their return and are able to take advantage of training schemes or education in preparation for return. In the return of Guatemalan refugees from Mexico in 1993 the refugees themselves were integral to the negotiations leading to the drafting of a four-way repatriation agreement between the governments of Mexico and Guatemala, the UNHCR and the refugees. In Switzerland, the – at times – close relationship between the Federal Office for Refugees and the LTTE, served to inhibit many Tamils from engaging in direct talks with the federal authorities and obstructed cooperation. One way of strengthening links between Swiss Tamil groups and Sri Lanka could be to encourage longer-term Tamil residents in Switzerland who are not immediately liable for repatriation, particularly those who are open to the idea of returning to Sri Lanka once the war has ended and democratic control returned, to actively invest their Swiss franc earnings in those Tamil areas to which failed asylum seekers are likely to resettle and in the training of returnees in skills that will be useful on return.

There are signs that a new approach to the return and resettlement of failed asylum seekers in Europe is emerging. The government of The Netherlands has recently initiated a development-oriented assisted return programme for asylum seekers from Angola, Ethiopia and Eritrea in which voluntary returnees will be prepared for return through training and are informed at regular intervals about the conditions in their countries of origin and what they could realistically expect on return. Once home, returnees may draw on a subsistence allowance, a grant, gift or loan to establish themselves in employment, business or training, and a further grant is made available for development initiatives that benefit the wider community into which returnees reintegrate. For a scheme such as this to work, it is essential that lines of communication are opened between governments and asylum seekers not just for the transmission of accurate and clear information, but also for the exchange of information (see Walsh et al., this volume). Development-oriented assisted return requires substantial financial backing, cooperation within governments but also between governments of sending and receiving states, and a thorough understanding of the risks associated with the reconstruction of returnees' livelihoods.

Meanwhile, whilst the Swiss–Sri Lanka–UNHCR return scheme for failed Tamil asylum seekers was about immigration control, the Dutch-Ethiopia (Angola and Eritrea) return programme is about development cooperation. If the latter model is to become the way forward then there will have to be a turnaround in the thinking of asylum receiving governments and among Western domestic NGOs who gear their activities to settlement in the place of exile as the only option. This turnaround can be assisted by detailed, comparative research that examines the range of resettlement and reintegration experiences (for example, see McDowell and Cernea forthcoming) and contributes directly to development and migration policy making.

Acknowledgements

I am grateful to Katherine Starup who commented on an earlier draft of this chapter.

9

The 'Self' in Self-Repatriation: Closing Down Mugunga Camp, Eastern Zaire

Johan Pottier

In mid-November 1996, after two years in exile, half a million refugees left eastern Zaire to return to Rwanda. Though sudden in some respects, this mass exodus in reverse followed a series of coordinated manoeuvres involving the strategic deployment of troops and aid. The return was planned and forecast, yet many questions surrounding the 'liberation' of the refugees remained, among them the thorny issue of whether the return had been voluntary. In view of the subtle changes that appeared in the international discourse at the time – in which terms like 'organised repatriation' and 'self-repatriation' came to be used – it is necessary to probe the mechanism that triggered the repatriation. Had refugees returned voluntarily or because of international collusion, or because of an extraordinary coincidence of extraordinary events?

Beyond these doubts, however, there was the certainty that refugees had returned in orderly fashion and that joy was expressed in many political quarters. The repatriation was a victory for the Rwandese Patriotic Front (RPF)-led regime in Kigali, the Alliance of Democratic Forces for the Liberation of Congo-Zaire (ADFL, or the Rebel Alliance), the U.S. Clinton administration, the 'new' South Africa and, according to many of its staff, UNHCR. Having long agreed that repatriation was the only solution, all these parties expressed relief and satisfaction on seeing 'the refugees' go home.

The crisis seemed to have ended. Moreover, as the return took place before the deployment of a multinational force, the repatriation could be portrayed as a victory for Africa, a victory with 'fairy tale' ending. On day two of the mass repatriation, Sylvana Foa, UN spokesperson for the Secretary General, captured the UN mood: 'The phrase you are hearing in the corridors of the UN today is "thrilled to death!" ... Hundreds of thousands of Rwandan refugees are voting with their feet'.[1] Despite lingering antagonisms, mainly between the Rwandan Government and the UNHCR, the publicly declared satisfaction was so extreme that several of the parties involved (particularly the U.S., but not UNHCR) hoped the world would buy the conclusion that Central Africa's refugee crisis had well and truly ended. Above all, the world needed to accept that this mass return had been 'a process of *self-repatriation*',[2] in which the refugees themselves had 'opened up the corridors' for a safe passage home.[3]

Euphoria aside, informed aid workers and analysts, UNHCR included, quickly realised that the crisis had not ended. There were missing refugees; not just a handful, but a high six-figure number. These refugees were at the mercy of belligerents reluctant to cease hostilities: the former Forces Armées Rwandaises (ex-FAR), the Rebel Alliance, the Forces Armées Zairoises (FAZ) and scores of mercenaries. Remaining refugees could be taken hostage and killed by their 'own' side or by 'the others'. In April 1994, the international community had stood and watched and filmed and written about the tragedy in Rwanda. It had acquiesced. In November 1996, when Mugunga camp was taken by the Rebel Alliance, that same international community was absent. Banned from Goma! Yet again, it accepted. A week before the refugees returned, Robert Gribbin, the U.S. ambassador in Kigali, acknowledged the U.S. would acquiesce: 'One has to work with the authorities who control Eastern Zaire'.[4] Differently put, let the Rebel Alliance, with the help of Kigali, find its own solution, let the international community believe in 'fairy tales'.

The 'fairy tale' so appealing to world leaders and opinion makers went something like this:

> After the massive slaughter of so many of their own ethnic kind inside Rwanda in 1994, a group of refugees, the RPF, conquered the country and took charge. They occupied the territory in record time, through

1. CNN, 16 November 1996.
2. Mike Hanna, CNN, 17 November 1996.
3. Ray Wilkinson, UNHCR, on BBC television, 16 November 1996.
4. *NRC Handelsblad,* 12 November 1996.

which some 1 to 1.5 million people fled abroad, mainly to Zaire. After living in exile for over two years, during which time this group was held hostage by the former extremist powers (ex-FAR and *interahamwe* militias), these new refugees were in turn liberated through yet other military groups, the Banyamulenge and the Mai-Mai warriors, so they could quickly return home where they would live long and happily-ever-after.[5]

Unlike most fairy tales, however, this one was riddled with questions too awkward to resolve. Did the returnees want to go back *that quickly*? Where were the roughly 500,000 'forgotten' Rwandan and Burundese refugees, and what about the 250,000 internally displaced persons (IDPs)? How many had died from exhaustion or been killed? And what about that snap decision by the U.S. to stop supporting the plan for an international intervention the very moment the mass repatriation began? Earlier, Clinton had declared the U.S. would not turn its back on desperate people and innocent children.[6] As neither observers nor cameras were allowed in the 'dungeon' that was Kivu, the international community was asked to pretend the dungeon was empty.[7] The purpose of this article is not to seek answers to all of the above questions, but to shed light on the making of the 'fairy tale' in order better to understand how complex African emergencies and solutions are internationally constructed.

Because of the international dimension of the 'fairy tale', I shall use as 'data' press cuttings and even some television interviews. The cuttings come mainly from Belgian, French, Dutch and US newspapers. The use of press cuttings as ethnographic data may be problematic, since there is editing and selection involved (Feldman 1991), first by journalists and then by myself, yet such materials do allow insight into the ways in which aid organisations, policy makers and politicians constitute the world they intervene in.

Repatriation from Mugunga: voluntary or involuntary?

Mugunga (population 200,000) became the world's largest refugee camp after the Rebel Alliance attacked surrounding camps in October 1996 (Figure 9.1). At this point, 195,000 refugees from Kibumba, 115,000 from Kahindo and an unspecified number from Katale (population 210,000) arrived in the relative safety of

5. Marti Waals, director Memisa-Belgium, *De Standaard,* 17 December 1996.
6. *International Herald Tribune,* 27 November 1996.
7. *De Standaard,* 17 December 1996.

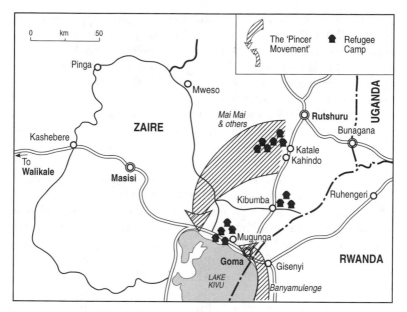

Figure 9.1 *The North Kivu Region*

Mugunga.[8] Of the Katale refugees, however, many were caught in the cross-fire between the ex-FAR and the Rebel Alliance. Unable to reach Mugunga, they made for Kisangani. Just before Goma fell to the Rebel Alliance on 1 November 1996, UNHCR and WFP pulled out of Kivu. The Government of Zaire then announced the imminent return of the refugees, a return it qualified as 'forcé et progressif'.[9] Being long discredited, the voice of Kinshasa fell on deaf ears. The media had more interest in Thabo Mbeki, South Africa's Vice-President, who defended his country's massive arms deal with Rwanda. Mbeki explained that the ex-FAR were ready to invade Rwanda. And Rwanda had the right to protect itself.[10]

But there was truth in Kinshasa's prediction. With the aid workers and journalists removed from the battle zone, Kabila declared a cease-fire on two conditions: first, that the FAZ must not launch a counter-offensive; second, that the Rwandan refugees had to use the opportunity to go home.[11] This second condition pleased UNHCR, as it had already stepped up its campaign to persuade refugees to

8. These figures are estimates, possibly on the high side.
9. *Le Soir*, 2-3 November 1996.
10. The statement in full: 'Rwanda [had] the right to protect itself against such an invasion. Otherwise, we [would] end up with another gigantic bloodbath' (Thabo Mbeki, *De Morgen*, 2 November 1996).
11. *De Standaard*, 5 November 1996

return. Via radio programmes and handbills airdropped over the camps, UNHCR had told refugees that going home was their only hope of escaping the war. The handbills depicted Rwanda as heaven and the camps as hell. UNHCR promised that returnees would receive two months' worth of food rations.[12] What would later come to be known as 'self-repatriation' was thus no more (and no less) than an order by Kabila, sweetened by the offer of food inside Rwanda.

By early November 1996 there was indeed no alternative, not even for food aid: the pipeline to Kivu was closed off. At this very advanced stage in the escalation of ADFL hostility against the Hutu camps, most organisations, including Caritas, agreed that repatriation had become the only solution.[13] This did not mean, however, that all aid organisations would remain silent on how and when the refugees should return. Many doubted the wisdom of an immediate, forced return. The U.S. and UNHCR, on the other hand, reacted swiftly and positively to Kabila's conditional cease-fire proposal. The High Commissioner for Refugees, Mrs Sadako Ogata, discussed 'humanitarian corridors' with the international community,[14] the purpose of which, American diplomats were quick to point out, was to make the refugees return without delay. The strategy was to make food, shelter and medical aid available only inside Rwanda.

One week before the first of the returnees re-entered Rwanda, the priorities of Washington (the Clinton administration), Kigali (the Rwanda government), Geneva (UNHCR) and Pretoria (the government of South Africa) converged openly and determinantly in a joint strategy for immediate repatriation. The strategy appeared unavoidable, even honourable, as the mass repatriation was sure to remove a key factor of instability. As a result, the impact of an immediate and massive repatriation on the prospect of long-term stability inside Rwanda was not addressed. The urgency also justified that little or no attention be paid to the protection of the refugees. Reminders of the Geneva Convention, however, came in fast. Emma Bonino, the EU Commissioner for Humanitarian Affairs, sharply attacked the U.S./Kigali/UNHCR strategy and declared:

> humanitarian aid must urgently reach the refugees where they are, that is, inside Zaire. We do not have the impression that these people want to be repatriated to Rwanda. No law can be evoked to force them to return, that would be deportation.[15]

12. *Knack*, 6 November 1996.
13. *Knack*, 6 November 1996.
14. *Le Soir*, 5 November 1996.
15. *Le Monde*, 6 November 1996.

Belgium's National Centre for Development Cooperation backed Bonino:

> According to the Geneva Convention, refugees have the "right" to protection and humanitarian aid. As far as repatriation is concerned, the principle of freedom [i.e., voluntary repatriation] has to be respected. The proposal to starve the refugees and thus force them to return to Rwanda flagrantly contravenes that principle.[16]

Others disagreed. Rwanda's Foreign Affairs Minister, Anastase Gasana, justified the plans for 'organised repatriation' – the term now favoured by UNHCR[17] – by emphasising that refugees could not return voluntarily as long as Zaire kept them hostage.[18] The refugees were Mobutu's political trump card. They were held hostage twice, once by their own leaders, a second time by the host country. Representing Rwanda's official position, Gasana implied (a) that 'the refugees' wanted to return unconditionally; (b) that the use of force (by Zaire) made voluntary repatriation impossible; (c) that the use of counter-force by the ADFL and its 'friends' was therefore legitimate; (d) that effective counter-force would truly liberate 'the refugees'.

UNHCR shared Gasana's stance, as did the U.S. Both took the view – a view never tested – that the stranglehold of the *interahamwe* on the refugee population had been continuous, even increasing, over the two years in exile. UNHCR's Ray Wilkinson most clearly expressed this view when learning that the Rebel Alliance had cut hundreds of thousands of refugees free from their intimidators. He reflected: 'the *interahamwe* continues its two-year long campaign and terror'. Hearing also that the *interahamwe* had shot and killed refugees who tried to flee to Goma, Wilkinson qualified the atrocities as 'an ominous sign that the *interahamwe still has a grip* on the refugee population, which makes our task very difficult'.[19]

Anonymous diplomats in Kigali supported the do-it-yourself (DIY) option. Africans using force on other Africans was more acceptable than a white-dominated international presence which would use force and bring home 'boys in bodybags'. As applied to eastern Zaire, however, DIY did include the help of the Rwandese Patriotic Army (RPA). RPA leaders strenuously denied being physically present in Zaire, but never hid their moral and logistical support. Kigali-based diplomats also condoned food aid being used

16. *De Morgen,* 6 November 1996.
17. *De Morgen,* 5 November 1996.
18. *Financieel Ekonomische Tijd,* 6 November 1996.
19. *NRC Handelsblad,* 11 November 1996, emphasis added.

as bait to induce repatriation. Some said: 'They [the refugees] will run faster if we provide food aid this side of the border'.[20] UNHCR delighted in the 'African solution' and preferred not to ask questions about wider international involvements. Despite the news blackout when Mugunga camp was taken, Wilkinson emphatically said about UNHCR: 'Our starting point is that the refugees are returning. To us it does not make any difference who is responsible for this'.[21] This sounded remarkably similar to what U.S. ambassador Gribbin had declared several days earlier.

At the end of the three-day exodus in reverse, Rwanda and the U.S. were eager to declare the refugee crisis over. Rumours of 'missing refugees' had to be smothered. Seth Kamanzi, political adviser to President Bizimungu proclaimed: 'We challenge the UNHCR to give us proof of where those [remaining] refugees are. Nowhere do the American satellite photographs show up any significant refugee concentrations'.[22] They were adamant that the world should listen and accept the Kigali/US verdict that 'those who remain[ed] in Zaire [were] criminals'.[23] The US ambassador in Kigali added his wisdom via the BBC world service: only a couple of tens of thousands of refugees remained in Zaire; certainly 'no masses'.[24]

The Kigali/U.S. interpretation of what the post-Mugunga satellite photographs had shown would be contested by Oxfam staff. In a widely circulated statement, Nicholas Stockton, the Emergencies Director at Oxfam U.K. & Ireland, recalls:

> On 20 November [1996] Oxfam staff were shown the original US aerial reconnaissance photogrammetry that confirmed, in considerable detail, the existence of over 500,000 people distributed in three major and numerous minor agglomerations. (Whether these were refugees or displaced Zairois could not be determined.) This information, also made available to the United Nations, was the non-attributed source of the UNHCR press release of 20 November that also identified the whereabouts of a very large proportion of the 'missing' population. Yet, incredibly, in a press conference in Kigali on 23 November, the U.S. military claimed that they had located only one significant cluster of people which 'by the nature of their movement and other clues can be assumed to be the ex-FAR and militias'. The press were given reassurances that this population appeared to be in 'good shape'. On the basis of this information and repeated assertions of the predominantly

20. *De Morgen*, 9-11 November 1996.
21. *De Morgen*, 16 November 1996.
22. *NRC Handelsblad*, 22 November 1996.
23. Rwandan Ambassador in Brussels, *De Morgen*, 20 November 1996.
24. *Het Volk*, 23-24 November 1996.

military composition of this group, proposals for the deployment of an international military force began to collapse ... We were asked to believe, and many did, that all the remaining Rwandese and Burundian refugees and displaced Zairois had disappeared from eastern Zaire without trace.

However, on the basis of the quality and authority of the information received by Oxfam on 20 November, we feel bound to conclude that as many as 400,000 refugees and unknown numbers of Zairean displaced persons have, in effect, been air-brushed from history (Stockton 1996: 2).

UNHCR did indeed issue such a statement, indicating that some 700,000 refugees remained in eastern Zaire. Spokesperson Melita Sunjic told the press:

We have located these refugees thanks to the satellite photographs and other information obtained during reconnaissance flights carried out in the region, and thanks also to other sources.[25]

As reported in the press, refugee and IDP concentrations had been found west of Masisi (50,000), north of Sake (100,000), north of Bukavu (200,000), south of Bukavu (250,000) and in the Fizi region (100,000). Rwandan officials sneered at the figures. Backed safely by the U.S. official declaration of what the reconnaissance mission had shown, Kigali officials retorted that UNHCR had a habit of exaggerating its figures, so why would anyone want to believe them this time round.[26] The Rwandan ambassador in Brussels used the occasion of the mass return to slam the international community:

The rebels have accomplished the task of the international community. The latter has been watching for the past two years, even though [back in 1994] we asked them to separate the armed forces from the civilian camp population. They did nothing. We are proud that *Africans themselves* have sorted things out. We have been misunderstood and disadvantaged ever since 1959. Everyone then knew about the genocide, but nobody did anything.[27]

The mixing of different forms of identity – 'Africans themselves' followed by 'We' [i.e., Tutsi] – raises questions regarding, firstly, the identity of 'the rebels' and, secondly, regarding refugee perceptions of the fall of Mugunga. Specifically, who 'liberated' Mugunga? and how proud were the returnees that 'Africans themselves' had sorted

25. *La Libre Belgique*, 22 November 1996.
26. *NRC Handelsblad*, 25 November 1996.
27. *De Morgen*, 20 November 1996; emphasis added.

things out? The phrase 'Africans themselves' is crucially significant to the 'refugee cycle' theme, as it suggests a wider conceptualisation of the term voluntary repatriation. The 'self' in 'Africans themselves', as in 'self-repatriation', no longer refers unambiguously to the refugees in question, but rather to a nonspecified body of 'Africans'.

The second question (how proud were the refugees?) will be answered first, since the first question requires a historical overview of the rebellion in eastern Zaire. As the following statements by refugees all make clear, their decision to return was a decision devoid of choice. The first testimony is by Nsengi Yumva, a carpenter from Kigali, who surely spoke for the majority of returnees when recalling that on Thursday, 14 November 1996:

> the *interahamwe* told us we had to leave our homes and follow them or we would die. ... We were so hungry that it was no use to keep on running away. I decided to stay and wait for the rebels' decision on whether they would kill me.[28]

The *interahamwe* did kill in Mugunga, as the militias had done also when fleeing other camps. Refugees returning from Katale and Kahindo regularly reported how the *interahamwe* had killed 'many' when the Rebel Alliance closed in.[29] Later investigations would put at several thousands the number killed, even though it could never be fully established whether the killers were *interahamwe*, ex-FAR or ADFL soldiers.

No running away, no choice. A woman who had left the refugee camps in advance of the rebellion made a similar point. On seeing the refugees come home, this woman, now a member of a local prison committee, said: 'There was no other choice. They have decided that a life in prison is somehow better than being adrift in eastern Zaire'.[30] It should be clarified at this point that the refugees were no longer in Mugunga when on Thursday 14 November 1996 the *interahamwe* ordered them to move deeper into Zaire. By then, Mugunga's refugees were already in Sake, west of Mugunga, where one branch of the AFDL, the feared Mai-Mai troops, had been instructed to cut off the escape route. Given the news blackout at the time, it is useful to be clear about the chronology of the fighting. The following testimony by Anastase Ziherambere, an engineer from Mugunga, is usefully detailed:

28. *International Herald Tribune*, 16 November 1996.
29. *La Libre Belgique*, 28 November 1996.
30. *De Morgen*, 18 November 1996.

The political and military leaders of the camp decided already on Friday [8/11] to make the move to Masisi. So on Saturday [9/11] we fled to near Sake, where we were stopped at the roadblocks of the Mai-Mai. We were caught. Before us were the Mai-Mai, behind us, in Goma, the Banyamulenge.[31]

The refugees were caught in a pincer movement and had no choice. Once caught, they were instructed to return to Rwanda. Kabila gave them their marching orders: it was a do-as-you-are-told repatriation. Off-camera, soldiers of the Rebel Alliance allegedly used megaphones to warn the refugees of what awaited them should they have second thoughts about returning. A voice in Swahili reminded of the real choice: 'Those who are not in Rwanda by tomorrow will be either imprisoned or killed'.[32]

Refugees returning during the initial three-day period had lived mostly in protective environments. They were in reasonable health and had not died of starvation. Those who returned later, however, often women from Katale who had failed to reach Mugunga, told a different story. Independently, many related how 'rebel' soldiers had arrested the men they were with – fathers, husbands, sons – to lead them away. A new chapter had begun. Associated Press correspondent Chris Tomlinson in Goma reported: 'A horrendous drama is unfolding. The rebels are killing off hundreds of men in the forests, … especially along the Bukavu–Walungu–Shabunda road'.[33] Other eyewitnesses also came forward, suggesting:

> for the first time that large numbers of people [were] dying and that soldiers, perhaps on both sides of the conflict, [might] be involved in atrocities. Conditions in the forests were appalling beyond description. One woman returnee said: 'We were all the same in there. We were all starving. When it rained we stood with our mouths open and our hands out.'[34]

But the voices of these women refugees did not alter the pride many officials felt. Nor did they change the elation of leaders like Seth Kamanzi, who had hailed 'the end' of the refugee crisis as 'a magnificent Christmas gift. The return of the refugees is our victory. We have always said that these refugees were being kept hostage. The world now sees we were right'.[35]

---

31. *De Morgen*, 18 November 1996.
32. *De Morgen*, 16 November 1996.
33. *Belang Van Limburg*, 26 November 1996.
34. *International Herald Tribune*, 26 November 1996.
35. *NRC Handelsblad*, 22 November 1996.

With few exceptions – Oxfam, Memisa, MSF, Christian Aid, and some others – the world did indeed see it that way. Many who had given so generously to emergency aid in 1994, now failed to respond. Lulled into complacency, they accepted that the strong-arm African solution was the only solution. And they accepted 'a price' had to be paid.

Who 'liberated' Mugunga?

Having established that the mass repatriation from eastern Zaire was shrouded in controversy and assertive language, to the point where its voluntary nature must be doubted, we now ask: who liberated Mugunga? Answering this question will enable reflection on the 'fairy tale' claim that the Rebel Alliance accomplished the task of the international community and taught that community 'a real lesson'.[36] For the sake of clarity, however, an overview of Rebel Alliance activities in Kivu in the second half of 1996 is necessary. This overview will shed doubt on the Alliance's allegedly local character.

After explaining how Mugunga refugees had been caught in a pincer movement, Anastase Ziherambere (above) gave further details about the battle for Mugunga.

> Initially, Hutu leaders tried to come to an arrangement with the Mai-Mai to allow the refugees a passage. ... The deal included many buses and a formidable amount of dollars. But the Mai-Mai did not keep their word. The roadblocks reappeared on the Wednesday [13/11]. At this point, the FAR encircled the Mai-Mai and killed a good number of them.

For the ex-FAR, it was a case of one battle won, but not the war.

> The following day refugees sobered up. Ziherambere: 'We had always thought we had a strong army. [Leaders] had always impressed upon us that one day they would retake Rwanda. But, when on Thursday [14/11] the Banyamulenge began their assault on the FAR headquarters at Nyamirambo, between Mugunga and Sake, it quickly transpired that there was no truth in that claim. FAR failed to take Sake and were easily outmanoeuvred by the rebels. It was then that the refugee stream got under way. People realised it made no more sense to follow these leaders.
> It seems, however, that nearly the entire FAR army escaped towards Masisi and Kisangani. They departed on Friday [15/11], in disarray, leaving equipment and vehicles behind. They escaped with their families, even though many soldiers mixed in with the refugee stream.[37]

36. *Le Monde*, 26 November 1996.
37. *De Morgen*, 18 November 1996.

The ambiguous stance of the Mai-Mai towards the ex-FAR and *interahamwe* should not come as a surprise. Whilst generally portrayed as firmly committed to the Rebel Alliance, Mai-Mai also pursued a *local* agenda quite different from that of 'Banyamulenge' fighters. This difference in agenda must be understood. For too long, the international community assumed that the people of eastern Zaire were taking up arms against the corrupt Mobutu regime. In reality, however, the notion of a cohesive rebel front was actively nurtured by the Kigali regime to give credibility to the story of a local Zairean uprising. By exaggerating the level of internal cohesion within the ADFL, by promoting the fantasy of uniform agendas and goals, Kigali effectively masked the extent of its own involvement. A look at the history of Kivu reveals a more diverse picture: thoughts of a single *local* agenda (i.e., Kabila's) quickly evaporate.

Kivu: historical developments

Before the arrival of the European colonialists, the sphere of influence of the *Nyiginya* Tutsi dynasty (in south-central Rwanda) stretched into parts of eastern Zaire, including the high plateau above Lake Tanganyika's western shore where Kinyarwanda-speaking Tutsi lived (Newbury 1988; Webster et al. 1992). The link between this plateau region in south Kivu and Rwanda's ruling dynasty was severed, however, by the Berlin Conference of 1885. The Conference made the plateau region part of (what would become) the Belgian Congo. Likewise, Rutshuru, in north Kivu, also became part of the Belgian Congo and its Kinyarwanda-speaking population, mainly Hutu, also stopped paying tribute to the *Nyiginya* king.

For the colonial period, an important difference between north and south Kivu must be noted. Whereas Banyarwanda ('people from Rwanda') in north Kivu comprised two ethnic groups (Hutu and Tutsi), those living in and moving to south Kivu were mainly of Tutsi origin. In the 1920s and 1930s, colonialists encouraged Rwandan Hutu to come to north Kivu to work in the coffee plantations, while Tutsi also emigrated there. Tutsi did so either to decongest Rwanda (in the case of herders) or to take up administrative posts. This huge influx of Banyarwanda, however, threatened to dwarf the presence of other groups in north Kivu; groups referred to as 'autochthonous'.

During Rwanda's Hutu revolution of 1959-61, several thousands of Tutsi again crossed into Kivu, mainly south Kivu, where they would settle and prosper like earlier migrants had done. But unlike the roughly 8,000 Tutsi whose ancestors had lived in the area for some two hundred years, many among the new Tutsi exilés, also referred to as '59-ers', joined the so-called 'Muleliste' movement in eastern Zaire. By 1964, many had moved into 'rebel'-held territory and joined the Armée Populaire de Libération, in which Laurent Kabila served under Soumialot. Exiled Tutsi joined on the principle of 'reciprocal assistance in the course of military engagements' (Lemarchand 1970: 213). Lemarchand specifies this important principle:

> There was a common awareness of the advantages that either party would draw from the realisation of the other's objectives: if the Congolese ['rebels'] were to gain permanent control over the [eastern] border areas, the refugees would then enjoy the benefit of a 'privileged sanctuary' for organising border raids into Rwanda; likewise, if Rwanda's republican [Hutu] regime should fall before the completion of their task, the Congolese could expect similar advantages for themselves (Lemarchand 1970: 213).

This remarkable passage explains in the most lucid terms why some thirty years later a Congolese rebellion could be launched from within a Tutsi-ruled Rwanda.

It was in the early 1960s then, in an atmosphere charged with local resentment against the Tutsi newcomers (Lemarchand 1970: 210), that long-term Tutsi residents in Kivu began to refer to themselves as Banyamulenge, which simply means the people of Mulenge (hill). A different, but not incompatible interpretation is that all Tutsi in south Kivu, 59-ers included, began using the term from about 1973 in order to mask their 'Rwandan' origins and justify their citizenship.[38] In 1971, President Mobutu had indeed granted citizenship to all Banyarwanda living in Zaire. This included the original Banyarwanda, the Rwandan economic migrants of the 1920s and 1930s, and the (Tutsi) refugees of 1959-1961. Importantly, however, Kivu's 'autochthonous' population (Bahunde, Banande, Batembo, Nyanga etc.) never accepted Mobutu's decision. Resenting the wealth of the Banyarwanda, and especially that of those who had arrived in or after 1959, 'autochthonous' leaders began a campaign of hatred against all Tutsi. The campaign peaked following the 'selective genocide' of educated Hutu in Burundi at the hands of the Tutsi-led army in 1972 (Lemarchand and Martin 1974), and remained acute throughout the decade. By 1981, a campaign to strip all Banyarwanda of their citizenship was under way. It called on Kivu's 'autochthonous' groups to step up the effort to reclaim ancestral lands lost to Banyarwanda.

38. *La Libre Belgique*, 30 October 1996.

Ethnic tensions were rekindled when the Rwandese Patriotic Front (RPF) invaded Rwanda in 1990. The reason was simple: young 'Banyamulenge', descendants of the so-called '59-ers', had joined the RPF; a decision which other Kivu residents interpreted as confirming that 'Banyamulenge' (in the wider sense) were not really *Zairois*. But the National Conference in 1991 failed to resolve the nationality issue. As confusion spread and the promised elections of 1995 approached, Kivu's autochthonous groups resorted increasingly to violence against *all* Banyarwanda, Tutsi and Hutu. Zairean politicians exploited the potential for violence, succeeding especially in Masisi and Walikale in 1992-93, when tens of thousands of Banyarwanda were killed in response to their civil disobedience campaign. The latter had disavowed the traditional chiefs to whom land taxes were owed. Following these killings, Hunde and Nyanga groups recovered some of the ancestral lands.

But fortunes would soon change again. The following year, Hunde and Nyanga faced a new threat when Hutu forces (Zairean Hutu and Rwandan Hutu refugees) combined for an all-out assault on Masisi. In contrast to 1993, this time the violence developed more along ethnic lines. This happened not just because of the Hutu refugee influx, but also because of the departure from Kivu to Rwanda of many influential Tutsi, mostly '59-ers'. These Tutsi were returning to Rwanda partly out of a concern for their safety in Zaire, partly because they wanted to return. Many Zaireans, though, felt 'cheated' by their departure, especially by that of 'Banyamulenge' known to have participated in the RPF invasion of Rwanda. Interestingly, whereas the international community (Kigali, the U.S.) time and again stressed that the 'Banyamulenge' were persecuted and expelled from Zaire because of their ethnicity, being given just one week to leave (on 8 October 1996), Kivu's non-Banyarwanda stressed the close Banyamulenge–RPF ties that had developed over a thirty-year period.[39]

The pincer movement: north Kivu's Mai-Mai guerrilla war

When Mugunga fell, its refugees were held in a pincer movement: Mai-Mai, sometimes referred to as Bangilima Mai-Mai, blocked the

---

39. After launching their second guerrilla movement in 1967, the People's Revolution Party (PRP), Soumialot and Kabila continued to work closely with exiled Tutsi soldiers (trained in China). The PRP's armed wing operated from Fizi and the Baraka mountains.

western axis; Banyamulenge soldiers attacked from the east. Mai-Mai guerrilla activities are often situated in the context of the 1993 Masisi-Walikale killings, when, for reasons already explained, the 'autochthonous' population began to cleanse Masisi–Walikale of its Banyarwanda. Little is known about the anarchic Mai-Mai. Simplified, the story goes that many

> years ago, [Hunde] let their more marginal lands in Masisi to Tutsi cattle keepers, often in return for a calf. The Tutsi then enriched these lands, which, over time, resulted in envy on the part of those who owned the land. Since the original owners failed to reclaim these lands when they needed them, they sent in the Mai-Mai warriors to fight the Tutsi.[40]

The story is more complex, though, and involved land leases agreed by Hunde chiefs originally appointed by the Belgian colonialists. With time, starting at independence but increasing after 1981, these leases came to be contested by a new generation of Hunde. In 1993, Hunde warriors, joined by fighters from other autochthonous groups, (re)organised as Mai-Mai to attack and dispossess all Banyarwanda.

For the dispossessed Banyarwanda, revenge became possible in 1994 when the refugee exodus split the Zairean-Rwandaphone Hutu from the Zairean-Rwandaphone Tutsi. The former aligned with the Rwandan Hutu refugees and were joined by paracommando elements of the Zairean army.[41] Pushing into Masisi between November 1995 and May 1996, this joint Hutu force purged the area of its Tutsi and 'autochthonous' Hunde and Nyanga. Thousands died, among them ten Hunde chiefs, while 15,000 Tutsi fled to Rwanda. Tutsi who reached Rwanda were welcomed as Zairean refugees, not fellow Tutsi who knew about genocide, for the Rwanda government wished to highlight the purely local character of the troubles in eastern Zaire. Inside Kivu, the plight of the 250,000 IDPs who streamed out of Masisi was ignored by the international community. IDP camps sprung up in places like Sake (18,000), Minova (15,000) and Goma (30,000). Hunde and some Tutsi also fled t Mweso, where they sought the protection of the Hunde king Bashali, thus indicating that people's relations and politics must never be reduced to essentialising ethnic categories.

Reacting to the displacement, 'autochthonous' Zaireans, especially Hunde and some Nyanga and Nande, once again sent in their Mai-

---

40. *De Standaard*, 26 November 1996.
41. One must not generalise about the Zairean Army. The Amnesty International report of November 1996 makes this clear: 'Whereas paracommando units were frequently accused of being "pro-Banyarwanda", other military units [e.g. the DSP] were collaborating with Hunde combatants to attack Kivu's Banyarwanda population.'

Mai guerrilla fighters. Not being a disciplined army, these Mai-Mai 'pockets' embarked on a campaign of blind terror, striking not just at Banyarwanda but at the entire Kivu population. The campaign focused on Rutshuru district, from where local people fled in vast numbers. On 10 May 1996, for instance, Mai-Mai set up base in Vitchumbi, a small fishing village on Lake Edward. For nine days they terrorised the village, looting, raping, and killing several Banyarwanda. Then on 19 May, Zairean soldiers of 'Operation Mbata' moved in to flush out the Mai-Mai. They killed a local pastor, raided and burnt houses, arrested and killed local men suspected of being Mai-Mai rebels (Amnesty International 1996). When Operation Mbata left Vitchumbi four days later, the security forces who had fled on 10 May returned to the village. They were violent and demanded protection money from the bewildered villagers. What happened in Vitchumbi also happened in a dozen other locations in Rutshuru.

Destabilising attacks on north Kivu also came from outside the country. In June 1996, Bunagana in Jomba parish was attacked by members of the Uganda People's Defence Forces (UPDF) acting in collaboration with the Tutsi-dominated RPA. Responding to this cross-border attack, local (Zairean) Hutu set upon (Zairean) Tutsi and killed thirty-six. When the violence against Tutsi spread all over Rutshuru, international observers 'saw proof' that the Tutsi genocide continued in eastern Zaire. Rutshuru suffered its most tragic night of ethnic cleansing when local Hutu aided by *interahamwe* and ex-FAR soldiers from Katale massacred Tutsi residents in the town. No Tutsi remained in Rutshuru after that night, but some managed to escape to Uganda and Rwanda.[42] The organisation Human Rights Watch (1996) accused the international community of silence and indifference, and France of continuing its aid to Zaire.

By mid-October 1996, roughly at the time that 'Banyamulenge' troops attacked towns and refugee camps in south Kivu, Mai-Mai began their assault on camps in the north. They targeted not only the camps but, importantly, also Zairean Hutu (Banyarwanda). The violence quickly revealed – but not, it seems, to the international community – that the Mai-Mai agenda was to cleanse Kivu of every form of Rwandan influence, an agenda diametrically opposed to that pursued by 'Banyamulenge' and the ADFL leadership.[43]

---

42. *Le Soir*, 16 July 1996.
43. There is a strong possibility that some Mai-Mai are paid by Banande chiefs and businessmen, as the 'autochthonous' Banande are particularly keen to see all Banyarwanda disappear from Kivu. Their weapons are most likely to be obtained from or via FAZ troops not allied to Hutu refugee leaders.

Given the three year (and more) Mai-Mai campaign of terror against Banyarwanda, Tutsi and Hutu, it was most surprising that Mai-Mai would fight alongside the Kigali-backed 'Banyamulenge' in their battle for Mugunga. How could this alliance be explained in the light of recent history? My own inclination was to think in terms of their common enemy: Hutu refugees. Another explanation, highly plausible, was that the Rwandese Patriotic Army (RPA) had enlisted and paid certain Mai-Mai groups to give the fall of Goma the local character it required if Rwanda (and the U.S.) were to be absolved of the suspicion of direct involvement. Journalist Stephen Smith developed the point. About the (Bangilima) Mai-Mai he wrote in early November:

> [this] small ethnic group from the north of Rutshuru has arrived on the scene over the past few days. In actual fact, what we are seeing is the presence of a 'Bangilima commando' which has liberated several hundred [Zairean] Tutsi held captive in Goma's church of the Holy Spirit. ... Certain witnesses, however, claim that the action was led by RPA troops. The Rwandan government has made use of Bangilima fighters to give the 'rebellion' in Eastern Zaire its 'autochthonous' character and thus mask its own direct military involvement.[44]

This made sense since Mai-Mai guerrilla groups had also fought in Lumumba's nationalist–Marxist movement in the 1960s. But few journalists understood the tenuous nature of the Bangilima–'Banyamulenge' alliance. They rather focused on the 'exotic' behaviour of Bangilima fighters: their going into battle naked, their ferocity, their sexuality, their 'irrational' belief in witchcraft.[45]

When the 'Banyamulenge' assault on Mugunga camp got under way, Mai-Mai fighters had taken up positions in and around Sake, west of Mugunga. Their objective, officially, was to cut off the western axis along which ex-FAR, militias and refugees would attempt to escape. Eventually though, following bribes and battle, Mai-Mai failed to stop the hard core of the génocidaires, who escaped towards Masisi and Kisangani. That Mai-Mai were reluctant, untrustworthy Alliance Rebels would be confirmed when André Kisasse Ngandu, the ADFL's second in command, later dismissed them as a negligible presence (see below).

44. *Libération*, 4 November 1996.
45. One (anonymous) Flemish anthropologist reacted to the media fixation, pointing out that '[when] we jump into our BMWs and turn the ignition key, or when we start up our computers, then we too appear to outsiders as people with strange practices, as witchdoctors. Africans say the same of us as we of them' (*Belang Van Limburg*, 7 November 1996).

The second pincer: south Kivu's 'Banyamulenge' uprising

After the RPF victory in 1994, many 'Banyamulenge' soldiers and their families arrived in Rwanda hoping to settle there. Others, however, stayed in South Kivu and organised themselves in self-defence against the Zairean army (FAZ) and later the regrouped ex-FAR. The government of Rwanda never denied it supported the 'Banyamulenge', but persistently denied that its own troops operated on Zairean soil. Self-defence pure and simple, is how Rwandan authorities portrayed the 'Banyamulenge' uprising. Officially, 'Banyamulenge' began their rebellion after south Kivu's vice-governor Lwasi Ngabo Lwabanji gave them seven days in which to leave the country. Kinshasa saw it differently and accused Rwanda, Burundi and the international community of destabilising Kivu. UN agencies and aid workers were condemned for collaborating with Kigali and condoning the presence of Rwandan forces in Kivu. Uganda's involvement in eastern Zaire also became a matter of intrigue, speculation and high probability.[46] Whether the 'Banyamulenge' uprising and Rebel Alliance constituted local movements, or whether they were *téléguidés* from Kigali, and ultimately Kampala and Washington, is an issue that still preoccupies analysts. Informed journalists, however, have eagerly reported how the Alliance Rebels speak several versions of Swahili; a diversity regarded as proof that the Kivu war could not be an internal affair. Many Alliance Rebels speak the 'elegant Swahili' from Uganda, Rwanda or Tanzania; a Swahili different from that of eastern Zaire.[47]

The Kigali regime, however, strenuously denied that 'Banyamulenge' were its 'fifth column'. In early November 1996, Rwanda's Foreign Affairs minister, Anastase Gasana, denied even having a link with Kabila. 'We do not have any special links with the Alliance

46. On 21 September 1996, after three days of heavy fighting between FAZ and Banyamulenge, some thirty-four trucks with Rwandan and Ugandan number plates crossed from Rwanda into Burundi and then into Zaire, bringing military equipment, troops and advisers. Inhabitants near the border post of Gatumba, Burundi, reported how the vehicles returned empty just four hours later. It was now a matter of weeks before the towns of Uvira and Bukavu would fall, and the refugees would be attacked and dispersed.

47. Alliance Rebels sometimes use Ugandan phrases: like '*Vipi?*' ('what news?'), or '*Bulingi Seko*' instead of the local '*jambo*', '*jambo sana*' or '*abarigani*'. Some soldiers mix a lot of Swahili in their Kinyarwanda, and speak this Swahili with an English accent (*Het Volk*, 2 November 1996). But there are reports of local boys who left Kivu for Rwanda in 1994 to come home in August 1996 (*Het Nieuwsblad*, 29 November 1996).

of Laurent-Désiré Kabila. These people have taken up arms to secure their own survival. We can understand this, because we have ourselves been the victim of genocide.'[48] Gasana categorically rejected any suggestion of Rwandan involvement: 'the events ... are to do with Zaire's internal problems and do not in any way involve Rwanda. The Banyamulenge are at home in Zaire. ... The issue is not a regional one.'[49] To this, Laurent Kabila would later add that 'Banyamulenge' had been joined by 'Zaireans from every corner of the country'.[50]

Throughout this episode, Paul Kagame, Rwanda's Vice-President and supreme RPA commander, remained diplomatic and aloof: 'Rwanda is not involved, but I, Kagame, cannot stop young Banyamulenge soldiers who wish to step out of the RPA to go home and fight their war.' Kagame pointed out, however, that if Zaire continued its aggression against Rwanda, it would have to become involved.[51] After Cyangugu was shelled from Bukavu, and the RPA fired back, Kagame said: 'S'il faut faire la guerre, je la ferai'.[52] Several months later, as Kabila's ADFL swept through Zaire, Kagame admitted he was holding back information on the extent of Rwanda's military support, and promised to tell all in about a year's time.[53]

For his part, President Pasteur Bizimungu was less circumspect about Rwanda's 'special link' with Kivu. He declared his interest in Kivu by suggesting that the Banyamulenge area was really part of Rwanda. Reacting to the expulsion order by Zaire, Bizimungu commented: 'if the Zaireans wanted to send the Banyamulenge back, could they not also then return their land?'.[54] In the same issue of *Le Soir*, Colette Braeckman, an RPF sympathiser, reported that the news from Goma did indeed suggest a more direct involvement by the RPA:

> The latest news from Goma is especially intriguing. It seems that the Rwandan army has not only attacked the refugee camps in order to cause their dispersion, but that it also attacked the [Zairean] military camp of Rumangabo in North Kivu.[55]

48. *De Morgen*, 6 November 1996.
49. *La Libre Belgique*, 31 October-1 November 1996.
50. *Le Soir*, 23-24 November 1996.
51. *NRC Handelsblad*, 30 October 1996.
52. *Figaro*, 31 October 1996.
53. *Le Soir*, 16 April 1997.
54. *Le Soir*, 31 October-1 November 1996.
55. Original text: 'Les dernières nouvelles en provenance de Goma sont également préoccupantes. Il apparaît que l'armée rwandaise ne s'est pas seulement contentée de tirer sur les camps des réfugiés pour provoquer leur dispersion, mais qu'elle a également attaqué le camp militaire de Rumangabo au Nord-Kivu' (*Le Soir*, 31 October-1 November 1996).

After Mugunga fell, Braeckman added to the growing suspicion of RPA involvement: Hutu militias and the ex-FAR had fled towards Masisi and Kisangani following their defeat at the hands of 'the "rebels" (and most likely the Kigali army)'.[56]

When he appeared on the scene, Laurent Kabila, too, was cautious always to stress the strictly internal character of his mission:

> The Alliance of the Democratic Forces for the Liberation of Congo-Zaire wages above all a national liberation war. [For the region we now occupy] our aim is to install a provisional government charged with the preparation of real elections. In the towns we have liberated – Uvira, Bukavu and Goma – we seek first to re-establish law and order, next, to install an administration of responsible people.[57]

For many, though, Kabila could only be the puppet of Kigali's RPF-led regime, a 'local hero' needed to persuade the world of Rwanda's noninvolvement. Zaire's ambassador in Brussels, Mr Kimbulu, clarified that the concept of 'Zairean Rebels' was wrongly constructed. These so-called rebels

> are used by Rwanda. They have been there [in Zaire] since the 1960s and now, all of a sudden, they are waking up to liberate Zaire! All of a sudden, they have tanks, mortars and rocket launchers! Besides the fact that one does not liberate Zaire from Rwanda, there are changes afoot in Kinshasa. There is no need for a war [orchestrated from Kigali] to force changes [within Zaire].[58]

The UN remained remarkably silent on the issue of Zaire's sovereignty. Only Erik Derycke, Belgium's Foreign Affairs Minister, reminded Gasana of 'certain fundamental aspects of international law, with direct reference to the sovereignty of Zaire'.[59]

The involvement of RPA troops in Zaire, and perhaps even U.S. advisers, is a topic for continued debate. Of late, confirmation rather than denial has been on the lips of many commentators, partly because of reports that three U.S. military advisers died in Kivu in early March.[60] The important point, though, is that the Rwandan Government backed the ADFL logistically and militarily (whether in situ or from a distance makes little difference) and that this backing

56. *Le Soir*, 16-17 November 1996.
57. *La Libre Belgique*, 5 November 1996.
58. *La Libre Belgique*, 8 November 1996.
59. *La Libre Belgique*, 8 November 1996.
60. *La Libre Belgique*, 29-31 March 1997; see also K. Austin in *NRC Handelsblad*, 7 November 1996.

enabled Kabila's ADFL to seize half a million refugees in a pincer movement to force them out of Zaire.

By late October 1996, when 'Banyamulenge' troops had moved up to within reach of Goma, there was agreement in the world of aid and diplomacy that 'organised repatriation' was the only solution. This consensus notwithstanding, the question remained as to why the refugees were still in Zaire more than two years after going into exile. Had there never been an earlier opportunity to separate the extremists from the main body of innocent refugees?

Refugees as hostages. Life in Mugunga, 1994-96

If outsiders failed to understand the relationship between (Bangilima) Mai-Mai and the Rebel Alliance, if they were also uncertain about the extent and nature of Rwanda's support to 'Banyamulenge' fighters, then the same must be said of how the international community understood life in the refugee camps. As I have argued elsewhere (Pottier 1996a; 1996b), international observers and aid workers alike were poorly informed about, and hardly interested in, camp experience and politics. This lack of interest – most clearly expressed in UNHCR's admission that it did not care about who made the refugees go home (Wilkinson, above) – deserves further comment. My focus here is on the widely held assumption that *continued intimidation* prevailed in the camps.

The portrayal of camp leaders as continuous intimidators permeated media reporting, too. In the *International Herald Tribune*, for instance, we read at the time of the mass repatriation, that

> [over] the past two years, the guerrilla leaders in the camps have fought to prevent refugees from going home, using propaganda and intimidation. In essence, they have held their own people hostage, playing on the sympathies of aid organisations for the refugees.
>
> They have also rearmed themselves, raising 'war taxes' by exacting payment from people working for the aid organisations and selling stolen food aid for weapons according to a recent UN report.[61]

While the stealing and the taxes (the latter known in the camps as *aide aux enfants abandonnés*) cannot be denied, one must be careful not to misconstrue, and generalise about, the nature and level of intimidation. The claim that extremist leaders waged their campaign of terror unabated over the two years in exile is at odds with the

61. *International Herald Tribune*, 14 November 1996.

'mood swings' the refugee population experienced. Essentially, violence and intimidation were discontinuous, even in Mugunga. There were moments when the grip of the militias was not as strong as it had been in the early days in exile. The more relaxed grip, however, tightened again in the four months preceding the 'liberation' of Mugunga, when the militias became more desperate and ready to use force on refugees. The impetus for this *resurgence* of extreme forms of intimidation and violence, including murder, can be traced back to August 1995, when Zaire forcefully repatriated 15,000 refugees. The combination of this forceful intervention and the harsh reduction in aid flows with which this coincided, meant: (a) that militias stepped up the armed struggle to conquer Masisi; (b) that military incursions into Rwanda accelerated, especially in the four months before Mugunga fell; and (c) that militias toughened up against disenchanted refugees suspected of wanting to go home.

That there were ups-and-downs in intimidation levels makes sense, since camp authorities, no matter how ruthless, cannot rule on the basis of intimidation and force alone. Even the harshest of regimes must hand out rewards some of the time. Once this is understood, it becomes easier to refute the simplistic view that Rwandan camp authorities were invariably intimidators who held refugees hostage *at all times*. Extremist leaders and the militias did resort to violence as a means of control, yet this violence and intimidation were not a constant feature of life in the camps. There are examples, for instance, of hard-line commune-level leaders moving away from their communes under pressure from 'ordinary citizens', especially after UNHCR withdrew 'salaries' for low-level authorities who worked as camp assistants (Pottier 1996b). Their luck had run out. There were also times when refugees returned to Rwanda regularly and in numbers. By mid-January 1995, UNHCR estimated that from the Goma camps alone some 200,000 refugees had successfully repatriated, meeting only little resistance from the militias.[62] The defiance of the militias in late 1996, in contrast, was a last desperate attempt to reassert their much weakened authority.

The faltering grip of the authorities and militias is most vividly portrayed in a diary kept by the ex-FAR officer who headed the 23rd Brigade. Found after the evacuation of Mugunga, the diary starts in the early days in exile and informs about both military plans and camp morale. In mid-1995, and again in September 1996, this FAR officer expresses concern over the 'gap', the apathy, that had developed between the armed forces and the refugee population:

62. *Gazet van Antwerpen*, 16 January 1995.

refugees were no longer fully behind their leaders. By mid-1995, the ex-FAR and former regime were going through a bad patch: the number of meetings at the ex-FAR headquarters had decreased, the armed forces were demoralised and, as I myself learned in Mugunga at the time, the civilian population had gained better control over food aid distributions (Pottier 1996a; 1996b). The officer voiced concern, too, about Madame Hélène, the Australian woman who wondered around Katale camp telling refugees she had had a vision of their imminent mass return to Rwanda. The officer:

> This woman preaches the return of the Rwandan refugees. She says it is God Almighty who has announced the event. Her presence is beginning to have a negative impact on the refugees. The worst consequence would be if many refugees went back as a result of this so-called message from God. For our enemies this would be a great political and media victory, to the detriment of the Hutu.[63]

The diary's authenticity rings through not just in the chilling details of incursions into Rwanda, but also in the assessment of the incursions by 'Rwandans' into Kivu; incursions aiming to sour the relationship between refugees and the local population. The officer:

> It is within this setting that soldiers infiltrate North Kivu, particularly those who came from that region before being drafted in to fight alongside the RPF when it began the war in October 1990. The aim of these infiltrations would seem to be to cause anguish in the hearts of the Zairean population, to raise the anger of the people, and to entice them to attack the Rwandan refugees.[64]

The psychological effect of such incursions on the camp population was devastating indeed, the more so since refugees knew about the demoralised ex-FAR. After two years of misery and waiting, without a solution ever coming in sight, many refugees declined to give much attention to the voice of authority. The officer's diary confirms what some refugees (see A. Zihambere, above) would later articulate: that by the time the 'Banyamulenge' offensive set in, the majority of refugees in north Kivu were more than ready to denounce the

---

63. *Le Figaro*, 20 November 1996.
64. *Le Figaro*, 20 November 96. Original text: 'C'est dans ce cadre que se font des infiltrations de militaires au nord du Kivu, surtout ceux originaires de la région, et qui ont été recrutés pour combattre à côté du FPR lors de la guerre d'octobre 1990. Ces infiltrations auraient pour mission de commettre des forfaits au sein de la population zaïroise, pour susciter la colère de cette dernière et la pousser à s'attaquer aux réfugiés rwandais.'

extremists and accept that repatriation was the only option remaining. By September 1996, the writing was on the wall. The officer:

> The population of Mugunga and Lac Vert is discouraged by armed banditry, warns a report dated 30 September 1996. This [banditry] is the reason why refugees are increasingly making their way to Goma. All this has been caused by a leadership vacuum in the camps ... Compared with the past, the refugees are returning [to Rwanda] in relatively large numbers, and they are not educated [*encadrés*] in matters of ideology.[65]

This last statement, and the diary as a whole, must stand central in any reconstruction of what happened in Mugunga. Here is a military leader who admits that refugees were ready to go back.

Repatriation was indeed what many refugees prepared for, mentally and practically. A man who returned to Rwanda in mid-November, Alois Karanbera, explained, for instance, that at Mugunga he had been involved in preparing children for their return to Rwanda. Children had been instructed that should they be separated from parents or guardians when fleeing Mugunga, they had to make every effort to run towards the Rwanda border.[66] Crucially, Karanbera's testimony confirms how 'ordinary refugees' distanced themselves from the extremist leadership, even in Mugunga.

But the story of the mass repatriation must not end here. There are two additional angles to be considered. Firstly, there is the issue of why no multinational force, preferably neutral, was ever mobilised to intervene, separate and disarm the Hutu extremists at times when it would have been possible to do so with limited loss of life. The first half of 1995 would have been ideal for such an intervention. As the do-nothing option was chosen instead, the local 'Banyamulenge' (a term to be defined most broadly) decided to take the situation into their own hands. They operated with the backing and guidance from Kigali and, as their strong signals reveal, with the approval of the U.S. The resulting mass repatriation, however, happened with such massive loss of life that the term genocide is certain to be used in future. Secondly, the half million or so refugees who returned to Rwanda from Goma were forced to return *at once*. The repatriation happened at gun point, and so cannot qualify as voluntary.

65. *Le Figaro*, 20 November 1996. Original text: 'La population de Mugunga et du Lac Vert est découragée par le banditisme armé, avertit un rapport en date du *30 septembre 1996*. C'est ainsi que *les gens s'exilent de plus en plus vers Goma*. Cela découle du manque de direction des camps ... Les réfugiés rentrent relativement nombreux comparé au passé, et ils ne sont pas encadrés, surtout en matière d'idéologie' (emphasis added).
66. *De Morgen*, 18 November 1996.

Conclusion: terminology in complex repatriations

The opportunity to send in an international force, preferably coordinated by the OAU, was lost irretrievably in the second half of 1996 when intimidation levels and violence in the camps started to rise again. Those responsible for the genocide in Rwanda knew they were cornered: they re-tightened their grip on refugees, stepped up their murderous incursions into Rwanda, and made (unrealistic?) plans to reconquer the country. It was this return to *intimidation and violence*, epitomised in the killing of refugees unwilling or unable to flee deeper into Zaire in November 1996, which 'confirmed' the less than accurate impression that militias and ex-FAR had maintained a continuous, unwavering grip on refugees over the entire time in exile.

Prepared to accept the Washington–Kigali–Geneva view that the refugees *of late 1996* needed help in their quest for repatriation, I nonetheless believe it necessary to consider further issues: first, whether the timing of the 'liberation' was right, and second, whether the refugees' desire to be free from the extremists implied a readiness to go home unconditionally and without delay. If the majority of refugees shared Kigali's wish for separation from the extremists, which they did, did it then automatically follow that they were ready to be herded back across the border in the way it happened? Was this return 'now and without conditions', with hundreds of thousands of refugees staying behind and facing death, a fair price to pay or was it, to follow through Emma Bonino's argument, a case of flagrant deportation rooted in international complacency?

As it happened, the returnees could not stray from the road that led to the Rwandan border once the mass repatriation had begun. Had the international community intervened to physically protect refugees, as it should have done in the spirit of the Geneva Convention and well before November 1996, then with time, resources and adequate information, many refugees would have gone home voluntarily. And some would have stayed. But the intervention force did not materialise. As a result, civilian refugees were separated from the extremists *voluntarily*, but repatriated *by force*. (This also happened in Tanzania, where the use of force by the Tanzanian army was more clearly in evidence.) To pretend that refugees would not have crossed the border had they not been 'absolutely sure that they [would] get proper treatment back in Rwanda'[67] is to want to contribute to fairy tales.

67. Baroness Chalker, British Minister for Overseas Development, CNN, 16 November 1996.

The refugees' fairly unanimous desire to part from the militias and ex-FAR did not coincide with a similarly unanimous wish for sudden repatriation. Without a humanitarian corridor, without a safe zone that would enable the returnees to think twice about immediate repatriation, there could never be 'voluntary repatriation with dignity', the ideal favoured by UNHCR and refugees worldwide (Harrell-Bond and Voutira 1992). That right was denied. Instead, the international community, the U.S. in particular, sided with the government of Rwanda and accepted that a 'higher need' (my term) overrode individual preferences and international conventions, thus making sacrifice acceptable. This 'higher need' was the need for national and regional security, for a buffer zone to protect Rwanda from its enemies in Zaire.

The role of the U.S. as a catalyst in the 'African solution' needs to be acknowledged here. Most noteworthy is that the U.S. abandoned its intention to send ground troops for the 'corridor' plan the very day the mass repatriation got under way. Following the 'liberation' of Mugunga, the American Embassy in Kigali issued a statement, through spokesman Paul Patin, making it clear that the very thought of an intervention was now 'bullshit'.[68] This was not such a sudden decision, though. As Joseph Ndahimana, spokesperson for the moderate '*Rwanda Pour Tous*', observed, what happened in the six weeks prior to the 'liberation' corresponded with what Richard McCall of the United States Agency for International Development (USAID) had proposed at the Geneva Round Table in June 1996: the camps in eastern Zaire would be closed once and for all.[69] For Ndahimana, the mass repatriation of mid-November was an American–Rwandan plan, with Ugandan and South African inputs, dressed up as an 'indigenous revolution'.

By early November 1996, if not before, UNHCR went along with the American–Rwandan plan. The Washington–Kigali Alliance was by then sufficiently strong, and Kabila's ADFL Alliance sufficiently comfortable on the battlefield, for UNHCR to drop its customary insistence on 'voluntary' repatriation. UNHCR now talked of 'organised repatriation'.[70] Although the concept was by then acceptable also to many aid workers, organisations like MSF-Holland continued to insist that the repatriation be 'progressive, not abrupt'.[71] In the same spirit, MSF, Oxfam, ICRC and some other agencies continued to call for a multinational military intervention even after the half million returnees had crossed back into Rwanda

68. *NRC Handelsblad*, 25 November 1996.
69. see *De Standaard*, 22 June 1996; *Financieel Ekonomische Tijd*, 21 December 1996.
70. *De Morgen*, 5 November 1996.
71. *De Morgen*, 5 November 1996.

(Stockton 1996). It was too late: the macabre fate of the missing refugees and many Zairean IDPs had been sealed.

Zaire's IDPs must not be excluded from the analysis of how the Rwanda refugee crisis 'ended'. Among the 'autochthonous' groups, hundreds of thousands had become displaced after the arrival of the Rwandan Hutu refugees in 1994. Following the departure of half a million of these same refugees, the IDPs would not now simply go home and live happily ever after. They too would need 'sorting out' by their new Banyamulenge/Banyarwanda masters. How the new masters will deal with the internally displaced remains uncertain at the time of writing, but may have been foreshadowed in the way the ADFL 'thanked' the Mai-Mai for their assistance. After the battle for Mugunga was won, André Kisasse Ngandu, Vice-President of the Rebel Alliance, had this to say:

> Yes, we found the Mai-Mai here when we liberated East Kivu. We told them at once they could not fight any further. Those boys have plundered and raped on a grand scale. We brought them together in a camp near Sake, where they are now being trained. After which they can join our liberation movement. As you can see, we are well organised.[72]

In the post-Mugunga days, it is conceivable that Banya-mulenge/ADFL will 'sort out' the autochthonous (mostly Hunde) IDPs to avenge the slaughter of Tutsi in 1993. It would be very short-sighted if analysts were to reduce the 'Banyamulenge' uprising to a movement aiming simply to reach Kinshasa and oust Mobutu. 'Banyamulenge' may have a *national* agenda as part of their ADFL affiliation, but they also have a (new) *local* agenda, which is to subjugate the autochthonous groups of eastern Zaire. The fraught relationship between 'Banyamulenge' and Kivu's 'autochthonous' groups, however, may also be the beginning of a new power struggle. In March 1997, the new governor of south Kivu declared that several 'Banyamulenge' had taken advantage of the confusion of war to move into high-level positions. He told them to step down and make room for 'autochthonous' Zaireans.[73] As international agendas become clearer, it is not unthinkable that the much applauded *local uprising* of 'the Banyamulenge' will disappear into the mists of history. One thing is clear, though. Awash with heavy weaponry and *new* reasons for antagonism between 'Banyamulenge', Banyarwanda and 'autochthonous' groups, Kivu's cycle of violence and displacement has certainly not come to an end.

72. *Belang Van Limburg,* 25 November 1996.
73. *Het Volk,* 18 March 1997.

The Rwandan refugee crisis and its 'solution' must not be glossed over in ahistorical, apolitical terms. It does not help to be vague. When Augustine Mahiga, UNHCR, referred to the events of November 1996 as *'une coïncidence malheureuse d'événements malheureux qui peut mener à une issue positive'*, he was sharply condemned by Faustin Twagiramungu, the Prime Minister of Rwanda's first RPF-led government. Twagiramungu interpreted Mahiga's statement as reflecting the complacency of the international community.[74] Such complacency is neither negligible nor new in the Great Lakes region. Back in 1972, following the selective genocide of educated Hutu in Burundi, during which 80,000–200,000 Hutu died at the hands of the Tutsi-dominated army, United States officials were conspicuous 'mainly by [their] sheer indifference' Chomsky and Herman 1979: 105, cited in Malkki 1995b: 35).

So long as the gruesome fate of the missing refugees and IDPs remains unsolved and unexplained, it will be difficult to share in Mahiga's hope that the multiple traumas of the Rwanda Crisis might have a positive outcome. His words, however, reflect the enormous complexity of the mass repatriation from Mugunga and the inappropriateness of using a simple label to describe what has happened in the aftermath of the 1994 genocide and war. Even the term 'complex repatriation', although an improvement on voluntary–involuntary dichotomy, cannot adequately describe the unique mixture of elements found in the repatriation that followed the seizure of Mugunga.

Postscript, July 1997

Paul Kagame, Rwanda's Vice-President and Defence Minister, has kept his word. On 9 July 1997, he informed *The Washington Post* that the Rwandese Patriotic Army had planned, led and fought in the rebellion that ousted Zaire's Mobutu Sese Seko. RPA troops had been centrally involved in the capture of Zaire's major towns, including Kinshasa. The Alliance of Democratic Forces for the Liberation of Congo-Zaire (ADFL), Kagame revealed, had been his creation. He, not Kabila, had taken charge. Set up in response to international indifference over continued Hutu aggression against Rwanda, the ADFL's objectives had been to dismantle the camps, destroy the structure of the ex-FAR and Hutu militias and, finally, to topple Mobutu and install Kabila.

---

74. *Le Soir*, 30 October 1996.

Facing allegations of human rights abuses and genocide against Hutu in eastern Zaire, now renamed the Democratic Republic of the Congo, Kagame denied that refugees had been systematically slaughtered. He dismissed the allegations as part of a UN smear campaign which aimed to 'deflect the blame' for their own failure to act in eastern Zaire. '[And] when things blew up in their faces, they blamed us.' Finally, Kagame commended Washington for 'taking the right decisions to let it proceed'.[75]

Acknowledgements

I thankfully acknowledge the insightful comments which René Lemarchand (University of Florida; USAID, Ghana) and James Fairhead (SOAS, London University) have made on a draft version of this article. Sincere thanks are also due to the Leverhulme Trust for the 1997 research fellowship which permitted the present materials to be analysed and prepared for publication. Responsibility for its content, however, must remain my own.

75. The very close relationship between the RPF-led government in Kigali and the U.S. military precedes the RPF attack on Rwanda in October 1990, when Kagame was still an officer in Yoweri Museveni's liberation army. On the second day of the RPF attack, after Major-General Fred Rwigyema died on the battlefield, Kagame hastily left the training centre at Fort Leavenworth, where Museveni's Banyarwanda officers trained, to assume the military command of the RPF (Prunier 1995: 92-96).

10

From 'Refugee' to 'Repatriate': Russian Repatriation Discourse in the Making

Hilary Pilkington and *Moya Flynn*

When the Soviet Union collapsed in 1991, Russia and the other newly independent states had no legislative or institutional framework for monitoring or managing large migrational flows, still less 'forced' migrations and refugee streams. During the Soviet period 'immigration' into the USSR had been virtually nonexistent and migration between constituent members of the Union ('interrepublican migration') was treated largely as an issue of rational economic planning.[1] In the post-Soviet period, however, Russia has found it necessary to develop rapidly legislative and executive structures to manage a range of population movements. More than one hundred migrational flows have been identified in the post-Soviet space, ranging from the organised and planned withdrawal of Russian military personnel from Eastern Europe and some of the Newly Independent States to the flight from ethnic and military conflict in many former republics (Tajikistan, Uzbekistan, Moldova, Armenia, Azerbaijan and Georgia) and within the Russian Federation itself (North Osetia, Chechnia). UNHCR estimates that there are currently nine million displaced people on the territory of the former Soviet Union.

1. Although there were a number of state-organised deportations of particular ethnic groups as well as flights from ecological catastrophe and ethnic conflict during the Soviet period, these were not recognised at the time as 'forced migrations'.

Table 10.1. *Types of repatriation in the post-Soviet space*

Type of 'repatriation'	Examples	Volume and direction
Return to 'ethnic homeland'	Armenians, Jews, Germans, Poles, Greeks.	Concentrated East–West flow from former Soviet republics to Germany, Israel, USA and Greece.
'Delayed repatriation'	Crimean Tatars, Volga Germans[1]	Movement within the former Soviet space primarily from Central Asia to Crimea and the Volga region of Russia as well as out-migration to Germany.[2]
Refugee repatriation	Georgia, South Osetia, North Osetia, Abkhazia, Azerbaijan, Armenia, Tajikistan, Chechnia	Acute outflows followed by slow process of return hindered by continued hostilities and political and institutional instability.
Postcolonial population movement	Ethnic Russians and Russophones in the former Soviet republics	Steady flow from former Soviet republics into Russia averaging 875,000 annually (1989–96) and peaking in 1994 at 1.14 million.

Sources: Shevtsova 1992; Terekhov 1994; *Demograficheskii Ezhegodnik Rossii* 1995: 402, 422; Aushev 1996; Grankina 1996; Michugina and Rakhmaninova 1996: 44; OSI Forced Migrations Project 1996).

1. Both these ethnic groups were originally granted their own autonomous Soviet Socialist Republics within the Soviet Union but were deported during the Second World War – the Volga Germans primarily to Siberia and rural Kazakstan, the Crimean Tatars to rural Uzbekistan.
2. Crimean Tatars have been involved in a spontaneous repatriation since rehabilitation but this became a mass movement only in the late 1980s following official permission from the Soviet government (in 1989) to return to Crimea. By 1996 250,000 Crimean Tatars had returned to Crimea (OSI Forced Migration Projects 1996). In 1992, following the relaxation of exit regulations, a record 195,000 Germans left the former USSR for Germany. However, discussion of the reestablishment of an autonomous territory in the Volga region and the allocation of German government funds to aid German settlement in the Volga region has generated a semi-organised repatriation movement within the former Soviet Union.

Classifications and typologies of these flows are as varied as the organisations and individuals monitoring them but at least four 'repatriation' movements are identifiable in the post-Soviet space (Table 10.1). Locating these four 'types' of repatriation within the categories generally employed in repatriation literature – refugee repatriation, return labour migration and post-colonial population movement – is problematic. Not only is there evidence of different types of repatriation in the former Soviet space, but individual migration flows themselves defy neat categorisation; rather they cut across and challenge these boundaries. The implications of this will be illustrated in this chapter through an examination of the largest repatriation in post-Soviet Russia – the movement of Russians and Russophones from the newly independent states to Russia.[2]

Returning Russians: repatriation theory confronts post-Soviet reality

Whilst the return of ethnic Russians to Russia may appear to be a classic example of post-colonial population movement, the actual migratory experience of those involved suggests it is more a process of *leaving* than of returning home. Returnees often feel themselves to be in refugee-type situations, forced to flee their homes due to ethnic conflict and overt or covert discrimination.[3] Since July 1992, the Federal Migration Service (FMS) of the Russian Federation has been monitoring migrational flows from the former republics and registering those who provide evidence that they were forced to leave their former place of residence as a result of persecution. Of the three million people who have moved from the former republics to Russia since then, by 1 January 1996 just over one million had been registered as forced migrants or refugees. The implication of this registration process is that the majority of migrants are moving *voluntarily*, deciding perhaps that their economic and social prospects would now be best served by returning to Russia.

2. The return of Russians from the former republics to their ethnic or historical homeland is the largest repatriation flow in the former Soviet space. This is because of the sheer size of the Russian 'diaspora'; there were 25.3 million ethnic Russians living in Soviet republics other than the Russian Federation at the time of the last Soviet census of 1989. A further three million people of non-Russian ethnic origin belong to ethnic groups whose homeland is part of the Russian Federation and, in total, 11 million nonethnic Russians living outside their titular republic are considered to have a primary cultural affinity to Russia and thus to be potential returnees.
3. Such in-migrants cite, in particular, the replacement of Russian as the official state language, the restriction of access to Russian language schools and universities and the reduction in availability of Russian language media as the reason for their exodus.

While this chapter cannot claim to include within its scope an adequate analysis of the diversity of experience of the Russians in the former Soviet republics, nor of their motivations for leaving, it is important to note that Russians began to migrate from the central Russian territories to the periphery as early as the sixteenth century. This means that some members of the current Russian diaspora have roots in their current places of residence which span a number of generations. It was in the Soviet period, however, that Russians, and other Slavic nationalities, were attracted in great numbers to the former republics as the tempo of agricultural and industrial development accelerated. In many cases this migrational movement acted as a rural-to-urban migration for newly trained and qualified personnel as they took advantage of the new employment and housing opportunities of the new cities of the 'periphery'. This wave of Russian in-migration to the former republics peaked in the 1960s when the number of Russians in the republics grew by almost one third (Zaionchkovskaia 1996: 7). As the cases of the Volga Germans and Crimean Tatars indicate, however, the migrational experience for some was not voluntary but one of forced migration to the former republics as members of ethnic groups deported *en masse* during the Second World War.

The same processes of modernisation in the former Soviet republics which had spurred in-migration by Russians are also cited as the reason for the beginnings of postcolonial return. The education and training of members of the titular nationality increasingly brought competition for urban residence and employment opportunities in professional, management and skilled labour sectors. By the end of the 1960s interrepublican migration data were indicating a process of return migration by Russians from the republics of Transcaucasia and by the second half of the 1970s this process had spread across the Central Asian republics. Repatriation had effectively begun.

From the late 1980s, however, the return of the Russians accelerated rapidly. The first to leave were ethnic Russians and Russophones resident in those former republics caught up in civil war: Tajikistan, Armenia, Georgia and Azerbaijan. Some fled war zones, others were driven out by anti-Russian sentiment and activity, while the majority simply saw no future for their families in what no longer felt like 'their' countries. By 1994, however, the chief region of exodus of Russians had shifted to the Central Asian states and Kazakstan (see Table 10.2) which, with the exception of Tajikistan, had not been afflicted by acute ethnic tension. Consequently the migration of Russians has been attributed increasingly to the relative

Table 10.2. *Number of refugees and forced migrants in Russia registered between 1992 and 1995 by country of origin*

	1992	1993	1994	1995
Armenia	126	1,864	3,382	1,653
Azerbaijan	32,860	44,479	13,751	12,968
Belarus	0	17	108	188
Estonia	56	1,992	2,784	3,171
Georgia	24,817	66,063	17,451	10,774
Kazakstan	283	7,665	63,533	88,681
Kyrgyzstan	897	20,074	32,588	17,767
Latvia	92	4,156	5,929	5,426
Lithuania	41	468	1,190	720
Moldova	10,341	4,323	2,682	2,688
Russia	21,826	91,125	23,040	34,868
Tajikistan	65,448	68,598	24,320	26,974
Turkmenistan	54	450	2,208	4,574
Ukraine	19	262	1,904	2,263
Uzbekistan	3,247	18,366	59,574	59,209
Not stated	234	690	74	31

economic stagnation of these former republics in comparison to Russia. It appeared from the outside that those who had sought professional advancement through positions on the periphery in the past were now undertaking return labour migration in order to preserve their standard of living.

Within the 'single' migration flow of Russians out of the former Soviet republics back to Russia, therefore, there are examples of the repatriation of those in refugee-like situations, of the simple acceleration of existing postcolonial repatriation and of return labour migration. The example of Russia thus raises questions about the meaningfulness of 'repatriation' in describing the return of Russians from the former Soviet republics. This chapter addresses these questions at two levels. Firstly, at the discursive level, the chapter charts the development of the migration regime in Russia from its original focus on 'refugees' and 'forced migrants' to current debates about 'repatriation' and asks how this positions returnees and potential returnees to Russia. Secondly, the chapter explores the individual migration decision in its social context. It describes the information flows and networks employed in the process of making and executing decisions to migrate and the importance of changing perceptions of 'home' and 'homeland' among returnees. It will be suggested that only through the analysis of both state discourse and migrant experience can the intricate and contextual nature of repatriation be captured and assumptions that 'returning home' is a 'natural' and unproblematic resolution of physical and cultural 'displacement' be challenged.

From 'refugee' to 'repatriate': the changing nature of the Russian migration regime

The migration regime in Russia has not only emerged in a vacuum but in an unstable vacuum. Post-Soviet Russia is undergoing rapid social change, institutional restructuring and relocation within the global environment and, consequently, migration discourse has proved to be highly dependent upon the wider sociopolitical environment.

The migration regime emerged in post-Soviet Russia in an initially liberal and humanitarian climate. In December 1992 Russia signed the 1951 UN Convention and 1967 Protocol on the Status of Refugees and this international legislation came into force on Russian territory from 4 May 1993. In February 1993 domestic legislation was passed which recognised and provided for refugees and forced migrants in Russia. The legislation distinguishes between a 'forced migrant' and a 'refugee' on the basis of citizenship; the former is a citizen of the Russian Federation, the latter is not. In practice, however, liberal guarantees of the right to apply for Russian citizenship effectively protected all former Soviet citizens.[4]

The institutional framework for handling refugees and forced migrants in Russia actually predated the legislation; the Federal Migration Service (FMS) of the Russian Federation was established by presidential decree in June 1992 and mandated to protect the rights of refugees and forced migrants and help in their resettlement. By April 1996 this unitary federal structure had regional branches in all regions and republics of the Russian Federation with a total staff of 3,697 and a Moscow-based headquarters employing 243 people.

The receptive climate towards those wishing to move to Russia from the former republics in the first part of 1992 indicated Russia's acceptance of the obligations as well as advantages of having

4. 'The Law on Citizenship' which came into effect on 6 February 1992 (being amended on 17 June 1993 and 18 January 1995) grants Russian Federation citizenship to all those permanently resident in the Russian Federation before that date. In addition Article 18 of the law allows all those who held USSR citizenship on that date and were resident in a former Soviet republic prior to that date to receive Russian citizenship if they applied within three years of the law's promulgation and were not already citizens of another republic. Amendments to the law on 18 January 1995 extended this three-year period for application to 31 December 2000.

become the 'successor' to the Soviet Union on the international scene, but also her readiness to downplay her own 'interests' in the former republics, leaving them free to form as separate nations, whilst concentrating Russia's foreign policy on swift acceptance into the global community. While 'repatriation' was absent from government discourse at this stage, President Yeltsin's declaration that Russia was 'looking forward to' greeting returnees from the former republics was understood by many to be a welcoming call home from the motherland.

The government policy agenda changed quite dramatically in the course of the latter half of 1992 and 1993. This came about largely as a result of pressure from parliamentary bodies calling for a tougher line on the rights of Russians in the former republics – articulated particularly via the parliamentary Committee on CIS Affairs and Relations with Compatriots. But it was also a result of real policy issues – the conflict in the Dniestr region of Moldova, the dispute with Ukraine over Crimea and the introduction of anti-Russian citizenship laws in Latvia and Estonia – which put increasing pressure on the Russian government to adopt a tougher line on the protection of the interests of Russians in what became known as the 'near abroad'.[5] This pressure intensified following the December 1993 elections, which returned a majority of communist and nationalist deputies, and led to a significant reorientation of the Russian migration regime.

The first indication of this was a shift in rhetoric on the part of both President Yeltsin and Foreign Affairs Minister Kozyrev who began to express their 'concern' about the status of Russian speakers in the 'near abroad' and to identify the protection of Russians' rights in the other former Soviet republics as 'one of the main strategic issues of Russian foreign policy' (Current Digest of the Post-Soviet Press 1994). The tough words were accompanied by a shift in Russian policy towards the Russians in the Newly Independent States. Policy became increasingly defined as dual track, that is, it was stated that the doors would not be shut to those who wished to return but, at the same time, there was a virulent promotion of their 'right to stay'. Subsequently, the December 1995 parliamentary declaration 'On the support of the Russian Federation for the Russian diaspora and protection of Russian compatriots' referred to a 'preferential regime' for returning Russians but only guaranteed the right to repatriation in cases of persecution.

5. The 'near abroad' is used to indicate all former Soviet republics and thus differs from the CIS (Commonwealth of Independent States).

Institutional and legislative changes codified this policy shift. The priority of the Federal Migration Service gradually shifted from its original role of developing universal aid programmes for refugees and forced migrants to immigration control functions. Meanwhile amendments to the Law on Forced Migrants, finally adopted in November 1995, sought to distinguish in legislative terms between economic and political migrants and specifically excluded economic migrants from forced migrant status.[6]

These developments herald a break in migration discourse in Russia on two fronts. The first is the movement from a humanitarian, protective discourse (the protection of the rights of 'forced migrants' and 'refugees') to a securitised migration discourse. The securitisation of migration is clearly, though alarmingly, articulated in FMS documentation which links what it terms 'uncontrollable migration' to disease, criminality and social tension in Russian cities (Informatsionno-analiticheskii Biulleten 1995). The perceived threat to security presented by such immigration has led the Federal Migration Service to incorporate in its remit the role of curbing 'illegal immigration' from outside the former Soviet Union (often 'transit migrants'), and fifty-three posts of immigration control are currently being put into operation at points of entry to Russia.

The second is the much clearer distinction between voluntary and involuntary migrants which underpins the process of 'securitising' migration. The Russian migration regime has increasingly distinguished between categories of incomers, and, in particular, between 'forced migrants' ('ours' since they are Russian citizens) and 'refugees' ('not ours'). Refugees have lost equal status with forced migrants (such as access to priority housing lists) and, in recent months there has been particular concern about the treatment of refugees from outside the former Soviet Union who are often expelled without being granted the opportunity to apply for refugee status and even returned to the country of flight in contradiction to international norms of non-*refoulement* (Korkeakivi 1996). This shift marks a significant retreat from the early humanitarianism of Russia and brings Russia much closer to the restrictive migration regimes of Western and Northern Europe.

Unlike Western European states, however, increasing differentiation between economic and political refugees is not being driven by

6. Point 3 of Article 2 states that persons who may be refused forced migrant status are those 'leaving their place of residence for economic reasons or owing to famine, epidemic or extreme situations of a natural or technological character' (see 'O vnesenii izmenenii I dopolnenii v zakon Rossiiskoi Federatsii "O vynuzhdennikh pereselentsakh"' 1995).

concerns about ethnic/race relations in the receiving country, but rather by an unlikely convergence of democratic and nationalist/ communist interests. The neo-imperialist lobby (which cuts across nationalist and communist political affiliations) would like to see the Russian diaspora remain *in situ* to allow Russia to justify her interference in the internal affairs of the Newly Independent States. Government supporters, meanwhile, are primarily concerned about the financial burden to the government of ongoing mass return and the potential tensions which could be caused by a sudden increase in competition for housing and jobs in regions of high immigration. At the current rate of immigration, the Federal Migration Service is able to meet only the immediate needs of those in the most difficult circumstances.[7]

The reverse side of the metamorphosis of the FMS from an aid to a policing institution is that, de facto, its former functions have been passed down to the NGO sector. As a consequence this sector has increasingly been able to act – at the policy-input level – as the voice of refugees and forced migrants. This provides a better institutional balance to the migration regime but it has also opened the way to the recognition of a mass of voluntary migrants requiring no targeted state assistance. If the bill on repatriation currently under discussion in parliament is adopted, it will undoubtedly lead to significant numbers of returnees, who under existing legislation would have been recognised as 'forced migrants', being labelled as 'repatriates'.

The roots of a 'repatriation' discourse

Talk of repatriation is not new in Russia but, until recently, it was primarily an academic discourse which sought to explain current immigration from the former republics as a continuation of 'decolonisation' processes already under way (see for example *Migratsiia bedstvie ili blago: materialy kruglogo stola po problemam vynuzhdennoi migratsii v Rossii* 1996; Fadin 1994; Okulov 1994; Vishnevskii 1994), an interpretation widespread in Western academic literature also (Messina 1994; Brubaker 1995, Codagnone 1997). Political support for the notion of repatriation came from the democratic camp in Russia which interpreted the causes of forced migration as a natural result of the collapse of empire for which the present Russian government should take responsibility. Particularly vocal promotion of this interpretation has emanated from

7. In 1995 the FMS was allocated only a quarter of calculated expected expenditure and received, in practice, only 42 percent of that.

representatives of two Russian NGOs, the Coordinating Council for Assistance to Refugees and Forced Migrants (CCARFM) and its sister organisation the Civic Assistance Committee, specifically the chair of CCARFM, Lidiia Grafova and legal expert Svetlana Gannushkina. The two organisations have also advocated the adoption of a 'repatriation' law, believing it would codify the right to return in the absence of persecution – not enshrined in current legislation – and Gannushkina drew up a draft of such a law.

Thus, while the roots of repatriation discourse run deep, until recently it remained very much a peripheral debate, more a subversive undercurrent to the mainstream discourse. In the Russian press, for example, the term 'repatriates' (*repatrianty*) has been used only rarely in articles concerning returning Russians; in the peak year of return (1994) a content analysis of central and local press revealed that the term 'repatriates' was used in just one percent of a total of 325 articles concerning migration from the former republics to Russia (Pilkington 1998). Ongoing reviews of the press debate from January 1996 to April 1997 reveal that the term is gaining in usage, being used in almost four percent of the articles over this period.[8] There has also been a marked increase in discussion of the experience of returnees after arrival in Russia and an increasingly positive portrayal of the contribution of migrants to the regeneration of Russia. This is another victory for the NGO sector and migrant associations which have persistently raised the question of the negative media reporting of the forced migration issue.

The centrality of 'repatriation' in current policy debates on migration is thus, partially, evidence of the growing ability of the democratically oriented NGO sector to influence migration policy. The voices of NGOs and migrant associations were increasingly heard in the early part of 1996 in a number of debates, most notably a round table session on the problems of forced migration, a Forum of Migrant Associations and, subsequently, the parliamentary hearings held in April 1996 as part of the preparation for the CIS Conference on refugees and migrants organised by the UNHCR and the International Organisation of Migration (IOM) in Geneva the following month. This process reflects a new stage of institutional cooperation and evolving dialogue to which repatriation is integral.

While this dialogue is certainly an encouraging sign, preliminary analysis of the emergent repatriation discourse suggests that far from an agreement on principles and policy on the question of the Russian communities in the 'near abroad' between parliament,

8. This analysis is based on fifty-two articles from six central newspapers.

government and nongovernmental organisations, the concept of 'repatriation' has forged an unlikely alliance of divergent interests.

Unpacking Russian repatriation: common language or unstable convergence of interests?

The bill on repatriation currently being considered by parliament was proposed by the State Duma Committee on the Affairs of the CIS and Relations with Compatriots and is set within a wider law on support for the Russian diaspora and the protection of Russian Compatriots and Repatriates.[9] However, the draft law reflects many of Gannushkina's suggestions, possibly since a leading figure in the drafting process is Vyacheslav Igrunov (of the democratic faction *Yabloko*) with whom NGOs have long had a good relationship. According to the bill, citizens of the Russian Federation living beyond its boundaries are entitled to repatriation as are Russian 'compatriots' (*sootechestvenniki*). Russian compatriots are defined as those without Russian citizenship but who have hereditary links with Russia or the former Soviet Union and who possess cultural and spiritual links with Russia.

Government willingness to contemplate a law acknowledging a new category of immigrant – the repatriate – is understandable. Set, as this draft is, in the wider context of the protection of Russian compatriots abroad, it effectively continues the dual track policy of 'right to stay' and 'right to return' promoted by the government since 1994. The recognition of the status of 'repatriate' has two additional advantages. Firstly it may smooth the conclusion of agreements at interstate level which are inhibited by reluctance on the part of the donor states to acknowledge the 'persecution' of Russians leaving, as is necessitated by current 'refugee' and 'forced migrant' legislation (Gannushkina 1996: 1). Secondly, the acceptance of repatriation as a process of *voluntary* migration relieves the Russian government of financial responsibility for the resettlement of the majority of returnees. A striking absence from the parliamentary draft law on repatriation is the Federal Migration Service. It is possible that a new executive structure to manage the repatriation movement is envisaged but it is more likely that welfare functions for repatriates will be accommodated within the general welfare system supported by nongovernmental migrant and refugee associations.

9. The draft discussed here is in fact the second proposed; an earlier version, submitted in November 1996, contained a number of proposals which were in contradiction with federal laws and the constitution.

While, on the surface, the representatives of fundamentally different political and moral positions might be applauded for having found a 'common language', these differences may yet unhinge the adoption of the repatriation bill. One issue which is certain to provoke substantive disagreement is the question of 'prioritisation' in the acceptance of repatriates. In particular fears have been expressed that priority would be given to *ethnic Russians* and that this might encourage the repatriation process to be hijacked by extremist, nationalist groups (Filippova 1996: 1).[10] Such concerns were fuelled by a proposal by the prominent politician Sergei Shakhrai that upon repatriation individuals should be required to swear an oath to the Russian state (*Migratsiia bedstvie ili blago: materialy kruglogo stola po problemam vynuzhdennoi migratsii v Rossii* 1996). In actual fact the current draft legislation makes Russian ethnicity neither a precondition for repatriation status nor a category for prioritisation. Rather the bill proposes eight categories of repatriate with the highest priority being accorded to those who qualify for forced migrant or refugee status but who are prepared to forgo this right if granted repatriate status. The reasoning behind this prioritisation is clearly pragmatic although its inclusion potentially undermines a key rationale of the bill; to differentiate between categories of migrant.[11]

There is also the important question of the impact that this change in Russian legislation would have on the position of Russians in the 'near abroad'. Whilst NGOs see the law as providing concrete procedures for the implementation of the hitherto abstract 'right to return' of Russians in the near abroad, others fear that such a law would be likely to force individuals into opting for repatriation as their position in the former republics would be compromised. They would become regarded as 'temporary residents' whose repatriation the governments of the republics would act to hasten. Clearly, if this were the case, the interests of the Duma Committee (set out above) would not be met since the legislation would protect only a section of the Russian communities abroad – those with a prior intention of leaving. The apparent 'inevitability' of repatriation enshrined in the draft legislation on repatriation might also trouble the government, since it implies a mechanism of reception which Russia may not be in a position to provide (38-41). Thus the government is likely to

10. A case for comparison is that of the *pieds noirs* whose return to France in 1965-8, at a time of general social and political upheaval, led to a swelling of the ranks of the extreme right (McMillan 1985:177).
11. The bill also allows for application for repatriate status following an unsuccessful application for forced migrant or refugee status.

ensure that 'repatriation' is firmly embedded in a wider law which seeks to protect the interests of *all* Russians in the 'near abroad'.

Current attempts to make room for 'repatriation' within discourse and policy reflect a changing balance of priorities within the post-Soviet migration regime. The demands, from the increasingly influential nongovernmental sector, for attention to be paid to the situation of returnees to Russia has meant the political issue of protecting Russian interests in the 'near abroad' has become more tightly bound to the social issue of their reception upon return, and the focus of policy has shifted to Russian territory. The shift away from 'forced migration' as the central concept of the legislative framework also bridges the – artificially constructed – gap between 'economic' and 'political' migrant by establishing a fundamental right to return irrespective of the reason for departure.

On the other hand, the promotion of voluntary return migration may facilitate the process of state withdrawal from welfare functions associated with resettlement. Moreover, if the return of Russians moves firmly into a context of repatriation, there will be repercussions for other migratory movements. Repatriation, with its focus on the return of nationals to their 'historical homeland', may reinforce the existing move away from general humanitarianism and, in the process, render refugees the object of 'monitoring' and 'policing' rather than the subject of positive aid policies.

The emergence of a repatriation discourse has proved to be a positive step in policy formulation in Russia in that it has revealed the scope for cross-institutional dialogue between governmental bodies, nongovernmental organisations and migrant representatives. However, concrete structures need to be formed to facilitate and continue this dialogue, to translate it into practical policy formation and implementation and thus to reduce the vulnerability of migration discourse in Russia to the vagaries of the wider political climate. The establishment of a stable and migrant-friendly discourse of repatriation is central to ensuring returnees are seen not as 'deserters' of Russian interests abroad but as a positive force for the regeneration and consolidation of the Russian nation.

'We rely only on ourselves': the state, the individual and the migrant collective in the repatriation movement

If the original outward labour migration of Russians to the former republics was highly organised, then the return movement is distinguished by the complete absence of state planning. Repatriation movements within the post-Soviet space – with the limited exceptions noted at the beginning of this chapter – are not of the organised kind but overwhelmingly of what is generally referred to as 'spontaneous'. In mapping the role of the state, the individual and the migrant collective in the process of repatriation in Russia we draw on a review of published and unpublished materials from academic and media sources, international refugee and migrant organisations, Russian federal level NGOs and locally based migrant associations and on an empirical study conducted in Russia between June and December 1994. During this fieldwork data was gathered from a total of 195 respondents (returnees from the former Soviet republics) who had resettled in Russia between 1988 and 1994.[12]

For the majority of returnees – including those officially registered as forced migrants or refugees – the place of resettlement is not chosen as a result of a concrete job offer or organised through state or professional channels. Rather decisions about return to Russia are taken quickly and often to the economic detriment of migrants. In particular the move often involves an urban-to-rural relocation which constitutes a major social downshift. However, in the majority of cases neither is the move one of flight; only six of the 195 respondents who participated in the empirical study said they had been directed to their destination by a state agency dealing with refugees and forced migrants. The move is, for most people, neither carefully planned nor spontaneous, neither wholly voluntary nor involuntary, but a traumatic upheaval into which much is invested economically and emotionally and which is undertaken with virtually no assistance from the state.

The empirical study showed that returnees were unlikely to have used either media or government information sources to locate an area for resettlement. During interviews questions asked about what information they had received in the process of making their decision to move and to which institutions they had turned before leaving the former republic and on arrival in Russia, revealed that the vast majority of people had received no institutional help at all in planning their move. One in eight of those settling in Orel region (see Figure 10.1) stated that they had arrived in the region completely 'by chance'.

12. Two fieldwork bases were used, one urban and four smaller rural bases and a mixture of semi-structured interviews and questionnaires in interview format was used to gather data. The majority (77 percent) of respondents had moved to Russia from Central Asia and Kazakstan, a further 15 percent had previously lived in Azerbaijan. 73 percent stated they were ethnic Russians while Tatars and Armenians constituted the main non-Russian nationalities. 62 percent of respondents were female. Unless otherwise stated empirical data is cited from this study.

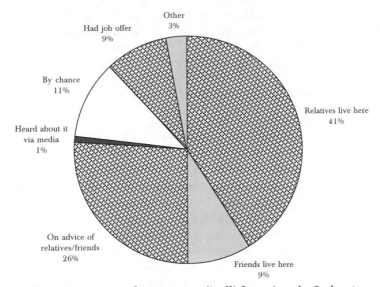

Figure 10.1 *Motivations for migration ('pull' factors) to the Orel region*

State indifference continues after the move. Quantitative indicators suggest that the majority of forced migrants and refugees receive very little of the material help from the state to which they are entitled according to the 1993 legislation, either in the form of a cash benefit or help with the cost of purchasing or building housing for themselves. Of the respondents interviewed in 1994, only 31 percent of forced migrants in the rural areas and 14 percent in the city had received one-off cash payments, while only four percent in rural areas and nobody at all in the city had received the centre-piece of FMS provision, the 'loan' for building or buying housing. Evaluations of help received by respondents during in-depth interviews, moreover, show that one-off cash benefits were universally considered laughable; typical statements were that they were enough to buy the kids chewing gum, or for a packet of cigarettes.

Knowledge about the 'benefits' of registering as a forced migrant or refugee with the local migration service is transferred through migrant communities quickly and has led to a significant decline in the numbers registering. Primarily this is because more money is spent gathering the necessary documents and making repeated visits to the regional centre in order to acquire official status than the financial gain received from that status.[13] Moreover, many respondents

---

13. More positively evaluated were other forms of 'help in kind' received mainly by those settling in rural areas, including the provision of 'rations' of meat, milk and sugar from the farm or temporary exemption from payment for electricity, or water.

noted the psychological impact of the indifferent or humiliating treatment received during this process. A fifty-three year-old woman who had arrived in Ul'ianovsk city from Uzbekistan at the beginning of 1993 described her experience of assistance to forced migrants thus:

> When I arrived I went round all the offices, and in one place I was even asked: 'What do you need a flat for? You'll be dead soon ...' We went to the migration service, they looked at us and did not even record us in the book. They said Ul'ianovsk does not give anything to refugees ...

In the absence of concrete state assistance, migrants employ a range of strategies to aid resettlement in the short term including the tactical use of state benefits, entrepreneurial initiative, collective organisation (legal and political) and on-migration. In the long term, however, the absence of accurate information about governmental assistance encourages a scepticism and alienation which does not aid adaptation to the new environment.[14] Whilst the very real financial constraints on the Federal Migration Service have been noted, the apparent fear that information about the availability of state assistance will increase the flood of returnees may be misplaced. In return migration to Israel in the 1960s, migrants stated that special benefits were not a major factor in deciding to return (Toren 1978: 53).

A second consequence of the growing awareness of the lack of state assistance is that migrants increasingly look to each other for mutual support and in some instances such migrant communities may take on an organisational structure. It is to these formations, at their various levels of formalisation and institutionalisation, that discussion now turns.

Migration networks: post-Soviet 'pioneers'

Migration decisions are not the enactment of an individual's 'dream' but are the product of the mediation of such aspirations by an awareness of the wider structural environment. The origin and reception of information is a major component in the way the repatriation process is developing in Russia.

The first waves of out-migration from the former republics were characterised by a heavy reliance on the presence of relatives and

14. The Federal Migration Service, for example, refuses to publish information about the sites of temporary accommodation centres for refugees and forced migrants for fear of being swamped with potential clients.

friends in the host country ,as the majority of returnees did not 'flee' in fear of their lives but nevertheless felt forced to move and were willing to accept any opportunity which allowed them to 'get out' rather than planning economically or socially advantageous moves. The majority of respondents in the empirical study in Orel region, for example, were attracted to the region of their resettlement by the presence or advice of friends, family or acquaintances (see Figure 10.1), knowing that this would provide a support network in the immediate period after arrival. Such networks are particularly important in urban areas of resettlement where the presence of relatives, friends or acquaintances is often the only means of gaining residence rights and a roof over one's head upon arrival.

For those settling in often depopulated rural areas, networks tended in contrast to develop in the sending country and often between first and later waves of returnees.[15] Among respondents in the rural fieldwork bases there was a greater tendency to follow neighbours, colleagues or relatives from the former republic of residence – to effectively move as a collective. These networks are primarily of an informational rather than survival strategy kind; first-wave resettlers provide information about job opportunities and, most importantly, housing availability, thereby attracting or deterring subsequent waves of migrants.

There is also a third level of more transient networks of chance acquaintances. These are often made on the so-called 'scouting' missions during which one or two members of a family or residential or work collective travel to Russia to locate a possible place for resettlement. On their travels they are told by chance acquaintances – other migrants or locals – where there might be housing or work and follow up these leads, make agreements with farm or factory directors and then return home with a 'concrete' site for resettlement in mind. The first families, or members of extended families, to move are referred to as 'pioneers'; a term which evokes not only Soviet 'Go West' mentality but also the original out-migration to the former republic.

The current deceleration of out-migration from the former republics has at least partially been precipitated by a change in the information received by the Russian communities in the near abroad; information which comes via the mediating institutions of government, nongovernmental bodies, and the media (Koser 1993)

15. Similar patterns of migration have been identified in the case of the *pieds noirs* from Algeria who settled in areas of southern France and Corsica where earlier repatriates were located (Hunt 1992: 563).

but also via migrant networks and returnees.[16] The growth of migrant associations has already established 'bridges' of information between communities who have resettled in Russia and those considering the move. In certain circumstances these 'bridges' are more than stepping stones to integration into the new community, becoming either the foundation stones of new migrant communities, or developing into more institutionalised, organised forms of networks. This constitutes a further level of networking and is discussed in more detail below.

Going home? Subjectivity and repatriation

For the reasons discussed in the first part of this chapter, 'repatriation' may be increasingly expressing the (diverse) interests of government, parliamentary and nongovernmental bodies. But to what extent does repatriation articulate the experience of returnees themselves? As the movement of repatriation infers the return to a homeland rather than just to a country of origin (Warner 1994) it is necessary to explore not only where home is, but what it constitutes (Zetter 1994). Many potential migrants in the former Soviet republics may have been born outside what is now the Russian Federation; in the empirical study cited here, 71 percent of respondents (126 of the 177 for whom birthplace data was available) had been born outside the Russian Federation. One Russian pensioner, who had settled in Orel region from Kyrgyzstan, expresses the resultant sense of loss:

> I was born there, lived there. Of course it is hard. You yearn ... for your native land. And that native land is there, there where you were born, in spirit you never leave ...

A similar problem was confronted by the Pontian Greeks who left the Soviet Union for a 'historical homeland' in Greece which they had never known (Glytsos 1995). In such cases, the significance of the 'imagined' homeland is intensified. However, ambiguous feelings about returning home are not confined to those who have never actually lived in their 'homeland'. Through the process of repatriation the 'imagined' community (Anderson 1991) is suddenly confronted in reality. This is illustrated by one female returnee from

16. Although 'return migration' (to the former republics) is beyond the scope of this article, it is apparent that it is a growing phenomenon and indicates the problem of both weak informational networks during the first waves of out-migration and of subjectivity and migration (the concept of 'home' discussed below).

Baku in her late twenties who, despite having no real 'love' of Azerbaijan, nevertheless found it hard to come to terms with the reality of the Russia she had imagined as her homeland:

> It isn't a very nice thing to say, of course, but all my life I have been a Russian, all my life I have wanted to go to Russia … [but] when I came to Russia and saw the dirt, the swearing, I hated it … I don't know where my homeland is now… I wanted to move to Russia because I thought it was my homeland. I was blonde, I was Russian, I talked about Russia all the time. [but when] I came to Russia, here I was an 'emigrant', a nobody …

The sense of cultural isolation expressed by this respondent is partially a result of the fact that her move to Russia was simultaneously an urban to rural move; in this sense her alienation may be as much from village as from Russian, culture. However, in urban areas of resettlement returnees also feel 'home' is elsewhere, as illustrated by the following statement by a woman refugee who arrived in the city of Ul'ianovsk from Tajikistan in 1992:

> It seems like we don't have a homeland, you had a homeland, or so it seemed … you were born somewhere, you knew it was your land, but suddenly … you feel cut off from something larger … you yearn all the same, my homeland for me is there, it is Tajikistan. I was born there, I grew up there, you can't get away from that.

It should be noted here that 'homeland' in Russian is rendered by the term *rodina* which fixes it linguistically as the 'place of birth'. It could be argued, perhaps, that culturally Russians feel their rootedness in relation to the land upon which they are born rather than an ethnic community to which they belong. Such a simple explanation of this lack of identification is difficult to maintain, however. Russians, even second or third generation migrants, do not fail to identify themselves as *ethnic Russians*, wherever they live. Rather, their lack of identification at the civic level is with contemporary Russia. This is linguistically conveyed by the differential use of *russkii/aia* and *rossiianin/ka*. The former denotes ethnicity and is rarely problematised by migrants – as is evident from the respondent's equation 'I am blonde, I am Russian' cited above. However, Russians in the 'near abroad' continue to identify at the civic level with the Soviet state and thus the term *rossiianin* was used by only one respondent to talk about themselves, even though all the respondents interviewed had already resettled in Russia and most had taken, or were in the process of taking, Russian citizenship. *Rossiianin* rather was used to denote the 'other', that is local Russians, who were seen as quite different from Russians from the 'near abroad' while civic identity among respondents remained firmly tied to a 'Soviet' community.

The problem is not that returnees had integrated fully into the former republics, but rather that the collapse of the *Soviet* state had inflicted upon the Russian community abroad a sudden disembodiment of their 'homeland'. The 'imagined community' (Russia) had been severed, suddenly, from the physical *rodina* (former republic) leaving the Russian diaspora culturally displaced.

Forms of resettlement: migrant associations and compact settlements

The process of resettlement is thus one of reimagining 'home'. For the Russian community in the 'near abroad' Russia was imagined as the great 'metropole', the example to which those in the republics should aspire. The reality of the contemporary rural and urban provincial Russia to which they return challenges that image and thus the journey's status as a return to a known, a 'home', is disrupted; the journey is rather one into an unknown wilderness. As one forced migrant from Shymkent put it:

> We thought that there was a lot more order in Russia, that the cultural level was a lot higher … but it turned out that in Kazakstan there was a lot more order and that people treated each other better … so all our images, our dreams about Russia have been … destroyed.

It is significant that much talk about 'local' (Russian) culture is expressed by migrants in terms of its alienness to established ways of life in the former republics, employing, in particular, the adjective 'savage' (*dikii*).

The profoundly disturbing process of the journey made by returnees causes migrants to seek ways of recreating 'home' in their new environments. The mechanisms of establishing a space which can be called 'home' in the process of repatriation by returnees themselves, however, may not always match the goals set for the management of repatriation by policy makers. There is often a mismatch between the official government programme (designed to resettle returnees in depopulated rural areas especially in the north and east of Russia) and the urban, professional skills the returnees bring with them. The post-Soviet Russian state also has a preference for the settlement of individual migrant families rather than compact settlements of migrants. However, migrants find it easier to share their feelings and problems with others who are experiencing a similar sense of displacement. This is witnessed by the following statement which was made by a migrant from Kazakstan who had resettled in Orel region:

> ... mostly we talk to the newcomers from Kazakstan, that is we understand each other better, better than talking to the locals ... they are closer, I don't consider them [the locals] to be our kind of people. But the newcomers, they are our kind of people.

Moreover, when forced migrants settle as individual families or ad hoc groups they complain that they become labelled as 'outsiders' by local communities and often meet with hostility.

In reality this 'otherness' is not only externally but internally imposed. In other words returnees are not only perceived as 'other' but perceive themselves as such. This is not surprising. The ambiguous relationship between an individual, a territory and the possibility of return is heightened by change over time and space (Warner 1994); migrants must confront changes which have taken place in the space to which they are returning both in actual terms and in relation to their image of that space. Reidentification with the new homeland is thus a process of 'becoming' which must take into account both the future and the past (Hall 1990). Russian returnees are indeed displaced in both time and space as their imaginations of Russia are tied to *Soviet* Russia. Much of their disorientation is thus related to an unpreparedness for the market culture of post-Soviet Russia, given that the pace of change in Central Asia has generally been far slower. Experience prior to repatriation profoundly shapes attitudes to return and perceptions about the future (Zetter 1994) and, in the Russian case, the past experiences of returnees have generated a feeling of superiority originating from the idea that it was often the 'best' who had been sent to the former republics. This encourages the formation of a strong migrant identity in the new homeland; a sense of being 'other' Russians[17].

The sense of 'community' generated among forced migrant groups often eases the adaptation process for returnees to Russia and has encouraged a type of self-organised repatriation through the formation of migrant associations and compact forms of settlement of returnees (see Figure 10.2). The promotion of 'compact settlements' was initiated by the Coordinating Council for Assistance

---

17. Voutira (1997) identifies similar feelings of superiority in the case of Asia Minor refugees returning to Greek Macedonia.

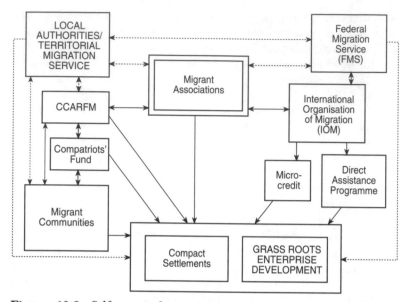

Figure 10.2. *Self-organised repatriation: major actors and types of resettlement in Russia*

to Refugees and Forced Migrants (CCARFM) and supported by a number of migrant associations as a 'realistic solution' to the problems of housing, employment and adaptation faced upon return which, for individuals, might appear insurmountable (Grafova et al 1995). Initial construction began at the end of 1991 and there are now sixty such settlements in the Russian Federation.[18]

CCARFM sees this mode of resettlement as being a resource haven for migrants in the immediate postmigration period as well as providing a necessary feeling of security and social inclusion. At a cultural level existing settlements have been successful in providing a link between the past and present for returnees. In economic terms compact settlements have had mixed fortunes. The most successful have been those situated in close proximity to urban centres since this allows the migrants to draw upon the existing infrastructure, provides a market for their produce and facilitates interaction with local residents which reduces feelings of isolation (Grafova et al. 1995).[19] Interaction and integration with the local community has been facilitated by small enterprise development designed to

18. This is the figure cited by CCARFM although other commentators estimate the number higher (ninety-two) (Kozlov in Pilkington 1998).
19. An example of such a settlement is that of Khoko in the town of Borisoglebsk, Voronezh region.

broaden opportunities for both migrant and local employment. Such grass-roots action has been encouraged by nongovernmental organisations at both the federal Russian (by CCARFM and the Compatriots' Fund) (Tishkov 1996) and international levels.

The International Organisation for Migration (IOM) is the major international actor at this level of resettlement, although the Red Cross has been involved in funding specific settlements, most notably the Novosel compact settlement. Through the Direct Assistance Programme the IOM aims to help migrant organisations make a start in successfully forming small private enterprises at the early stages of settlement through the provision of equipment. The programme began in 1993 and by the end of 1995 the IOM had assisted seventy-five migrant enterprises in twenty-five regions of the Russian Federation (IOM 1995). The programme's objectives are to generate economic development, promote the migrant group as a positive force and reduce the danger of social tension through the provision of employment. The IOM is also keen to promote the use of 'micro-credit' (adopted as part of the Programme of Action of the CIS Conference on Migration, May 1996) – a system of small-scale loans to migrants to develop enterprises. This has received initial support from other international organisations including the Open Society Institute and the UNHCR.[20] This kind of direct assistance approach effectively targets the migrant in the process of resettlement whilst emphasising the importance of cooperation and interaction with the local community.

The Federal Migration Service has been more cautious about, initially even hostile to, the idea of compact settlements. The chief objection has been that compact settlements potentially encourage the exclusion of migrants from Russian society by concentrating migrants with similar mentalities from the same republic and, in this way, fostering feelings of superiority among migrants over local Russians. Although the FMS is not alone in voicing such concerns, the perspective it takes is that of the wider, receiver community, whereas other commentators, whilst recognising the short-term social and cultural advantages they offer migrants, acknowledge that separate, enclosed settlements might encourage their long-term social exclusion.

20. There has been some uncertainty over whether the micro-credit idea will work in Russia where the economic situation differs from other areas where the strategy has proved successful (Latin America, Africa, Asia) and the IOM is currently concentrating on providing nonreturnable *grants* for the purchase of equipment . However, loans are being offered by 'Opportunity International', an American NGO, which says it has already issued 1,270 micro-credit loans ranging from $350 to $20,000 in Russia since 1993 (Open Society Institute 1997).

However, the new cooperation between NGO and government agencies in resettlement appears to have encouraged a more positive approach by the FMS (Airapetova 1996). In the amended Law on Forced Migrants a need is identified to co-operate with migrant associations in helping to construct compact settlements and the FMS claims to have helped financially in constructing housing and establishing a social and engineering infrastructure in 107 compact settlements.

Compact settlements are not the only form of self-organisation in the migrant community; looser networks of migrant associations and communities are actively promoting migrant interests. Such groups may form in the country of origin – some associations have their origins in work or residential collectives existing long before any plan to migrate to Russia – or emerge in the new place of settlement. Today there are more than a hundred recognised migrant associations and the number of migrant communities involved in some form of housing, construction, production, commerce or social and welfare activity is estimated to be as high as 1,000. A number of the larger associations have developed into nongovernmental-type organisations providing support for smaller migrant communities and representatives from these larger associations are acting as a lobbying force on migrants' behalf at the parliamentary level. The recent Forum of Migrant Associations (see above) illustrated the progress made in organisational terms; it was now possible to talk about a network of regional organisations which would transform the current 'chaos' into a migration 'movement'. The forum also made concrete legislative proposals including legislation on migrant associations, tax privileges for migrant associations, the creation of a migrant bank and repatriation legislation.

The growth and increasing organisation of the migrant associations and their networks is the reverse side of the withdrawal of the state from welfare functions in relation to returnees. In many ways it is a response to that state indifference. However, the growing confidence of the larger associations and their cooperation with federal-level nongovernmental organisations and local state structures indicates the way in which migrant-led associations can not only influence the migration regime but are a part of that regime. 'Self-organised' repatriation, in its many forms, thus reflects not self-exclusion by migrants but an active response to the social exclusion which returnees currently face and a mechanism of interacting with local communities whilst retaining a distinct identity for themselves within the new society.

Conclusion: Repatriation discourse, one step forward, two steps back?

Repatriation movements are relatively rarely subjected to theorisation or conceptualisation in migration literature (Basok 1990; Rogge 1994). Since repatriations are, by definition, journeys 'home', it has been largely assumed that such movements are familiar and unproblematic; a belief embodied by UNHCR's notion of voluntary repatriation as the optimal 'durable' solution.[21] In this chapter we have attempted to add a Russian voice to the recent questioning of the unproblematic nature of journeys 'home'. In so doing we have employed a conceptual framework which seeks to place the individual within the context of the wider macro environment (Bascom 1994). We have also drawn on recent attempts within migration theory to employ Giddens' theory of structuration (Goss and Lindquist 1995; Phizacklea 1996; Schwarz 1996) to suggest that the potential repatriate is not the object of state or international refugee programmes but acts within a framework of both constraining and enabling factors (Bakewell 1996). The discussion has shown the importance of analysis of individual agency and how action at this level can shape the development of policy and structures at the wider macro level. Indeed the possibilities presented by structuration theory to unfix the boundaries between structure and agency are essential to understanding the process of return to Russia, given the empirical difficulty of separating voluntary and involuntary migration and the fluidity of migration discourse.

At the structural level the possible emergence of 'repatriation' as a central part of migration discourse in post-Soviet Russia recognises the return of Russians from the 'near abroad' as a distinct migrational process and is potentially liberating in its recognition not only of a refugee movement but also a postcolonial population movement in the post-Soviet space. The displacement of the 'refugee/forced migrant' by the 'repatriate' in migration discourse would help many returnees regain a positive sense of self and of their potential contribution to Russian society. It also provides for a range of experiences of 'return' without making any primary distinction between forced and voluntary migration. At the same time the application of the notion of 'repatriation' within the existing

---

21. Official refugee documentation supporting repatriation as the optimal solution is the 1969 OAU Convention on Refugee Problems in Africa Article V Voluntary Repatriation and Annex II 1980 UNHCR Executive Committee 31st Session, No. 18 Voluntary Repatriation (Goodwin-Gill in Loescher and Monahan (eds) 1990: 287-9).

migration regime may effectively exclude ever more returnees from even the current pitiful levels of state assistance. Redefining 'forced migration' in terms of a post-colonial population movement could also be manipulated in such a way as to prioritise acceptance of returnees on the basis of ethnicity – a temptation which hitherto Russia, to her credit, has fastidiously avoided – or encourage forced migrants and refugees to accelerate their return by waiving the right to material assistance.

While repatriation discourse positions returnees in distinct ways *vis-à-vis* the Russian state and the host society in general, repatriation itself is also an act undertaken by individuals in possession of at least some of the facts. The study of the individual experience of returnees suggests the power of constructions of nationhood, evident in affection for a 'historical homeland' and hence the prioritisation of the 'return'. At the same time the process of resettlement itself reveals the deeply ambiguous relationship between nationality, citizenship, territory and identity and the conflicting feelings of belonging and exclusion which do not necessarily correlate with bounded physical territories. In Russia, at least, the notion of repatriation – return to homeland – may indeed be a concept too tied to a discrete physical space to adequately conceptualise return migrations in conditions of the unprecedented mobility of the late twentieth century (Gupta and Ferguson 1992; Warner 1994). The experience of Russian returnees suggests that 'home' is not a physical space which can be 'returned to' but an imagined community which requires both physical and cultural reconstruction by migrants upon return. The study of repatriation should reflect this experience, making it the study not of a bounded, unidirectional migrational movement but of a process of cultural reconstruction undertaken by both migrants and host societies.

PART FOUR

FROM REPATRIATION TO RECONSTRUCTION?

11

Why Angolan Soldiers Worry about Demobilisation and Reintegration

Art Hansen and *David Tavares*

In the immediate postwar period, the vast majority of people migrating, resettling and reconstructing civil society are civilians. Yet demobilising soldiers and reintegrating them into civil society are key steps, and sometimes necessary preconditions, in the processes of demilitarisation and postwar social reconstruction. In Angola, the failure to demobilise after the 1991 Bicesse Accord facilitated the return to war in 1992. Demobilisation in Angola entails merging two armies and then sending around 70,000 soldiers back into civil society. As of November 1997, this process was still far behind the schedule predicted when the Lusaka Protocol was signed. Who are these soldiers, and what is their future in civilian life? Why do they worry about demobilisation? This chapter presents data collected by the authors in a survey of 500 soldiers (250 from each side) from both armies in April 1995. It discusses the social profiles of these soldiers, their postwar expectations, and some of the problems in fulfilling these expectations.

Since the 1960s, the southern African region has been profoundly affected by forced displacement from widespread warfare and politically-related governmental programmes. Millions of refugees fled wars in Angola, Mozambique, Namibia and Zimbabwe to crowd border villages, designated rural settlement areas, small towns, and cities in neighbouring countries. Even more people were internally displaced within these four countries by warfare and official villagisation (or *concentração*) programmes that were instituted to contain anti-colonial forces. Similarly, millions of people were displaced within the Republic of South Africa, by its programmes to channel or stop political change by territorially separating racial and ethnic categories.

The Mozambican, Namibian and Zimbabwean wars are over; the long-anticipated political transformation within South Africa is under way; and at the time of writing, the civil war in Angola appeared to have ended. However, the aftermath of war includes massive population shifts, widespread changes in settlement patterns, problems associated with demilitarisation, reconstruction, and a reshuffling of priorities affecting all of the countries. In particular, the transition from military to civilian status involves a period of risk and uncertainty. Some of the worries soldiers express about reintegration are shared by civilians who are reintegrating into the same post-war conditions, whilst other concerns are more specific to soldiers.

Angolans have experienced almost continual warfare during the past thirty-five years, beginning in 1961 with the anti-colonial war against the Portuguese. After initial attacks in Luanda and in the northern coffee country, the main eastern front opened in 1965-66. The conflict then evolved into civil war in 1975, the year of Angolan independence, and continued until the Bicesse Peace Accord was signed in 1991. This peace lasted more than a year, but war resumed in September 1992. The ensuing phase of devastating urban warfare continued until the Lusaka Protocol was signed in November 1994. Although the cease-fire was signed more than three years ago, the peace process continues to be tentative and hesitant.

In analysing the failure of the 1991 Bicesse Accord to ensure a sustainable peace, the United Nations recognised the significance of their failure to fully demobilise the armies. With the signing of the Lusaka Protocol in 1994, the UN had a second opportunity for peace in Angola. Determined not to repeat the mistakes of 1991, and learning from its experiences in ending other wars around the world, the UN contracted a team of social scientists to develop a psychosocial profile of the soldiers of both armies, identify soldiers' socioeconomic expectations, and help plan programmes that would encourage demobilisation and diminish ex-soldier frustration during their reintegration into postwar Angolan society. The authors (an American anthropologist and a Portuguese sociologist) were members of that team (the first author heading the team); the other members were a Zimbabwean economist and an Argentinean expert in information systems.

This chapter focuses on some of the highlights of what we learned about those soldiers, and some of the problems to be faced in meeting their expectations. The central question we address is: why do those soldiers worry about demobilisation and reintegration?

Demobilising and reintegrating soldiers

An army is a complex organisation that is dedicated to producing force or security; the army's division of labour is organised around military technologies in a distinctive hierarchical structure. The demilitarisation of a state and polity involves diminishing the size and dominance of the army (and, in the case of Angola, of actual warfare). According to Cilliers (1995: 5), 'demobilization is the process through which armed forces of a government and opposition parties shed themselves of excess personnel after a period of conflict.' This is the military equivalent of 'downsizing' or 'rightsizing' that occurs in civilian corporations (Motumu and Hudson 1995). According to Luckham (1994: 23), 'the production of security involves not only relations of force and surveillance, but also meanings and identities.' Therefore, the processes of demilitarisation and demobilisation also include diminishing the importance of symbols and values that validate military power and status (Luckham 1994: 22-24). What do these sociopolitical and sociocultural changes mean for the men (and, sometimes, women) who are demobilised?

Most of the literature on demobilisation is recent. The studies focus on: (1) the economic relationship between demobilisation and development; (2) planning new demobilisation and reintegration programmes; or (3) the failure of past demobilisation and reintegration programmes.

The first set of studies emphasises the need to spend less on the military, thus seeing peace and demobilisation as ways to shrink a bloated government payroll and release funds for economic development. Thus according to the World Bank (1993: v), 'it has become painfully clear that the insecurity and diversion of fiscal resources caused by civil war represent the primary roadblock to a return to economic and social development'.

The second set are planning documents, which are usually policy-oriented or management-oriented reports rather than academic articles (IRG 1994; UCAH 1994; Clark 1996). These reports vary in their evaluations of previous programmes from being positive – as with Clark who concludes for USAID that 'demobilization and reintegration efforts have been successful' (Clark 1996: ii) – to being much more cautious, as in the case of the International Resource Group's evaluation of demobilisation and disarmament in the Horn of Africa.

The third set (studies of failure) view the process largely from the perspectives of excombatants and paint a dismal picture of unkept promises and forgotten veterans. For example, Musemwa (1995: 44) bemoans how 'more than 25,000 ex-combatants have become progressively more destitute in Zimbabwe', whilst Cock (1994: 5) argues that 'benefits and procedures were complicated and cumbersome and created confusion and disappointment'. Viewing the Namibian experience of demobilisation of soldiers, Shikangalah (1995: 70) notes how 'many ... swelled the ranks of the unemployed'.

This chapter views the process of demobilisation from the perspective of combatants, but at an earlier phase – before they are demobilised – and in a country where demobilisation and reintegration are protracted and still in progress. In the Angolan case, the goodness of fit between soldiers' desires and skills, on the one hand, and the employment possibilities in a war-ravaged economy, on the other hand, have an impact on the willingness of soldiers to demobilise.

Methodology

The team of social scientists made two trips to Angola. The initial trip (late October through to early December, 1994) was only partially successful because we were unable at that time to interview any active soldiers. An unexpected delay in signing the cease-fire meant that the war continued during the first month of our stay, and the ensuing peace was too tentative for the generals to permit us access to their troops. Finally, in April 1995, the two authors returned to Angola and surveyed 250 soldiers in the government army (*Forças Armadas Angolanas*, or FAA) and 250 serving with the main opposition (*União para a Independência Total de Angola*, or UNITA). Travelling around in small planes for two hectic weeks, we surveyed FAA soldiers in four cities (Luanda, Lubango, Luena and Menongue) and UNITA troops in three cities (Bailundo, Mavinga and Negage). We used both a written questionnaire and small informal focus groups.

The data from our survey are valuable, but must be interpreted with caution. Clearly, these soldiers were not an unbiased representative sample. Instead of being selected by the UN in a random or stratified way, the samples were selected by the two armies. Not knowing their criteria, nonetheless we assume that they wanted us to survey their better and more politically-aware troops. We know the troops were briefed by their officers before the survey. Another limitation is that our research ignored those soldiers who belong in the category of 'vulnerable groups'. Most visible and noteworthy for Angola are the physically mutilated (losing feet, legs and arms) by land-mines and other explosives. We did not study these (*mutilatos*) soldiers because the UN had commissioned another team for that purpose.

Another concern is that the FAA and UNITA samples cannot simply be compared against each other. The samples are not symmetrical and do not represent the proportional composition of the populations of the two armed forces. As an example, there is a disproportionately large number of sergeants in the FAA sample (37 percent, compared to nine percent in the UNITA sample), and a disproportionately large number of officers in the UNITA sample (42 percent, compared to 15 percent for the FAA sample).

There was also a problem with confidentiality. The interviews were deliberately conducted in an open (or in UN jargon, a 'transparent') manner. Officials of the army whose troops were being interviewed were present during the interviews, often listening to the informal focus group dialogues, even sometimes assisting the troops to fill out the questionnaires where there were problems in understanding questions. This transparency was purposeful, so that everyone realised our neutrality, but the lack of confidentiality obviously diminishes the possibility that respondents would voice any opinions that their officers might criticise.

The social profile of Angolan soldiers

Given these qualifications, our survey provides valuable insights into the socio-economic features and expectations of FAA and UNITA troops. The sampled men were diverse in many ways, but most of them had spent all or most of their adult years (after eighteen years of age) in the army, and had little or no experience as independent working adults before joining the military (see Table 11.1). When they were recruited, one-half of the FAA and two-thirds of the UNITA troops were students, two-thirds of the FAA and three-quarters of the UNITA troops living with their parents. About three-quarters of the men in both armies wanted to demobilise, even in the face of considerable uncertainty about their future as civilians. Even

Table 11.1. *Pre-military experience of Angolan soldiers*

	FAA troops (%)	UNITA troops (%)
Were students when recruited into military	50	69
Were living with parents when recruited	68	77

Source: Authors' survey, 1995.

those who wanted to remain in the army were split, with many not wanting to remain for a long time, but hoping to receive some training (*formação profissional*) or education in the army before they were demobilised.

The soldiers were asked whether living together with ex-soldiers from the other army would be easy, possible, difficult or impossible. A minority believed that it would be easy (Table 11.2), but the majority (65 and 84 percent respectively) believed that it would be possible or easy. Only a few people on both sides thought that it would be impossible. However, the UNITA troops were more optimistic than the FAA. Almost one-third of the FAA troops believed that living together would be difficult. Comparing these findings with studies conducted in 1992 shows that there was less confidence by 1995 in the ease of coexistence, but that there remained a strong majority opinion that it was at least possible (Tavares 1993a; 1993b; 1993c; 1994).

On the question of whether the troops came from – and might wish to return to – rural or urban areas, our findings did not confirm common assumptions about UNITA troops. Thus most observers believe that the majority of UNITA's soldiers are rural and farming-oriented, with strong ties to family, agriculture and land. This means that agricultural programmes are seen as appropriate for the economic reintegration of most UNITA soldiers, and that there will be less demand by them for education or occupational training. Our findings suggest that these estimates are seriously misleading. The UNITA troops we interviewed were as urban-oriented as the FAA troops, and the premilitary backgrounds were found to be similar

Table 11.2. *Attitudes towards postwar coexistence amongst Angolan soldiers*

	FAA troops (%)	UNITA troops (%)
Believe that living together will be easy	28	19
Believe that living together will be difficult	31	9

Source: Authors' survey, 1995.

Table 11.3. *Origins and intended future place of residence of Angolan soldiers*

	FAA troops (%)	UNITA troops (%)
Born in rural municipalities	69	76
Want to return to home province to live	69	67
Want to live in a rural municipality after military	49	47
Want to live in a smaller provincial capital	23	9
Want to live in one of the five largest cities	25	34
Want to live in the capital city, Luanda	4	9

Source: Authors' survey, 1995.

(Table 11.3). Almost the same percentage of FAA and UNITA troops were born in rural municipalities, and wanted to return to their home province to live after demobilisation. However, a major shift from rural to urban orientation has occurred for both groups. Slightly less than half of the FAA and UNITA troops interviewed wanted to live in a rural municipality after being demobilised. The major difference between the two armies was in whether they wanted to live in smaller provincial capitals, the five largest cities, or in Luanda, the capital city. Many more of the FAA troops wanted to live in the smaller provincial towns, while more of the UNITA troops wanted to live in the five large cities or in Luanda.

Almost all of the troops could understand spoken Portuguese (Table 11.4). Non-Portuguese speakers were usually monolingual in an African language, usually Ovimbundu. FAA and UNITA troops had about the same degree of illiteracy, but among the FAA troops, this was found almost exclusively amongst the regular soldiers (*brazos*). In the UNITA sample, more than one-third of the sergeants and one-eighth of the officers were also illiterate. The FAA troops on

Table 11.4. *Literacy and education amongst Angolan soldiers*

	FAA troops (%)	UNITA troops (%)
Cannot speak the Portuguese language	4	9
Are illiterate in the Portuguese language	14	20
Illiteracy amongst sergeants	2	35
Illiteracy amongst officers	0	13
Completed primary school or higher	78	60
Reached middle or secondary school	70	34
Completed some or all of secondary school	37	13

Source: Authors' survey, 1995.

average had more education. In terms of formal schooling, the UNITA troops were distributed fairly evenly from illiteracy through primary into middle school. Only one-third of UNITA troops had reached middle or secondary school, compared to more than two-thirds of the FAA troops. Three times as many FAA troops had attended secondary school.

Many soldiers in Angola had never earned their own living before entering the military. Almost all of them appear uncertain about how they can earn a living outside of the military, and they feel unprepared for civilian life. Their uncertainty is exacerbated by the realisation that Angola's economy has been destroyed by the decades of warfare and neglect, and there are few, if any, employment opportunities in industry or commerce. The only obvious source of employment and livelihood for large numbers of people in Angola is agriculture. There is plenty of farmland available, and subsistence and commercial agriculture historically had supported most Angolans, and had been profitable.

For these reasons, many observers believe that soldiers will want to return to farming after demobilisation. However, our survey clearly demonstrated the unpopularity of farming. Only one-eighth of the FAA troops wanted to be farmers, and fewer of the UNITA troops (Table 11.5). Many soldiers said they had learned, or become familiar with, skilled occupations (as mechanics, drivers, radio operators, etc.) during their military service, and that becoming a simple farmer would be going backwards, They had progressed beyond village life. However, more of them said they would become farmers if they could receive tractors, or access to tractors. Sometimes, this was expressed as combining farming with being a tractor mechanic, or being involved in a tractor hire programme.

Table 11.5. *Economic aspirations of Angolan soldiers after demobilisation*

% wishing to be:	FAA troops (%)	UNITA troops (%)
Farmers	13	6
Mechanics	22	17
Drivers	20	10
Teachers	5	12
Health workers	4	15
Businessmen (in the informal economy)	14	2
Middle-level professionals	10	1
High-level professionals	9	25

Source: Authors' survey, 1995.

This corresponded to the popularity of becoming mechanics and drivers, popular future career choices for both FAA and UNITA troops. Becoming health workers and teachers were also popular career choices for UNITA troops, but not for the FAA sample. These careers can utilise military-related experience or training, and many of the UNITA troops' fathers had been health workers or teachers when their sons had entered the military.

After that, however, some UNITA soldiers expressed very unrealistic aspirations that were related to their belief that they deserved to be rewarded with higher status and higher-paid work because of their years of wartime service. Few UNITA troops chose business or middle-level professions as occupations, but one-quarter wanted to become high-level professionals, such as physicians or engineers. These career choices would require much formal schooling, which these UNITA soldiers lacked. On the other hand, the higher aspirations of the better-educated FAA troops seemed to be more realistic. One-quarter of them favoured more accessible occupations, such as becoming businessmen, or middle-level or technical professionals (accountants, journalists, telecommunications technicians, etc.).

The soldiers interviewed were asked to select their highest priority for help with postwar reintegration: help with immediate employment, education or training, housing, or receiving tool kits. Troops on both sides emphasised training, with the second choice being help in finding employment (Table 11.6). This priority was anticipated for the FAA troops, but the UNITA soldiers contradicted the widely-held assumption that they are rural-oriented and primarily want help in reestablishing themselves as farmers.

Demobilisation and reintegration are times when soldiers confront changing situations and have to make decisions that have major impacts on their lives and futures. Each decision has to be made with inadequate information, so there is always uncertainty and risk. Active soldiers were aware that the soldiers who were demobilised four years earlier (1991-92, after the Bicesse Accord) were ill-treated and felt

Table 11.6. *Priorities for postwar reintegration amongst Angolan soldiers*

	FAA troops (%)	UNITA troops (%)
Highest priority is advanced training	43	52
Highest priority is help with employment	36	35
Believed had learned useful skills in military	45	30

Source: Authors' survey, 1995.

abandoned or forgotten (*abandonado*). The soldiers interviewed in 1995 were clearly seeking any help that might give them an advantage in civilian life, and reassurance that they would not be abandoned. The emphasis on *formação* (training and education) and employment reflected soldiers' worries. In this sense, the importance of these programmes and promises of help with employment can be seen as much as an emotional as a financial issue.

Those soldiers who thought they had learned a skill in the military that they could use to earn a civilian living (i.e., a 'useful' skill) wanted help finding employment. Unfortunately, only a minority thought that they had learned a 'useful' skill (Table 11.6). Those who did not think that they had learned a useful skill wanted programmes to focus on training, housing, or tool kits. Soldiers most concerned about receiving more education or training generally wanted to live in urban areas. Those with less education were more likely to want to return to their original homes.

Problems in meeting soldiers' expectations

Some of the problems in meeting the expectations of soldiers as expressed through this survey are obvious. The Angolan economy has been ruined through decades of warfare. Towns were destroyed, cities besieged, and roads mined and impassable. Markets have collapsed: industrial production essentially has stopped; agricultural production has plummeted. Approximately one-quarter of the population was internally displaced by the war, and many people continue to depend to some extent on international food aid. There are few opportunities for employment, and a fantastic rate of inflation has impoverished almost everyone, especially those relying on salaries and wages. The government has bankrupted itself fighting the war, and probably has mortgaged several years of oil revenues.

How can the future livelihoods of demobilised soldiers be guaranteed when the entire economy is in a shambles? How can educational and training programmes be established when few schools are operating, and teachers are not being paid, or are receiving a salary made worthless by inflation? Where are the opportunities for employment? Who will start industries and commercial firms until the peace is more certain, the roads have been de-mined, and the safety of transport is guaranteed? Reintegration programmes need money to provide financial support to ex-soldiers and establish training and employment programmes.

Even though the UN has issued appeals for international help in funding the reintegration programmes, few donors have subscribed.

Conclusion

The process of postwar reconstruction is just beginning in Angola, and the future of the peace process is uncertain. One reason why the previous period of peace (1991-92) was shattered by a resurgence of warfare (1992-94) was because the two armies had not been demobilised. With a second chance for peace with the Lusaka Protocol of November 1994, the UN is trying to speed demobilisation and the subsequent reintegration of ex-soldiers into civilian society. Nonetheless, at the time of writing, the demobilisation process remained far behind schedule.

The decision to demobilise, and the speed with which that is conducted, are affected by many factors, but this chapter does not examine the political motives that may be impeding demobilisation. Instead, our focus has been on the soldiers involved, trying to understand their perspectives and worries. Soldiers are trying to make their own decisions about what is best for them, in a 'return' process that parallels that of refugees. Their decisions, whether to demobilise, and if so, where to go, and what to do, are surrounded by uncertainty and worry about being able to make a living (or a good living) in civilian life. The survey revealed realistic bases for these worries. The soldiers are heterogeneous in many ways, but many of the soldiers have little or no experience as working adults outside the military. Many have little education. Few learned useful skills in the military. Most know that the soldiers who demobilised in 1991-92 think they were essentially abandoned by the government.

In most wars, there will not be a uniform response to demobilisation or reintegration by either side, no matter how well-disciplined its members are. However, one clear message emerges from our survey: awareness that reintegration programmes exist to help them will encourage more soldiers to demobilise and this will further the peace process. International funding for such programmes is important in Angola for the peace process to continue.

Acknowledgements

This is a revision of a paper presented by the senior author at the 5th International Research and Advisory Panel Conference on Forced

Migration (IRAP) held at Moi University, Eldoret, 9-12 April 1996. Data for the chapter were collected whilst the authors were conducting research for the United Nations Coordinating Unit for Humanitarian Assistance in Angola (UCAH 1995). UCAH forms part of the UN Division of Humanitarian Assistance. The research team was attached to UCAH with the financial support of the United States Agency for International Development (USAID). Dr Holly Ann Williams at the University of Florida helped to analyse the data.

12

Repatriation and Everyday Forms of State Formation in Guatemala

Finn Stepputat

Introduction

The return of Guatemalan refugees from Mexico after more than ten years in exile is one of the cases that contributed to the designation of the 1990s as the 'decade of voluntary repatriation'. This repatriation exercise is an example of the contemporary concerns to promote the process of repatriation and to 'push' refugee assistance back across the border in order to prevent the further production of refugees. The lasting aim was to contribute to the formation of a modern, democratic state.

The process of how repatriation links up with the (re-) formation of states has rarely been examined. The present chapter focuses on this process by drawing upon a more general debate on state formation. The process of repatriation in Guatemala is demonstrated to have increased the presence of the 'state' in the former areas of conflict, but at the same time to have enhanced the possibility of new conflicts. After presenting an analytical framework for the study of state formation, the chapter articulates the relationship between repatriation and state formation by focusing on three issues, namely: the arrival and forms of intervention of 'waves' of relief and development agencies; the conflicts over access to land and other resources which are related to the recategorisation of the social landscape, and finally the arrival, capacities and strategies of repatriates and returnees who regard themselves as a social force of modernisation.

The chapter draws upon one year of fieldwork that was undertaken between 1994 and 1996 in Nentón, a rural township in Huehuetenango in northwestern Guatemala. During 1994-5, the incidence of armed encounters had reduced to one per month, and by late 1996, the 'Voluntary Committees for Civil Self Defence' – the backbone of the army control of areas of conflict – had been disbanded.[1] Returned refugees and other displaced persons make up more than 40 percent of the 20,000 inhabitants in Nentón. The fieldwork applied an inclusive, regional approach which did not focus exclusively on the returning refugees. Rather I sought to follow the conflicts and changes in a cluster of villages and settlements on both sides of the border between Guatemala and Mexico.

Background

The Guatemalan refugees became recognised as such by UNHCR in 1982, when they had fled the armed conflict between the military government and a front of left-wing guerrilla groups, known as La Unidad Revolucionaria Nacional de Guatemala (URNG). As many as 150,000 people fled Guatemala, but only 46,000 were recognised and assisted as refugees in the settlements controlled by the Mexican government. Ninety percent of the refugees spoke Mayan languages while 10 percent were *ladinos*, non-Indians. The government conditioned the presence of the refugees in terms of 'temporary asylum' and restricted their mobility and integration (Aguayo et al. 1987; Stepputat 1992; Hernandez et al. 1993).

While many Guatemalans have filtered unnoticed back across the border over the years, a formal agreement on assisted repatriation was signed by UNHCR and the governments of Mexico and Guatemala in 1986, when a civilian government was elected in Guatemala. The scheme provided repatriating households with transport, some food, seeds, tools and cash for building materials. However, by 1992 only a small proportion of the refugees had repatriated under this scheme. Continued human rights violations, compulsory participation in the armed patrols for civil defence, and problems of recouping prior land titles kept most refugees from repatriating and prompted the formation in 1987 of a refugee organisation, the Permanent Commissions (CCPP). Refugees in

1. The final peace accord was signed in December 1996.

more than a hundred settlements elected the members of the CCPP, which was commissioned to negotiate the conditions of an 'organised, collective return' of the Guatemalan refugees. Among the demands were access to land, freedom to choose where and how to settle, and non-presence of the army in the return settlements. 'Repatriation' vs. 'return' became a politically loaded distinction, the former being organised for the refugees; the latter being a sign of resistance against the Guatemalan government in general and the army in particular.

Repatriation came to constitute an important element of the peace negotiations and a central element in international involvement in the peace process in Guatemala, as it did in Central America in general.[2] In the face of this pressure, the Guatemalan government negotiated directly with the CCPP and eventually on 8 October 1992 the parties signed an agreement. This agreement gave the refugees access to land and to the establishment of segregated return settlements, most of them in the areas of former conflict. As of mid-1997, 18,800 refugees had returned 'collectively' while 17,400 had repatriated 'individually'. Many inter- and nongovernmental agencies have been keen to support the process of resettlement and reconciliation in Guatemala. The ferocity of the army's counter-insurgency campaign, the general interest in the upsurge of Mayan identity, and the preparedness of the returnees to modernise and organise for the reception of assistance are among the factors that have drawn attention to the aftermath of the violent conflict in Guatemala.

Everyday forms of state formation

How do we analyse the relationship between repatriation and state formation in the current global context of humanitarian interventionism? The three conventional levels of analysis – global, national and local – interact and need to be combined in considering how everyday forms of state formation are articulated through repatriation and resettlement.

In a highly polemical article David Slater refers to the current politics of humanitarian interventionism as the 'Occidental will and capacity to intervene … and subvert other sovereignties' (Slater 1995:

2. Displacement was an issue in the Esquipulas II peace agreements between the five Central American presidents in 1987. The UN Special Programme for Economic Assistance to Central America (PEC) gave top priority to displacement and return, a priority that was formalised through the International Conference on Refugees in Central America (CIREFCA).

371). This subversion, however, is somewhat paradoxical since the stated purpose of the interventions is to restore or create modern and coherent (nation-) states and reinforce the governments' ability to exercise 'good governance'. The Guatemalan return movement is a good case in point of the paradoxical nature of intervention. In a recent paper Thayer Scudder suggests that resettlement schemes always entail the possibility of reinforced state control over the groups resettled (Scudder forthcoming). In contrast, return and resettlement as directed by the CCPP and supported by the international community, was explicitly anti-governmental. Governmental agencies have deliberately been kept at a distance, and the returnees have only accepted support from intergovernmental agencies, NGOs and popular movements. Thus, the segregated return settlements may be interpreted as representing a kind of trans- or postnational space where state control is challenged or subverted (Appadurai 1993; Stepputat 1994).

Such an interpretation, however, depends on a conventional, dualistic understanding of the 'State' vs. (civil) 'society' in which the state is seen as a more or less coherent, autonomous and calculating political subject, centred in the government and state institutions. But the 'state' can also be conceived of as an idea – a claim to unity, coherence, structure and intentionality – with material effects. In this sense, the 'state' lives in and through its subjects (Abrams 1988; Joseph and Nugent 1994; Sayer 1994). The effectiveness and projection of this idea of the state is contingent upon the development of a grid of modern rationalities, techniques and practices which render the regulation and administration of everyday life desirable, feasible and even (possibly) legitimate. This is what the Foucauldian notion of 'governmentality' deals with: the modern governmentality is the particular way of thinking about the kinds of problems that should be addressed by social authorities, which emerged together with an ensemble of means to manage 'populations' during the seventeenth and eighteenth centuries in Europe (Miller and Rose 1990; Foucault 1991). These means included the conception and exploration of new objects of knowledge and intervention – such as economy, society, poverty and population – as well as modern techniques of administration, calculation and surveillance.

These everyday forms of state formation, that is, the embedding of ideas and practices of 'state' in the everyday life of the state's subjects, takes us into the 'local' level of analysis. As Henrietta Moore argues, the rationalities which sustain discourses and practices of government are global in scope, but they are always developed in specific contexts by politicians, academics, media and ordinary people

(Moore 1996: 12). As I understand Moore, she argues against the idea that there is one (European) centre for the production of these rationalities. The will to modernise works in many different localities, and among many different actors. Following Wagner (1994), we may for example distinguish between 'modernisation offensives from above' – carried out by an élite, a bureaucracy or an army – and 'modernisation offensives from below' that are promoted by, for example, groups who have been disadvantaged or excluded by 'modernisation offensives from above'.

Thus, when we are talking about everyday forms of state formation, it is important to note that the modern rationalities, techniques and practices that underpin state formation are not necessarily imposed. Modernisation offensives from above and from below entail an element of disciplinisation as well as of liberation from previous hegemonic limitations. Discipline works in schools, clinics, workshops and other bounded spaces, but discipline can also be, for example, 'a countermove against external impositions by means of establishing capable collective agency' (Wagner 1994: 26).

'Institutions' and modernisation from above

Institutions (*instituciones*) abound in Nentón. *Instituciones* is the common indigenous term to designate governmental, inter-governmental and nongovernmental agencies of relief and development which have positioned themselves in the township during the 1980s and 1990s. The distinctive trait of 'institutions' is that they are external agents in control of resources to which persons, groups and in particular communities may negotiate access, if they fit the categories managed by the institutions, and if they master the language and codified practices of the institutions.

'Institutions' are explicitly distinguished from 'organisations' (*organizaciones*). The latter are seen as something 'amongst ourselves'. Even though they have been introduced by people from other places, 'organisations' are seen to involve serious commitments on behalf of people in the villages. While they regard 'institutions' as legal and apolitical entities, the status of 'organisations' is less clear. People relate 'organisations' to the movements which preceded or directed the popular insurrection from the late 1970s onwards, and '*the* organisation' used to be synonymous with the guerrilla movement. The army apparently warned people in a village neighbouring the return settlement in Nentón not to mix with the returnees because 'they bring back their organisation that started the problem'.

The armed conflict has brought several new elements into the everyday life in the Nentón area. Apart from new social actors – the institutions, the organisations and the army – and the visible resources they have distributed, such as tin roofs and roads, the armed conflict has also engendered a new set of categories that have structured the work of the institutions and increased the complexity of the social landscape. The categories of 'displaced', 'repatriates', 'returnees' and 'locals' complement and cut across other sets of categories that used to circumscribe entitlements, belonging and social relations, such as 'tenants', 'individual landowners', 'holders of communal land', 'holders of national land', Indians and *ladinos*, and the names of the townships and villages of origin, all of which define important identities. This reconfiguration of the social landscape can be illustrated by focusing on two different sets of institutions which arrived in Nentón in the 1980s and the 1990s respectively.

In January 1982, the army evacuated the population of the township capital of Nentón. Return movements later that year occasioned intensified state presence. As a former teacher explained:

> Before 1982, only the Ministry of Education was present here in Nentón. But when we returned with the army to repopulate the town in 1982, all the institutions of the government arrived. Before, they didn't even know that Nentón existed. We, the teachers, were sent out to clear the bush and construct rustic schools.

Across the whole of Guatemala a first 'wave' of mainly governmental agencies accompanied the army's counter-insurgency campaign in 1982-84. The campaign was launched under the new doctrine of 'security and development' which was supposed to win 'the hearts and minds of the population'. This doctrine urged the army to become aware of, and respond to, the sufferings of the civil population, in particular to the 'displaced', 'a new actor in the Guatemalan scenario' and 'a new expression of the social costs of the armed challenge to the government' (Gramajo 1995: 192 and 198).

However, sensitivity to the sufferings of the civil population was clearly subsumed by security imperatives. During the campaign more than four hundred villages were massacred and destroyed, and the army reorganised and relabelled the population according to spatial criteria. While many fled into 'the wilderness' (*el monte*), those who stayed were considered subjects of the state and concentrated in villages where armed civil defence patrols could be organised and sustained. Those who had fled and were living either in Mexico or in *el monte* were excluded from the authorised national space, that is, the network of armed villages. They were deemed 'subversives', '*guerilleros*', 'non-Guatemalans' or '*canches*'.[3] The civil patrols and the network of villages constituted a near perfect system of social surveillance and information on movement for the army and other state agencies. The excluded non-subjects of the state – the refugees and displaced persons – who could only be 'helped' if they submitted themselves to the army's rituals of reinclusion by applying for amnesty and passing through re-education camps before resettling in armed villages or in one of the new 'development poles' which were designated for displaced people and refugees (AVANCSO 1990; Wilson 1991; Stepputat 1997). In some cases they received some relief items before resettling, but before the repatriation scheme of 1986 this seldom occurred in any systematic way.

These strategies were based on the concept of a growth- or development-pole, whereby the idea of development could be radiated from one point of intervention or investment. In Nentón, the 'development pole' of Chacaj was established on a plot of land which had been abandoned by refugees, and during the 1980s development efforts in the township were concentrated here. The institutions there included the army's civil affairs office, several ministries, a Taiwanese mission for agricultural development and a few North American NGOs. Most of these worked in a paternalistic fashion. Meanwhile army-employed teachers taught the population how to become 'good patriots' and officers trained them for the civil defence patrols. 'Growth' or 'development' did not radiate from the efforts concentrated in Chacaj; in fact all that radiated was the rumour that people in Chacaj were spoiled by all the assistance they had.

The first wave of institutions was part and parcel of the attempt to secure direct state control of the population and its movement, but an attempt that was inscribed in the development discourse. The ritualised labelling of returning refugees as subversives was abandoned in 1986 when they were no longer required to sign a petition for amnesty when entering the country. But at village level repatriates would have to 'follow the custom', including taking orders from the army-authorised leadership, joining the civil defence patrols and often being refused the return of their land rights. It was in the context of this hegemonically controlled form of repatriation that refugees in Mexico formed the CCPP. Their return became a lever for the introduction of a different

3. *Canche* is an old Quiché word for 'yellow skinned' Spaniards (Zur 1993) and has been a popular nickname for blue-eyed foreigners and guerrillas alike. It has been used consistently by the army to delegitimise the guerrillas as foreigners and foreigners as guerrilla supporters.

type of relief and development agency which, in some respects, challenged the sovereignty of the Guatemalan state.

The second wave of institutions that reached Nentón from the late 1980s onwards was mainly internationally induced. Expectations of a massive repatriation to the border region attracted the attention of international donors and organisations, in particular after the much publicised 1992 accords on the 'organised return'. International funding was channelled through the President's office, through the new Ministry of Development or through transnational NGOs. Many foreign donors also sought to channel their support for reconstruction and return through national NGOs in order to strengthen NGO-capacity and the 'civil society'. UNHCR and the donors paved the way for major participation by NGOs in a context where the latter from the outset were not welcomed at all by the government. In the field, UNHCR effectively became an 'umbrella' for NGOs.

The modes of intervention of the second wave of institutions changed, *grosso modo*, from paternalistic, army-centred interventions that viewed civil patrols as extensions or representatives of the army's authority, to a mode of intervention that sought to induce nonmilitarised forms of organisation, such as 'development committees' or regional 'associations', serving as entities for negotiation with governmental and other agencies. Even though many programmes and projects did not focus specifically on repatriates, settlements and villages with returned refugees were usually given priority. While this was also true of the first wave of institutions, the discourse of intervention of the second wave of institutions changed from the security-centred discourse – depicting refugees and displaced people as subversive non-Guatemalans – to a postconflict discourse that depicted the same people as disadvantaged Guatemalans in need of assistance.

For the national NGOs in particular, the return movement represented an opportunity to enter the former zones of conflict which had been 'no-go' areas for more than a decade. They saw return settlements as 'bridgeheads' for further activities in areas that hitherto had been dominated by the army and evangelical churches. From these bridgeheads would be dispersed self-centred development; awareness of human rights, environment and gender issues, and non-governmental forms of organisation. 'Organisation and popular power' would spread at the 'local level' resulting in 'the opening of a field of pressure and demands towards the state' (CCPP 1993: 3).

Although these two waves of institutions differ in many aspects, they have several common features, particularly when viewed from the perspective of everyday life in Nentón. Even among village leaders in Nentón, the difference between governmental and nongovernmental may pass unperceived. They are all 'institutions' and the persons embodying them are all 'employees' or *licenciados*; the local employees of several consecutive institutions may well be the same non-Indians from the township capital, and they all try to teach the villagers new ways of doing things.

Another continuity between the two waves are labelling practices arising from the provision of resources, the elicitation of information on the categories defined for and by the intervention ('displaced', 'repatriates' etc.) and the tendency to focus interventions spatially in points from where 'development' or alternative ideas will radiate. These practices of intervention have the possibility of creating tensions as labels and strategies interfere with existing social identities and trajectories. Thus, for example, 'refugees' who returned from Mexico in 1984, 1990 and 1994 have received very different attention: while the 'subversives' of 1984 received a bag of beans, the 'repatriates' of 1990 received maize and beans for six months, as well as corrugated tin sheets for their roofs, and the 'returnee' of 1994 additionally received very soft credits for land, house and income-generation.

Visible difference: 'sadly remembering the conquest'

The resettlement of repatriates and displaced persons engenders a reorganisation of the social landscape and existing entitlements. As the following examples show, the new categories and entitlements nurture conflicts in which different identities and social memories are brought into play. Just as the visible individual assistance to repatriates before 1992 created resentment between them and their neighbours, the even more conspicuous assistance to the return settlements has created resentment and conflicts. The basic issue of most of these conflicts is the access to land that the 1992 accords provided, including the possibility of escaping existing communal hegemonies by establishing autonomous settlements.

Nentón provides two examples. One is the case of Pocobastik, where a group of repatriates bought a piece of land, which was also claimed by their former neighbours in Trinidad, the private estate that they all came from. Before the armed conflict they were all classified as tenants (*mozos colonos*); when the war started they all supported the guerrillas and they all fled to Mexico. But they went back at different times, under different conditions, and since the most recent group of repatriates had access to credits, they had won the land. Upon the return of these repatriates, earlier returnees to Trinidad – among them cousins and uncles of the repatriates – visited them and 'displayed threatening attitudes', according to observers from the Guatemalan refugee commission.

In the negotiations that followed, the people from Trinidad presented themselves as tenants. Long before the war they had the permission of the *patrón* to work the land 'as if it is your own', in exchange for defending the land against 'unknown' intruders. Their subsequent defence of the land during the war, and the lives of those who died in combat on this land, now entered the argument. They also resented the fact that the repatriates would not 'recognise the place where they were born' and come and live together with them in Trinidad. The repatriates, on the other hand, invoked ownership, laws of private property, and their right to settle wherever they wanted. Their claim to the land, based on the new category and the governmental accords, was modern and historically 'thin'.

The other example involves returnees in *Nueva Esperanza*, an autonomous settlement for returnees, where a land conflict with the neighbouring village Aguacate was inherited. Interestingly, a previous division in Aguacate between earlier 'repatriates' and people labelled as 'displaced' was healed and a united front presented to the 'returnees' in *Nueva Esperanza*. Adding to the complexity was the fact that several families from Aguacate had returned from exile to *Nueva Esperanza*, rather than back to Aguacate.

Having a communal land title, Aguacate claimed part of the land registered as the property of the returnees. In 1996, having obstructed the authorised remeasurement of the returnees' land, a large group of people from Aguacate, some of them armed, invaded the land, cleared some forest and planted their corn. Later the group started constructing houses on the land. The well-connected returnees in *Nueva Esperanza* attracted the support of the UN Human Rights mission (MINUGUA), the governmental Human Rights attorney and a number of NGOs. The army and the Governor also intervened, unsuccessfully, to resolve the discord.

In presenting their case, Aguacate representatives established their entitlement through the story of one of their grandfathers who had managed to obtain a title for the land from the government and had Aguacate declared a village (*aldea*). Struggle for the land and recognition by authorities, even in the distant past, are customary means of 'place-making' which legitimised the claims of Aguacate. At a meeting with foreign NGOs, representatives of the Aguacate land committee ended their presentation as follows:

Sadly it is as if the external assistance is putting a little pressure on us, it makes us remember the Conquest which the Spaniard carried out, because at that time they came and put the yoke on our Mayan ancestors, invading and removing their belongings, just as the situation we are experiencing now. Thus, this makes us remember the violations that the conquistadores committed in the year 1492. Hopefully this violation will cease since we now have these human rights ... we want that our rights be respected. We have already suffered a lot because of the violence. Here in this village the *guerilleros* have bothered us quite a lot, they have murdered several people. We have endured (*soportado*) this ... Why? Because here we were born, here we live, and here we will stay. We don't want to inflict damage on the people who travel (*caminan*), we don't want to be assailants. What we want is to show our children how to make a living with sweat on the brow, so they become honest people.'

The statement has a modern orientation, for example through references to 'rights' and the 'Mayan' ancestors.[4] But the way in which the new categories are made intelligible and negotiable is by applying the binary, colonial opposition between *indios* and *ladinos* with the returnees in the position of the *ladinos*, and Aguacate in the position of the *indios*. The latter are represented as the legitimate heirs to the 'Mayan ancestors', the victims of the conquest who had their land taken away. The inhabitants of Aguacate are the ones who have endured the suffering, who have worked long hours on the land, and who have a continuous presence from the past and into the future. Among the elements which position the returnees as *ladinos* are their 'conquest' of land; their abilities to communicate with 'institutions', *licenciados* (educated urban people) and *canches* (blue-eyed strangers); their access to urban style dwellings; their absence and failure to contribute to the defence of the land during the conflict, and their lack of local knowledge.

In both the above cases of conflict the less privileged party – the locals already in Guatemala when the newcomers arrived – represented the returnees in terms of spatial, social and cultural differences. Continuity, belonging, roots and their historical relations to the authority of the government constituted the locals' principal claims to the land. The newcomers, in contrast, represented the locals in terms of a difference in development, in modernisation and in time, thus constituting their claims on the basis of a break with tradition – an awakening.

4. A few years ago nobody in the area identified themselves as 'Mayan'. The Mayan movement is a new, postconflict phenomenon.

'Formal people' and modernisation from below

While their claims to the disputed land are based on the memory of (recent) violence and exile, the accords of 1992, and the formal acquisition of a deed, the returnees' representations of themselves *vis-à-vis* the local people are structured by a developed/ underdeveloped, or modern/traditional dichotomy. These distinctions revolve around the issues of livelihood, violence, language, education, as well as 'reason', as illustrated in the following excerpt from a representative's speech to a foreign ambassador who visited *Nueva Esperanza*:

> Those from Aguacate destroy the forest, they only leave fallow bush. If this land had not been *finca* (private estate), they would have destroyed the forest here as well. Their destruction is a problem because our estate depends on forestry. There will be undernourishment amongst our children, maybe the youngsters will become delinquents. It is a pity because we came here to make development. Here, in *Nueva Esperanza*, the families are thinking about how to develop every day. In Aguacate they only want to spill the blood ... They haven't got any education; 90% of them speak in dialect, and only the leaders speak Spanish. You cannot reason with them (*a ellos no llegan razón*). They do not want to accept the authorities, neither the Human Rights attorney, nor the INTA,[5] nor the Governor ... They have a problem with us, they threaten us. This situation reminds us of 1982, when we had to leave the country. (Transcript, November 1996)

The young representative, who was himself born in Aguacate, reasons within discourses of modern knowledge (environment, undernourishment, delinquency, percentages of monolinguism) and emphasises the distinctiveness of the returnees' will to develop, to become modern. This is their common project and an important collective identity which is based on the incorporation of a new set of ethics. Vehicles for these ethics are 'ideas', 'examples' and 'advice' which have 'woken us up', 'opened our eyes' and 'made us aware'. They are products of specific techniques for the making of subjectivities, self-perceptions and meaning – in Foucault's terminology 'pastoral techniques'. Throughout their trajectory returnees to Guatemala, and particularly their leaders, have received 'ideas' from Catholic and Protestant missionaries, in cooperative settlements in the lowlands, from peasant unions, from the guerrillas, and from relief agencies and solidarity workers in the refugee

5. The Institute for Agrarian Transformation, responsible for registration, redistribution and surveys of land.

settlements in Mexico. These 'ideas' have worked as blueprints for new modes of living.

The refugee 'camp' was thus one of several spaces in which new sets of ethics were developed. The 'camp' was a 'disciplinary space' (Foucault 1977), embodying a detailed structuring of time, space and social relations; while permitting observation and regulation. When incorporated in a relief regime, the refugees became subjected to headcounts, registers, measurements, classifications, listings, queuing and other procedures of logistical management. These procedures are techniques developed for the government of populations. But to a large degree in the case of the Guatemalan refugees, they themselves took charge of these tasks. In the words of the Mexican coordinator of a large settlement in Mexico, 'this is seen by the government as a major experiment in self-government'.[6]

An equally important experience from the refugee camps included the incorporation of formal procedures, for example, for democratic elections, the development of cooperatives, project management and workshops. A common denominator of most of these practices is that they are based on formalised operations, formalisation being 'a way of re-interpreting the world and re-classifying its elements with a view to increasing manageability' (Wagner 1994: 26). As Wagner points out this formalisation does not necessarily increase the general knowledge of the conditions under which we live, but it does entail a 'belief in the *knowability* and, following from it, in the *mastery* of the world by means of *calculation*' (Wagner 1994: 26).

Formalisation has become incorporated in the returning refugees' understanding of themselves and their encounters with their environment. As a leader from Pocobastik said to a government official while they were waiting for the civil patrollers to arrive for a meeting: 'Ahh, don't believe they're formal people like us (*gente formales*); they're like animals'. To become 'formal' is certainly a pervasive ambition for returning refugees in Pocobastik. They want to have 'formal houses', to have an officially sanctioned and technically impeccable 'urban layout' (*trazo urbano*), to follow prescriptions for meetings, to elect 'administrators' for the settlement and to have written regulations.

Even more pervasive is the formalisation of the return settlement *Nueva Esperanza* and its one thousand inhabitants. First it is criss-crossed by systems of representation based on diverse criteria such as neighbourhood, religion, age and gender. Secondly it is organised

6. It is important to note that there were major differences between the experiences of refugees in the larger camps in the interior of Mexico and those in the smaller and less established border camps.

as a cooperative 'peasant enterprise' where the management of different sectors of the economy is separated from the management of 'communal services' – the social sectors. The wall charts and filing systems in the cooperative's office are a far cry from the small desk drawer in the deputy mayor's desk in Aguacate and Trinidad. Obviously NGOs have been involved in the establishment of these organisational structures, but the ambition of the returnees to become formalised permeates the whole enterprise.

Seen in this perspective, the return settlements are dense packages of modern rationalities and techniques of government, or rather self-government. Although modern techniques of government are mastered in other places as well, the perception of return settlements as new beginnings invites the wholesale introduction of modern rationality (Riesco 1995). Within an encompassing project of modernisation and guided by a fairly rigid ideological blueprint, the CCPP and their national and international supporters have deployed the techniques which were experienced in exile. However, while procedures and formalised modes of operation *in abstracto* are transportable assets, they do not automatically lead to the practical knowledge which is necessary in order to survive on marginal lands in a poor region with a very limited market. After two years, *Nueva Esperanza* had not become self-sufficient in subsistence crops, and 20 percent of the returned households had left the settlement. Others relied on food donations or salaries from construction projects, while some continued to engage in migrant labour in Mexico.

In addition to the enormous task of re-establishing their own livelihoods – a process which often entails impoverishment (Cernea 1997) – the returnees and their supporters have set themselves the task of improving conditions in the whole return area and of achieving self-government. 'What we want for us we want for everybody' is one of the slogans of the CCPP. They see the return settlements as bridgeheads and themselves as promoters of human rights, gender and environmental issues, as well as of new practices of organisation and political action. In the sense that the politics of the return movement are directed against the state and the élite, the returnees indeed engage in a 'modernisation offensive from below' (Wagner 1994).

Settling people, settling conflict? Dimensions of postconflict state formation

The main argument of this chapter is that repatriation can have a potentially stabilising effect in terms of state formation. Repatriation in Guatemala has been demonstrated to have contributed to the social construction of peace and to the development of a 'common discursive framework' which includes the extension of a network of modern rationalities through which techniques of government work, as well as to the diffusion of specific ideas and languages of 'state' and 'civil society'. At the same time the Guatemala case study illustrates ways that repatriation may have destabilising effects (Sepulveda 1995).

Before the repatriation and resettlement in Guatemala, the state apparatus had little presence outside the cities in highland Guatemala. Systems of indirect rule through private estate owners were predominant, and the majority of the population, in particular the 'Indians', were excluded from citizenship and from the political sphere. In the countryside the state was generally perceived of as a distant source of authority and occasionally a source of violence. One way that the politics of repatriation might be described as affecting state formation in Guatemala was the closing of this gap between the state and the people through mobilising intervention.

In the wake of the counter-insurgency campaign, the army and the agencies which accompanied the process of resettlement gave the state apparatus a more continuous presence in the area of conflict where they offered, if not citizenship, then at least 'patriotship' to the male members of the civil patrols. The case of Nentón illustrates how displacement and resettlement became associated with waves of interventions, first for 'security and development' and then for 'peace and development'. Development interventions in turn necessitated the settlement of people in legally and physically defined places. A fixed and formalised spatial organisation seems to be essential for the construction of the state as a vehicle for human progress.

A second interaction between repatriation and state formation might be described as the 'modernisation' effect. Once settled, the repatriates and returnees involved themselves ('modernisation from below') and become involved ('modernisation from above') in the production of networks of rationalities, which are prerequisites for the extension of modern forms of power. Techniques of physical control were gradually substituted with techniques of containment operating through processes such as credit-schemes, licences, regulations and democratic systems of representation.

Even though the politics of the return movement was directed against the government and the élite, they contribute to the production of specific ideas of the state, the public sphere and the content of citizenship. This is a third aspect of the interaction between repatriation and state formation. Before the conflict, the image was of a predatory state. Particularly in association with the second wave of institutions, however, the state has come to be perceived as a more benign actor. Through their constant evocation of the 'state' and 'public' responsibilities, and through their ability to engage in a dialogue with representatives of the state, returnees in particular have contributed to the production of an image of the state as a body with powers and rights to intervene in society. Perceptions of the state have at the same time become more 'layered' and sophisticated. The distinction between governmental, inter-governmental and nongovernmental agencies was not very meaningful to most people in the villages. They were all seen as providers of resources, representatives of urban lifestyle and power, and promoters of formalised procedures. In contrast the returnees have become acutely aware of different types of agencies, and particularly the distinction between 'governmental' and 'nongovernmental'.

Overall, the return movement can be considered to have contributed to the formation of a 'common discursive framework' in contemporary Guatemala, defined as a 'material and meaningful framework for living through, talking about, and acting upon social orders characterised by domination' (Roseberry 1994: 361). The framework provides practices and discourses of (legitimate) intervention by governmental and other agencies, as well as a 'language of contention' through which subjects of the state can criticise and engage in negotiations with these agencies. According to Carol Smith, such a hegemonic construction has not existed in Guatemala since the days of the colonial regime (Smith 1990). It might be a conclusion that the political effects of the numerous assistance projects for returnees in the former areas of conflict in Guatemala have been more significant than their economic effects (cf. McDonald and Gatehouse 1995).

The increased local presence of civil authorities and the 'rule of law' has, however, gone hand in hand with the perpetuation of previous conflicts, or the creation of new conflicts over resources and identities. The interventions described involved the introduction of new categories and boundaries which redefined the social landscape. They have been targeted mainly on the displaced, repatriates and returnees and have thus created new differences and provoked or magnified conflicts over resources and entitlements. The people who were present before the repatriates and returnees arrived have reacted to the visible or perceived privileges of the returnees by delegitimising the newcomers as intruding foreigners, guerrilla-supporters and/or representatives of the non-Indian national society – as the heirs of the *conquistadores*. In the context of the local conflicts over resources, they legitimise their actions with reference to their roots and their defence of the land during the conflict. The recently returned, on the other hand, have constructed themselves as developers – as modern 'formal' people, and have privileged access to development agencies.

The local conflicts that have emerged in the process of repatriation to Guatemala are not the same as national-level conflicts. They are best understood as conflicts over access to resources, communal leaderships, ethnic identities, and the exclusions and inclusions which accompany repatriation schemes and modernisation offensives. The Nentón case provides several reasons to believe that these local conflicts do not persist over time, and shows how the different parties can enter new tactical alliances. There is a persistent danger, however, that the kinds of conflict which have accompanied local return can be exploited by actors in the national conflict.

13

Examining the Discourse of Repatriation: Towards a More Proactive Theory of Return Migration

Laura Hammond

In the study of repatriation, the lion's share of attention has been placed on examining either the decision to repatriate (particularly identifying the factors that go into electing to return and determining whether such decisions are voluntary), or the actual repatriation movement from the country of exile to the country of origin. While such areas of enquiry are obviously valid, there has been a virtual neglect of the later stages of repatriation, in which returnees attempt to establish themselves socially, economically and politically in their areas of return. Failing critically to consider these later stages can lead to the erroneous conclusion that with physical repatriation comes the end of the migration or displacement cycle. In fact the end of the process may still be years away for some returnee populations. As scholars and practitioners attempting to understand this process from the point of view of the repatriates, we need to question our assumptions about the meanings we give to concepts of 'return', 'home' and 'place' while at the same time reassessing the terms we use to describe postrepatriation life.

In this chapter I argue that our understanding of the sociocultural and economic processes in which returnees become involved following repatriation is handicapped by our use of biased and inappropriate terminology. Lacking precise conceptual tools for examining what returnees do once they get down from the trucks that brought them back to their country of origin, aid providers are largely shooting in the dark when they try to develop assistance packages or to evaluate repatriation operations. Social scientists, who use misleading terminology borrowed largely from the international aid regime, its subdiscipline disaster management, and outdated migration theories, also fail to appreciate the lessons that returnees can teach them about culture change, the construction of communities, and the multiple meanings of, and connections between, notions of identity, culture, home and geographical place.

Some of the recent literature on repatriation draws attention to the challenges that people commonly face after repatriation to their country of origin (Larkin et al. 1992; Allen and Morsink 1994a; Allen 1996). These challenges are particularly problematic in contexts where refugee movements have been spurred by civil conflict and where the period of exile has been prolonged. In such cases, return to the communities from which refugees originally fled may not be possible or even desirable. People who have lived as refugees for several years typically find upon return that they have lost their property and land rights in the country of origin. Whether they return to their birthplace or to a different area within the country of origin that is new to them, they often face intense competition with local residents for resources, social services, employment and educational opportunities. Population pressure and the fact that certain areas have become uninhabitable due to continuing conflict or the danger of land-mines may make it difficult or impossible for a country or region to absorb the returnee population. Without taking proper preparedness and social security measures (such as constructing schools and clinics, creating employment opportunities, and providing other services), repatriating large numbers of people to an area of chronic poverty and food insecurity may accelerate the general slide of an already poor population into a condition of even greater economic vulnerability. In such instances, repatriation may be a major contributing factor to the recurrence of disaster and of stress migration (Jackson 1994).

Consideration of these difficulties leads us to consider what sort of future is possible and viable for returnees. I argue here that the terminology we use to describe the social, political and economic behaviour of returnees obfuscates our understanding of the processes that are actually at work following repatriation. It reflects the assumption that refugees represent 'matter out of place' and thus that returnees should be put back into that place, in this case meaning their birthplace (usually assumed to be the site from which people flee to become refugees) (Douglas 1966, cited in Malkki 1992). Such an assumption holds that refugees are people whose 'natural' tie to their birthplace, and therefore to their culture, lifeblood and ethnic identity, has been broken and should be reestablished following repatriation. The argument assumes that for its subjects, repatriation is a return to a way of life and an association between identity and place that is familiar, and therefore qualitatively better, than either remaining in exile or being resettled to a third country.

In this paper, I offer an alternative to the 'repatriation = homecoming' model. I show that the assumption that it is desirable and possible for returnees to regain that which they had before becoming refugees is flawed. Whether a returnee comes back to his or her birthplace or settles in an entirely new environment, he/she considers return to be more of a new beginning than a return to the past.

The Tigrayans with whom I lived between 1993 and 1995 returned from the refugee camps in eastern Sudan to a part of Ethiopia unfamiliar to them. Prior to return, they were informed by their local leaders and representatives of the United Nations that the communities in their areas of origin could not accommodate them and that the land they had left behind had been reallocated in their absence. They therefore agreed to be resettled in the western lowlands of Tigray, an area that more closely resembles the environment of the refugee camps in which they had spent the previous eight years than it does the areas they fled during the war and famine of the mid-1980s.

In accepting the option of returning to Ethiopia but settling in a new area, these returnees reinterpreted their definitions of *person, culture, identity, home* and place in the context of their postrepatriation environment. For them, repatriation involved opening a new chapter of life and was not in any significant sense a 'homecoming'. In the context of movement to a new place, notions of *identity, community* and *home* were transformed. Such concepts were conditioned by the economic realities people found in the area to which they were settled and even four years later continue to shape the way that repatriates formulate their goals and expectations for the future.[1] Just as world views, visions of the future and strategies for social and economic survival in the returnee settlement reflect the opportunities and constraints presented by that environment, I suggest that these forms of culture change and community formation may be similarly constructed even for those who do return to their birthplaces.

1. The bulk of the data for this article is based on fieldwork that was carried out from November 1993 to July 1995. I also returned to Humera/Ada Bai in February 1996 and May 1997 for short visits.

Sedentarism and the discourse of repatriation

Despite the sometimes elaborate information campaigns that are conducted in refugee communities prior to registration for repatriation, the expectations that governments and assistance providers have of what will happen to returnees following repatriation usually differs vastly from what potential returnees expect will happen to them.[2] This divergence is reflected in the difference between, on one hand, the set of labels which I call here the 'discourse of repatriation' imposed by external actors, and on the other the testimonies and descriptions given by returnees themselves about their post-repatriation lives. Working with a conceptual framework that does not recognise real experiences of returnees, we run the risk of providing assistance that is inappropriate and of allowing legitimate needs for integration to go unrecognised and unmet. As scholars, we miss an important opportunity to further our understanding of social change and community creation, both in general and in the specific contexts of war, famine and migration. A thorough examination is thus warranted of this discourse of repatriation, its etymologies, hidden and not-so-hidden agendas, and practical implications for repatriates.

Terms to be found in the discourse of repatriation include: *reintegration, rehabilitation, reconstruction, rebuilding, readjustment, readaptation, reacculturation, reassimilation, reinsertion, reintroduction, recovery* and *re-establishment* (Gmelch 1980; Allen and Morsink 1994; Allen 1996). Among the most problematic terms of the repatriation canon are the very words *return* and *returnee*, which imply that by re-entering one's native country a person is necessarily returning to something familiar. These terms are riddled with value judgements that reflect a segmentary, sedentary idea of how people ought to live, what their relation to their 'homeland' should be, and ultimately how they should go about constructing their lives once the period of exile ends.

The implication of these terms is that returnees should seek to move backward in time, to recapture a quality of life that they are assumed to have enjoyed before becoming refugees or that those who remained behind currently enjoy. Because postrepatriation life, or 'home' in the discourse of repatriation, is rooted in the country of origin it is considered by outsiders to be necessarily better than the life in exile. The implied parallel between 'nation-state' and 'home' is peculiar,

2. Information campaigns typically involve representatives of UNHCR, the host government, and the government of origin/return presenting information concerning conditions in the country of return, assistance that may be expected by returnees, and logistical procedures for registration and repatriation.

particularly in Africa where many ethnic groups do not recognise national boundaries and where some groups can even become officially recognised refugees without leaving their ethnic territories.[3]

For some refugees, repatriation may entail an improvement in living conditions and the degree of protection made available, and also may involve the unification of kinship units (whether households or more extended relations) that were dispersed during the period of exile. In such cases, while repatriation may be the most desirable option, it still involves dramatic changes in economic strategies and the positioning of the returnee in the context of kin, community and the wider spheres of region and nation.

In the case of the returnees with whom I lived, however, repatriation was not viewed as a clear choice in upward mobility. While the memory of the war and famine that necessitated their flight from Ethiopia has been permanently and painfully etched in their minds, they insisted that once the initial famine emergency had passed, their time in the Sudanese refugee camps was a 'golden age,' where generous aid and income-generating opportunities gave them more food and money, and better health care and education, than they had ever known before or will be able to realistically expect during their lifetimes now that they are back in Ethiopia where the social service infrastructure is far less developed and does not single them out for special assistance. Repatriation has meant a significant drop in the availability of health care and educational services as well as a severe reduction in household food security levels. In a world where development, modernity and progress are given high priority, it is ironic that returnees should be expected to choose to forgo a higher standard of living for the 'pleasure' of going back to their country of origin. It is also disappointing that repatriation has tended not to be seen as an opportunity for development of the local economy and infrastructure in the country of origin.[4] Such

3. An example is Somalis who are given refugee status because they have crossed from Somalia into Ethiopia even though they remain in the territory of their clan. It should be noted that the Tigrayans who fled to Sudan were fleeing to a culturally dissimilar area, so for them the national border was culturally as well as politically significant.

4. One of UNHCR's most important roles is to ensure the voluntary nature of repatriation, guaranteed in the 1951 Convention Related to the Status of Refugees and its 1967 Protocol. Individuals sign a form stating that they freely choose to take part in the repatriation programme. While it is usually (but not always) true that refugees are not physically coerced into repatriation, the voluntary nature of the decision to return may be difficult and even impossible to distinguish in cases where those who opt not to repatriate face closure of camps, cessation of aid, and harassment by local security forces. Those who choose not to return may also face harassment and intimidation from the host government or political groups in the country of origin whose interests repatriation may serve.

development could be used as an important mechanism to prevent the recurrence of future flows of refugees.

Malkki (1992; 1995a; 1995b) has shown that deeply held sedentarist beliefs about the inseparability of identity and culture from place or 'roots' have become expressed as what she calls the 'territorialisation of national identity'. We use botanical metaphors to describe refugees: they are *uprooted, displaced, transplanted.* 'The territorialising metaphors of identity – roots, soils, trees, seeds – are washed away in human *floodtides, waves, flows, streams,* and *rivers'* (Malkki 1995b: 15-16). Their supposed natural tie to the land having been broken, refugees are considered to be deterritorialised, without culture, and suffering from a pathological condition due to the loss of their individual and/or collective identity (e.g., Daley 1991). They present a problem, are dangerous to their hosts, and are therefore quarantined in camps in order to control their polluting power (Douglas 1966; Malkki 1992; 1995b; Kearney 1995; Kibreab 1989).

In a similar vein, Appadurai has observed that heretofore anthropologists have bound people to place: 'natives are not only persons who are from certain places, and belong to those places, but they are also those who are somehow *incarcerated,* or confined, in those places' (Appadurai 1988: 37). Applying the analogy to refugee/returnee populations, we might say that those who have fled their native country must be returned to it in order to restore the proper 'order of things'. The implicit assumption is that the categories imposed upon migrants that bind them to their countries of origin are shared by the migrants themselves.

This is not to say that refugees who flee do not miss, or want to return to, their countries of origin, nor that they do not perceive a change in their conceptualisations of identity and place as a result of their forced migration. The individual's tie to his or her homeland may be mutable. It is a mistake, however, to assume that the experience of becoming a refugee is necessarily experienced as deculturing, deterritorialising, or dehistoricising, or that the connection is necessarily between person and nation, rather than person and area (region, village, etc.). Links may be recreated or shaped in new ways.

The present anthropological moment, with its 'recognition that people are increasingly 'moving targets' (Breckenridge and Appadurai 1989: I; Malkki 1992: 25), and the shifting of its lens of enquiry to examine peripheries, boundaries, borderlands, migrants, and processes of apparent flux and disorder (Malkki 1992: 25; Rosaldo 1989; Alvarez 1995; Limón 1989; 1994), provides an opportunity to reassess the conventional consideration that refugees inhabit a dangerous, decultured, liminal space (Turner 1967; van Gennep 1960). Instead, refugees may be understood as people who maximise the social, cultural and economic opportunities available to them while in exile. They learn skills, adopt new vocations, and develop new social frameworks. These influences become components in evolving senses of individual and collective identity, *vis-à-vis* new world views which are neither entirely like nor entirely unlike the identities and world views that people held prior to fleeing from their country of origin. Global culture has an increasing influence on local lives, through contact with the assistance regime, the media, and the expanding network of friends and relatives who leave the refugee camps to resettle in third countries.

If we take 'back across the border' the challenge of the assumed natural, immutable link between person and place and culture and geography we can see that the sedentarist bias is equally influential in prescribing 'cures' for refugees. One of the reasons that repatriation has not been problematised is that its goal has been defined primarily as the need to put people back into 'their place', defined in most cases as their birthplace. It is assumed by practitioners involved in repatriation programmes, whether governmental, nongovernmental or UN personnel, that once returnees are back in their native country, their roots will be reestablished. Like seedlings replanted in the earth, they will grow and thrive with a minimum of maintenance or attention. Once the natural tie between person and place is reestablished, it is expected that other challenges (attaining economic self-sufficiency, building social networks, and becoming active and valued citizens of the community, the region and the nation) will be met *ipso facto.*

The reasons for maintaining this position say much about the organisational self-interest of the agencies involved. To recognise the problems that repatriates often face after returning to their country of origin is to call into question the assumption that repatriation is the best available 'durable solution' to the refugee 'problem'. If repatriation is not the best solution, then the other solutions, of local integration or third country resettlement, must be examined more closely. For reasons which are primarily, but not only, financial, host and donor governments are loathe to do this.

Even if repatriation may be, as UNHCR recently admitted, 'the least worse option' in a 'no win situation' (UNHCR 1997c), a multitude of questions must be asked. *Where* in the host country should refugees be repatriated to? What kind of assistance (if any) should they be given? Who is to be responsible for ensuring their protection and welfare following repatriation? For how long should they be considered a 'vulnerable group', possibly deserving of specially targeted assistance? And, most importantly, who should decide the answers to these questions?

If the answers to these questions demonstrate repatriation to be more complex simply than the transportation of people from one side of an international border to another, then there is a challenge to UNHCR, other UN agencies, NGOs and governments of return countries to provide more assistance to help absorb these returnees or to find an alternative to repatriation. Lacking sufficient resources to perform the functions with which they are presently charged, let alone to provide additional services, these actors have (in many cases deliberately) chosen not to look closely at the medium- and long-term experiences and needs of returnees. In the aid world, to understand is often to recognise, and to recognise is to take responsibility. From the myopic point of view of assistance providers looking for a 'way out' of expensive refugee care and maintenance programmes, it is too expensive to take on added responsibilities. In this way opportunities for sustainable development and preventive action to prevent future refugee flows are left unexploited.

Building houses versus building lives: the discourse of disaster management

Many of the words used to describe postrepatriation social change (e.g., *rehabilitation, reconstruction* and *recovery*) are borrowed from the discourse of disaster management. Disaster management has become a subdiscipline of the applied social sciences, not to mention a growth industry for development consultants. Its conceptual frameworks are used to analyse and recommend ways of preparing for, preventing, responding to, and recovering from natural and human-made disasters. Herein lies a problem, for the same frameworks are often applied by self-declared disaster management 'experts' not only to the reconstruction of physical infrastructure, but also to the 'social recovery' of a community after a war or following displacement. There is little or no recognition on the part of most of these specialists that the 'relief to development continuum' which provides the basis for most disaster management studies, may not be applicable to individual or collective human actors in the same way that it is to physical objects, nor that the 'community' in question may not even exist as such any longer (UNDP 1993).

A building destroyed by an earthquake may be rebuilt so that it resembles its previous form. A field may be replanted after its crop is destroyed by a flood. When the damage affects human lives, economies and communities, however, the type of response required may be different from that which is needed for physical or structural damage. In particular, where disaster leads to displacement, most responses have sought to help migrants return to their places of origin to resume the lives they 'left behind' when they fled; to reconstruct the community as it existed previously. Little consideration is given to whether people want to or are able to return to their birthplaces, or whether they might not be better off migrating to a place where they may have greater economic opportunities, less conflict with other communities, and be accorded greater respect with regard to political, religious and human rights. The trap that many disaster management specialists fall into is to view displacement as similar in type to other forms of natural disasters.

Many returnees, in fact, do not see the object of repatriation as the 'rebuilding' or 'reconstruction' of their lives. Likewise, they often do not aspire to reclothe themselves in the culture of the past or to rejoin the community that they left. Even those who do return to their birthplaces know that their move is likely to be a return only in terms of geographic placement. Real return to the life they left may not be feasible or even desirable. Instead, they may see the experience of repatriation as an opportunity to position their social, cultural and economic selves in such a way as to effectively exploit the possibilities afforded in a new area. In many cases, returnees only 'return' insofar as they return to their country of origin; the actual place in which they choose to settle or to which they are settled may be a place to which they do not even have ancestral or kinship ties. To develop strategies for building a life that is economically viable as well as socially and culturally fulfilling, they use the knowledge, skills, and social networks they gathered in exile together with some of those they practised prior to becoming refugees.

1993 Repatriation to Ethiopia

The overwhelming majority of returnees with whom I lived in the Ada Bai settlement in northwest Ethiopia spent eight years living in refugee camps in the Sudan, having fled war and famine in their native region of Tigray in 1984-85. With the overthrow of the Dergue military dictatorship in 1991 by a government closely associated with the Tigrayan People's Liberation Front (TPLF), the way was cleared for most of the Ethiopian refugees living in the Sudan to repatriate. The first convoys brought approximately 12,000 people back to Ethiopia in June 1993. Repatriation brought these returnees to a place that bore little resemblance to the land they had fled nearly a decade before.

Ada Bai, like the other returnee settlements areas around the town of Humera, is situated in a hot, dry lowland environment close to the borders of Sudan and Eritrea. Climatically, agriculturally and culturally, the area is more similar to the refugee camps from which people repatriated than to the small highland farms from which they originally migrated. Prior to repatriating, refugees were told by Ethiopian government officials that if they chose to move to Ethiopia they would be resettled in the western lowlands because there was a shortage of available farmland in the central, eastern and southern highlands of Tigray. They were promised that they would be allocated farmland and that there was plenty of seasonal employment available on the large commercial sesame and sorghum plantations. In addition to plots of land ranging from one to three hectares, additional assistance would include tractor ploughing for the first harvest, one year's food ration, and a clinic and elementary school in each of the three settlements.

While conducting fieldwork in Ada Bai, the largest of these settlements, one of my major research aims was to determine how people considered this new place. Did they consider it a stopping-off point on the way to the highlands, or did they see it as their new, permanent, home? Responses to my queries fell into three basic groups, differentiated generationally. Analysis of these responses illustrates the shifting importance of home for returnees at different stages of their lives.

Many of the older residents of Ada Bai (aged over forty) insisted that they wanted to die in their birthplace, to be buried with their families and remembered in a proper funeral ceremony by their neighbours and kin whom they had known, and been known by, for their whole lives. They held this sentiment, which is common throughout Africa (Harrell-Bond and Wilson 1990) despite the fact that it does not correspond to the official contemporary teachings of the Orthodox Christian Church, of which most residents of Ada Bai are followers. Current Church doctrine holds that as long as a person is given an Orthodox Christian burial in any sanctioned graveyard, it does not matter if he or she is buried far from his or her birthplace. Funeral ceremonies can even be held in the birthplace of the deceased (at the home of the closest kin) even if the body is buried elsewhere. This position is probably a recent innovation of the Church, developed in response to increasing rural to urban migration and the high costs and logistical difficulties of transporting bodies, particularly during wartime. Despite the Church's assurances that a person buried in any official cemetery will be granted entrance to Heaven, most people still insisted that given the opportunity, it would be better to die 'close to the place where your umbilical cord is buried'. One man explained one of the problems of displacement to me thus:

> If you don't know where your parents' grave is (it is said that) you are not human; you are like an animal which dies anywhere (it falls).

The oldest people in Ada Bai had the most difficulty reconciling the idealistic notion of return to the reality that such return is not possible. One man in his seventies told me:

> Your birthplace is the place where you grew up and played with your friends, even where you quarrelled. Whether (the memory) is bad or good the area itself never disappears from my eye, even now. Here in Ada Bai we are saying that this is Tigray so it is our place (our home). But it has a very great difference with my birthplace and I will never see it as the same. Even (as) the sun rises and the sun sets, and the moon rises, they (look) different (to me here).

The same man spoke resignedly, however, of his expectation that he would live out the rest of his days in Ada Bai. There was an apparent contradiction between people's ideals and their practical behaviour, which is probably attributable to the economic constraints that prevent their return to their birthplace.

The younger and middle-aged adults (aged 15-39), particularly those who left Tigray as small children and came of age in the refugee camps, were content to stay in Ada Bai and establish their families there. For them, highland Tigray was significant because it was their ancestral home. It was not, however, a place to which they wanted or needed to return. The experience of exile involved the construction of a new social and moral community within the camps, which operated on different principles from the highland communities of origin (Malkki 1992; 1995a). Although the older members of the community also participated in these structures, the younger adults found it easier to shift their notions of home to the new place to which they had repatriated than their parents did.

During the course of their stay in the Sudan, people built social networks and occupations that revolved around life in the refugee camp. They quite deliberately reproduced many elements of these structures in Ada Bai so as to be able to exploit the opportunities that such structures afforded them. In the highlands, houses were

d across the hillsides and the weekly markets were often
l several hours' walk away. In Ada Bai houses are packed
tightly together, each on a plot of 16 x 20 metres, and the market is a
ten-minute walk from the furthest point in the settlement. Most of the
younger generation appreciated Ada Bai's large town characteristics,
with its clinic, elementary school, church, mosque and market.
Nearby irrigated sesame, cotton and sorghum plantations provided
an important source of employment, and the proximity to the
borders of Sudan and Eritrea also presented a trade opportunity.

In Ada Bai, the transformation that was started in the Sudan of the
younger generation's association between the ancestral home and
identity continues, albeit in a form that reflects the social, economic,
and environmental constraints and opportunities in the area of
return. While living as refugees in the camps in the Sudan, people
were organised into 'neighbourhoods' according to the areas of
Tigray from which they had come. This arrangement allowed those
who had lived close to each other before fleeing their country to
maintain something of the social and economic mutual assistance
networks in which they had participated prior to flight. People who
had not known each other in the highlands but were from the same
general area found it easier to forge new relationships, since they
tended to trust those who came from their home areas more than
they did 'strangers' from other parts of Tigray.[5] These links were
actualised and perpetuated by parents' tendencies to look within
their own neighbourhood for spouses for their children when
arranging marriages, and for newly married couples to establish new
households within the neighbourhood.

Rather than wanting to go back to their ancestral homes, children
and young adults chose to forge a connection to a new social space
bearing the same name that of the neighbourhood within the refugee
camp. A girl whose family came from Axum still derived an identity
as an Axum girl (though she may have no memory of that place and
may even have been born in the Sudan), but her representation of
Axum was based on the community in which she lived in the
settlement and was only remotely linked to the area that her family
had fled in the highlands of Tigray. In the Ada Bai returnee
settlement, this neighbourhood network has been reproduced. It was
further strengthened by the feeling, common among many residents,

5. Strangers are considered dangerous because it is impossible to know who is a *tebib*,
   or carrier of the Evil Eye. Many people recalled that when they first arrived in the
   Wad Kowli refugee camp in Sudan they were forced to share tents with strangers and
   many people, particularly children, became sick and died as a result of being 'bitten'
   by a *tebib*. The Evil Eye, or *buda*, is one of the most feared forms of spirit possession.

that they were a closer-knit community because they had the shared experience of having lived together as refugees for such a long time. Extended kin networks were redefined and understood as being much closer than they really were in the absence of nuclear and other close relatives, who had either remained in the highlands or who had died during the war and famine. This new definition of kin and social networks allowed people to feel that because they were with kin – their people – it was not necessary to return to their birthplaces. The tie between 'kin' and 'home' was thus defined anew by recasting the connection between social relationship and geographical place.[6]

The response of one of my neighbours aptly demonstrates this shift in the association between birthplace and home. This woman, in her early forties, belonged to one of the poorest households in the community; its members supported themselves through occasional waged labour on large commercial farms in the area, selling firewood, and cultivating a single hectare plot with another household. I asked my neighbour whether she thought that she would be in Ada Bai in five years' time. 'Of course', she snapped, amazed that I would ask such a question, 'Where am I going to go?' She said she would not try to go back to Axum, her birthplace, because there was no farmland there. 'But what,' I asked, 'if there was farmland?' Return to the highlands was still out of the question for her. 'Well, then we have no ox,' she said. 'No, this place [Ada Bai] is better than Axum. We lived in Sudan so long that that became like our home. Now we are here and this will become home. Aside from the heat, this is a good place for a farmer.'

It is this juxtaposition of aspirations, of wanting to return to one's birthplace versus making the most of where you are, which illustrates the ways in which economic realities can condition idealistic preferences and practical actions. Despite what middle-aged adults might want in an ideal world, the economic difficulties of return condition their goals in such a way as to produce a reformulation of the connection between identity and place, a reformulation which differs from that of their children. Returnees are experts at assessing a situation and adjusting their plan of action accordingly. As refugees dependent on the host government, aid providers and camp

6. A small subset of young adults has abandoned the virilocal pattern of marriage and residence. These marriages tend not to be arranged and the couple is typically older than with arranged marriages. In addition, one or both of the newly married often have no family living with them. Their tie to the homeland is weaker, and their ability to develop Ada Bai identities is faster than those who have several family members from the homeland living with them in the returnee settlement.

managers for their survival, they quickly learned how to make the most of ration cards, trading opportunities, health care services, and social networks to improve their security. While some middle aged adults with whom I lived appeared to be involved in a struggle between their idealistic preferences and practical options, others indicated that they had started their lives over so many times that for them the concept of 'going back' to a life they had once known was so unpractical as to be unthinkable. One man told me:

> We see our life as two lives. The life before 1977 [Ethiopian Calendar, which corresponds to 1984 in the Gregorian Calendar, when they fled to the Sudan] and the life after. The life before was better because we were in our homes. But this is a new life and we must try to make it as complete as possible.

Another told me that he viewed his life as three lives: one in the highlands, one in the Sudan, and one in the lowlands of Ethiopia. He said that he had no desire to go back to the highlands. Since leaving he had had numerous occupations, married a second time, had several more children, and made a complete break with his family in the highlands. These men were typical of the middle-aged group which had chosen to begin a new life in Ada Bai without apparent regret.

Members of this cohort who were parents of small children said that they expected their children eventually to develop an identity as Ada Bai people. A woman from Abi Adi (a town in the central highlands, not to be confused with Ada Bai) said that her children:

> ... know that they are from Abi Adi by story (i.e. they have heard me talk about the place), but they don't know it so they can say 'Ada Bai is our home'.

Another man said:

> We are teaching our children now to be Ada Bai people. They should say they are from Ada Bai when someone asks them.

When I returned for a brief visit to Ada Bai in May 1997, several of the children I knew who had been born in the refugee camps in the Sudan had actually travelled to the highlands to see their grandparents, uncles and aunts. They told me that while it had been interesting for them to see this place that they had heard about for so long, they preferred Ada Bai. One seven-year old girl reported to me with a frown of disgust:

> Axum is full of stones. You have to walk so far (to get from the village where the road ends to their house)! Ada Bai is better.

Impressions from visits notwithstanding, the process of fully adopting Ada Bai as home is more complicated. In addition to the first name, which is given to them by their parents or the local priest or *sheik*, Tigrayans bear the names of their father and grandfather. Many parents therefore said that to really feel that one belonged in Ada Bai, and not to another place, would take three generations. At the point when a person is able to say that their father and grandfather were both born in Ada Bai, then they will be a true Ada Bai person. Others saw the process as being even more prolonged. Incest prohibitions stipulate that a man and woman cannot marry if they have had any common ancestors within the past seven generations. Returnees said that when all relatives in the seven generation lineage were Ada Bai residents, then the tie to the highland home would truly be broken. In reality, however, most people can only recount their lineage as far back as four or five generations, and in any event it is rare for the rule of endogamy to be followed so closely that the entire lineage could be traced to a single locality. Local politicians, eager to develop a sense of Ada Bai identity among the younger people, encourage marriages to be made between people who come from different parts of Tigray. Most of the community do not yet accept this idea.

1994–1997 Repatriation to Tigray: a case in contrasts

After the first 15,000 returnees were repatriated to the northwest lowlands in 1993 and 1994, the Ethiopian government changed its policy and told potential returnees that if they returned to Ethiopia they would be required to go to their birthplace or place where they had lived prior to exile. For the vast majority this meant returning to the Tigrayan highlands, where few had any remaining claims to land, where there were no employment opportunities and where there is a chronic vulnerability to drought and famine. In the information campaign that was conducted in the camps in the Sudan, refugees were informed that they would be given 1500 birr cash (about U.S.$250) as well as nine months' food rations, plastic sheeting and a box of kitchen utensils.[7] No significant training schemes or employment opportunities would be made available specifically to returnees. In addition, no special assistance would be given to the local ministries of health or education to construct new

7. It is not clear whether the aid that refugees expected to get on return to Ethiopia was the major factor to encourage their repatriation. Certainly, the Sudanese government's plan to close the refugee camps and its increasingly hostile treatment of refugees had influenced many people's decision to repatriate.

clinics or schools. It was assumed that communities would be able to absorb the returnees and that regular development aid offered through international and indigenous NGOs and informal mutual assistance networks would be extended to assist them, in addition to everyone else in the region who faced food insecurity and poverty.

Fearing that the returnees might try to move into the lowlands to get farmland once they were back in Ethiopia, the local administration in Humera (the administrative centre of the lowland area) warned that no land would be given to the new returnees. Despite this warning, the population of Humera town has doubled in the past two years. UNHCR officials working in the reception centre close to Humera, where returnees being transported across the border since 1995 have to spend their first night at a reception centre, told me that they observed returnees hiring trucks to bring their furniture and other personal property to town to be stored while they collect the aid that is waiting for them in the highlands. Returnees whom I interviewed in 1996 said that they had brought their cash grants to Humera and planned to rent land from the large farmers. With one good harvest they calculated that they could recoup enough from their investment to be able to establish themselves permanently in the lowlands. Returning to the highlands was pointless, they said, because there was no land and no work available.

In this case, as with the Ada Bai returnees, the economic realities of return have conditioned ties to the ancestral home and resulted in the creation of different priorities, and even different loyalties, such that new ties to new places may eventually take precedence over the original association of identity and place.

To date, no assessment has been undertaken by UNHCR, the government, or the indigenous NGO working in Tigray to determine what happened to the returnees who actually did return to their birthplaces. Such data would offer important evidence to my argument, but might also reveal to assistance providers additional needs which have not been met, which might be why they have preferred not to know.

Towards a new discourse of repatriation: construction, creativity, innovation and improvisation

The individual's reinterpretation of his or her birthplace allows for a reconceptualisation of the goals of post-repatriation life. For the people of Ada Bai, life since repatriation bears little resemblance to that which they left in the highlands a decade previously. Exploiting the opportunities afforded by living close to both Eritrea and Sudan, and by the commercial farming in the area, returnees have developed a 'border culture' (Alvarez 1995; Limón 1989; 1994). They are not tied as strongly to their own land as they were before they left – even the farmers tend to work on someone else's land for wages for at least part of the year. They see themselves as much more closely tied to the market, where cross-border trade, smuggling, and entrepreneurial activities are essential sources of household income. Rather than reintegration, reconstruction, or rehabilitation, the operative principles of social change are *construction, creativity, innovation* and *improvisation* (Gmelch 1980; Rosaldo 1989). New rules of social organisation are being invented in an accelerated process of community formation.

Repatriation policy and assistance to returnees that follow the paradigm from which the old repatriation discourse is derived are not workable in many situations – that has already been demonstrated and documented (Allen and Morsink 1994a; Allen 1996; Zetter 1991). Returnees who genuinely need assistance are overlooked, and opportunities for promoting national or local development are lost when we fail to understand the experiences of people who have re-entered their country of origin. I am suggesting that a paradigm shift needs to be made in the way that we conceptualise returnees' experiences and the structuring principles with which they face their postmigration lives (Capra 1982; Kuhn 1970). Adoption of a new discourse that recognises and creates room for new forms of social identity, organisation, practice and meaning allows for the emergence of explanatory models that can inform decisions about assistance. Governments in countries of origin and the assistance communities (both international and national) have an obligation to ensure that the human rights of returnees are respected, with regards not only to protection, but also to a minimum level of physical security and dignity. UNHCR should not bear the burden on its own. Other international organisations must acknowledge their responsibility for helping to provide returnees with their basic requirements. The United Nations Development Programme and UNICEF, in particular, should play pivotal roles in assisting returnees so that repatriation becomes an opportunity for promoting sustainable development.

Assistance policies which recognise that returnees are facing a whole new world with new possibilities, opportunities and problems, will help them maximise the opportunities that exist, even if they are new opportunities; will be much more successful in facilitating returnees' attainment of economic self-sufficiency, and will place less of a burden on local (nonmigrant) communities.

Acknowledgements

This research was made possible by a grant from the International Institute of Education's Fulbright Program and funds from the United Nations High Commissioner for Refugees' Regional Bureau for Africa and logistical support from the United Nations Development Programme/Emergencies Unit for Ethiopia. I would like to extend my thanks to these bodies for supporting this research even in the face of criticism. Such openness gives me hope that the alternative discourse of which I write here might find some support where it is most urgently needed. I would also like to thank Richard Starkey for his exhaustive editorial assistance.

Notes on Contributors

Richard Black is Senior Lecturer in Human Geography in the School of African and Asian Studies, University of Sussex, and co-director of the Sussex Centre for Migration Research. He has researched forced migration, environmental and development issues in sub-Saharan Africa, as well as the integration and return of asylum seekers in Western Europe. He is author of *Refugees, Environment and Development* (Longman, 1998), as well as co-editor of *Southern Europe and the New Immigrations* (Sussex Academic, 1997), *Geography and Refugees* (Belhaven, 1993), and the *Journal of Refugee Studies*.

Chris Dolan worked from 1992 to 1996 in South Africa and Mozambique, studying, among other things, the changing status of Mozambican refugees in South Africa (University of the Witwatersrand, Rural Facility) and reintegration of ex-combatants in Mozambique (University of Oxford, Refugee Studies Programme). He is currently working as a Research Officer for ACORD, researching local level responses to Complex Political Emergencies in the Great Lakes region. He continues to teach 'Refugee Livelihoods' for the Oxford Refugee Studies Programme and is Honorary Researcher at the University of the Witwatersrand.

Marita Eastmond is Associate Professor at the Department of Social Anthropology at Göteborg University, Sweden. Her main research area is forced migration, involving the politics and culture of exile and diasporas, and responses to organised violence and displacement. Some of this work has focused on Chileans in exile, and more recently on refugees from Bosnia-Herzegovina, as well as the repatriation and reintegration of Cambodian refugees in 1993-94. She was Research Fellow at the Refugee Studies Programme, University of Oxford, and has taught there on various occasions since.

Moya Flynn is a Research Associate at the Centre for Russian and East European Studies, in the University of Birmingham. She is currently involved in research for her Ph.D. which explores the position of forced migrants and the development of migrant resettlement policies in contemporary Russian society.

Laura Hammond is a graduate student in Anthropology at the University of Wisconsin-Madison. She has carried out extensive field work in Ethiopia, including twenty months' research on the repatriation of refugees from Sudan to Tigray. In addition she worked for two years in other parts of Ethiopia as a development consultant for a wide range of international organisations.

Art Hansen is Associate Professor and coordinates the graduate programme for the Department of Anthropology at the University of Florida (U.S.A.). He is an applied economic anthropologist concentrating on Third World development and the behaviour of people in crisis situations, with special interest in the displacement and involuntary resettlement of refugees, internally displaced people, people uprooted by development projects, demobilising soldiers, and famine victims. He is the President of the International Association for the Study of Forced Migration, is co-director of the University of Florida's Displacement and Resettlement Studies Program, and is on the International Editorial Advisory Board of the *Journal of Refugee Studies.*

Khalid Koser is Lecturer in Geography at University College London. He was previously Research Fellow in Migration Studies in the Sussex Centre for Migration Research. His research experience includes work on the repatriation of Mozambicans from Malawi, and of Bosnians and Eritreans from European countries. He is co-editor (with Helma Lutz) of *The New Migration in Europe: Social Constructions and Social Realities* (Macmillan, 1998), and has published widely on refugee issues.

Peter Marsden has worked as Information Coordinator for the British Agencies Afghanistan Group since the beginning of 1989. He has contributed to the development of a consensus amongst the agencies in relation to the major issues which concern their operations and has also informed their strategic and day-to-day planning through the provision of information on the political, military, security and humanitarian situation in Afghanistan. He has worked closely with UN agencies throughout this period, monitoring their changing policies, and has undertaken a large number of studies relating to repatriation and reconstruction.

Christopher McDowell is an anthropologist currently based in Ethiopia, working on migration and resettlement issues in the south of the country. He has undertaken research on refugee repatriation in Sri Lanka, Western Europe and East Africa, and on the resettlement of people involuntarily displaced by planned development. His publications include *A Tamil Asylum Diaspora: Sri Lankan Migration, Settlement and Politics in Switzerland* (Berghahn, 1996), and edited volumes on development-induced displacement and resettlement, and environment in southern Africa.

Lucia Ann McSpadden is Research Director at the Life and Peace Institute, Uppsala, Sweden. Dr McSpadden, a cultural anthropologist, is a founding member of both the Committee on Refugee Issues of the Amercian Anthropological Association, and of the International Association for the Study of Forced Migration. Prior to her field research in the Horn of Africa, Dr McSpadden carried out research on the resettlement of Ethiopian and Eritrean refugees in North America. Currently she is the project leader of a multinational field study on the role of NGOs in the repatriation of refugees.

Joakim Öjendal is Lecturer in the Department of Peace and Development Studies at Göteborg University, and is currently Research Fellow at the Göteborg Centre for East and Southeast Asian Studies (GESEA). He worked as a volunteer with the United Nations during its transition year in Cambodia, and has since researched and written on political and economic development in Cambodia. He is currently concentrating on water management strategies.

Hilary Pilkington is Senior Lecturer in Russian Politics and Society at the Centre for Russian and East European Studies, in the University of Birmingham. She has published widely on issues of youth and gender in contemporary Russia and is author of *Migration, Displacement and Identity in Post-Soviet Russia* (Routledge, 1998), which charts the experiences of returnees to Russia from the former Soviet republics.

Johan Pottier is Senior Lecturer in Anthropology at the School of Oriental and African Studies (SOAS), University of London. His main interest is rural development and food security, and he has conducted long-term fieldwork on this topic in Rwanda since 1982. He worked on postfamine recovery in Kivu (Zaire) in 1988, and was a member of the Joint Evaluation of Humanitarian Assistance to Rwanda in 1995. He is editor of *Practising Development* (Routledge, 1993) and author of *Migrants No More* (Manchester University Press, 1988).

Rosemary Preston is Director of the International Centre for Education in Development at the University of Warwick. In countries of Latin America, southern Africa and the South Pacific, she has undertaken research on human resources in contexts of labour and war-related migration, and in consultancy as a transitional mechanism in development research.

Finn Stepputat is Senior Researcher at the Centre for Development Research in Copenhagen. His training is in geography and cultural sociology. He is currently working within the framework of the research programme 'Livelihood, Identity and Organisation in Situations of Instability'. He has published on refugee issues and is currently working on postconflict reconstruction in Mozambique, Guatemala and Mexico.

David Tavares teaches at the Escola Superior de Educação Jean Piaget and the Centro Interdisciplinar de Estudos Económicos, both in Lisbon. In addition to the research reported in this volume, he also conducted studies on demobilised Angolan soldiers in 1992 for a group of European and Angolan NGOs that were planning reintegration and development programmes.

Martha Walsh is a political scientist, and was formerly Research Officer in the Centre for the Comparative Study of Culture, Development and the Environment at the University of Sussex. She has worked on women's organisations and employment prospects in Bosnia, as well as women's political participation in Cambodia. She currently works as a consultant on issues relating to gender, democracy, and postconflict reconstruction.

Bibliography

Abrams, J. (1988) 'Notes on the difficulty of studying the state',
    Journal of Historical Sociology 1(1): 58-89.

Aguayo, S., Christensen, H., Dogherty, L. and Varese, S. (eds)
    (1987) *Social and Cultural Conditions and Prospects of Guatemalan
    Refugees in Mexico.* Geneva: UNRISD.

Airapetova, N. (1996) 'Migratsiia ne dolzhna byt' begstvom',
    Nezavisimaia gazeta, 2 April: 3.

Akol, J.O. (1987) 'Southern Sudanese refugees: their repatriation
    and resettlement after the Addis Ababa Agreement', in Rogge,
    J.R. (ed.) *Refugees: A Third World Dilemma*, New Jersey: Rowman
    and Allenheld.

—— (1994) 'A crisis of expectations', in Allen, T. and Morsink, H.
    (eds) *When Refugees Go Home*, London: James Currey, pp. 78-95.

Allen, T. (1993) *Social and Economic Aspects of Mass Voluntary Return of
    Refugees from Sudan to Uganda between 1986 and 1992*, Geneva:
    UNRISD.

—— (ed.) (1996) *In Search of Cool Ground: War, Flight and
    Homecoming in Northeast Africa*, London: James Currey.

Allen, T. and Morsink, H. (eds) (1994a) *When Refugees Go Home*,
    London: James Currey.

Allen, T. and Morsink, H. (1994b) 'Introduction: when refugees go
    home', in Allen, T. and Morsink, H. (eds) *When Refugees Go
    Home*, London: James Currey, pp. 1-13.

Allen, T. and Turton, D. (1996) 'Introduction: in search of cool
    ground', in Allen, T. (ed.) *In Search of Cool Ground: War, Flight and
    Homecoming in Northeast Africa*, London: James Currey, pp. 1-22.

Alvarez, R.R. Jr. (1995) 'The Mexican-US border: the making of an
    anthropology of the borderlands', *Annual Review of Anthropology*,
    24: 447-70.

Amnesty International (1987) 'An update to AI's continued
    opposition to *refoulement* of Tamils to Switzerland', External
    Document, London.

—— (1996) 'Zaire: lawlessness and insecurity in North and South-Kivu', External Document, London.

Anderson, B. (1991) *Imagined Communities*, London: Verso.

Appadurai, A. (1988) 'Putting hierarchy in its place', *Cultural Anthropology*, 3(1): 36-49.

—— (1993) 'Patriotism and its futures', *Public Culture* 6(5): 411-29.

Ardittis, S. (1995) 'Exchange of experience between the Russian Federation and Southern European regions in the field of migrant reintegration policies', *International Review of Migration*, 29(4): 1049-56.

AVANCSO (Associación para el Avance de las Ciencias Sociales) (1990) *Assistance and Control: Policies toward Internally Displaced Populations in Guatemala*, Washington: CIPRA/Georgetown University.

Aushev, M. (1996) 'Nasledie imperii', *Nezavisimaia gazeta*, 28 November: 2.

—— (1997) 'Migratsionnaia situatsiia vzryvoopasna', *Nezavisimaia gazeta*, 9 January: 3.

Bakewell, O. (1996) 'Refugee repatriation in Africa: towards a theoretical framework?', Occasional Paper 04/96, Centre for Development Studies, University of Bath.

Banister, J. and Paige Johnson, E. (1993) 'After the nightmare: the population of Cambodia', in Kiernan, B. (ed.) *Genocide and Democracy in Cambodia*, Yale: Yale Center for International Area Studies, pp. 65-139.

Bascom, J. (1994) 'The dynamics of refugee repatriation: the case of refugees in Eastern Sudan', in Gould, W.T.S. and Findlay, A.M. (eds) *Population Migration and the Changing World Order*, Chichester: John Wiley and Sons, pp. 225-48.

—— (1995) 'The new nomads: an overview of involuntary migration in Africa', in Baker, J. and Akin Aida, T. (eds) *The Migration Experience in Africa*, Sweden: Nordiska Afrikainstitutet, pp. 197-219.

Basok, T. (1990), 'Repatriation of Nicaraguan refugees from Honduras and Costa Rica', *Journal of Refugee Studies*, 3(3): 281-97.

Bernander, B., Charny, J., Eastmond, M., Lindahl, C. and Öjendal, J. (1995) *Facing a Complex Emergency. An Evaluation of Swedish Support to Emergency Aid to Cambodia*, Stockholm: SIDA Evaluation Report No 4.

Black, R., Koser, K. and Walsh, M. (1997) *Conditions for the Return of Displaced Persons from the European Union, Final Report*, Luxembourg: Office for Official Publications of the European Communities.

Blaeser, M. (1990) *Thailand: Technical Mission to Co-ordinate the Inter-agency Workshop on Education for the Cambodian Repatriation*

Planning, Geneva: United Nations High Commissioner for
Refugees, PTSS Mission Report, 90/28.

Breckenridge, C. and Appadurai, A. (1989) 'On moving targets',
Public Culture, 2(1): i-iv.

Brett, E.A. (1996) 'Rebuilding war-damaged communities in
Uganda', in Allen, T. (ed.) *In Search of Cool Ground: War, Flight
and Homecoming in Northeast Africa,* London: James Currey, pp.
203-19.

Brown, S. (1993) 'The contribution of local and international
agencies', in Preston, R. (ed.) *The Integration of Returned Exiles,
Former Combatants and other War-affected Namibians,* Windhoek:
Namibia Institute for Social and Economic Research, pp. 4/10-
4/58.

Brown, S. and Dix, T. (1993) 'Political prisoners and detainees in the
Namibian liberation struggle', in Preston, R. (ed.) *The Integration of
Returned Exiles, Former Combatants and other War-affected Namibians,*
Windhoek: Namibia Institute for Social and Economic Research,
pp. 8/1-8/71.

Brubaker, R. (1995) 'Aftermaths of Empire and the unmixing of
peoples: historical and comparative perspectives', *Ethnic and
Racial Studies,* 18(2): 189-218.

Capra, F. (1982) *The Turning Point: Science, Society and the Rising
Culture,* New York: Bantam Books.

CCPP (1993) 'El papel del retorno y la situación actual del Ixcán'.
Unpublished circular: Guatemala.

CERA/PGE (EPLF) (1992) 'Current status of the repatriation
programme and the way forward,' Conference paper, Asmara,
Eritrea, April 29.

Cernea, M. (1997) 'Understanding and preventing impoverishment
from displacement – reflections on the state of knowledge', in
McDowell, C. (ed.) *Understanding Impoverishment. The
Consequences of Development-Induced Displacement,* Oxford:
Berghahn, pp.13-32.

Chanda, N. (1986) *Brother Enemy – The War after the War,* New York:
Macmillan.

Chingono, M. (1995) 'Post Lancaster House: return to Zimbabwe,
1980-1983', Case Study XI in Quick, S., Chingono, M. and
Preston, R. (eds) *Social Applications of Refugee Law Repatriation in
Safety and Dignity,* IRLP, University of Warwick, International
Centre for Education in Development, Vol. 2, unpublished
report.

Chomsky, N. and Herman, E. (1979) *The Washington Connection and Third World Fascism*, Boston: South End Press.

Christensen, H. (1985) *Refugees and Pioneers*, Geneva: UNRISD.

Cilliers, J. (1995) 'Preface', in Cilliers, J. (ed.) *Dismissed, Institute for Defence Policy*, South Africa: Halfway House, pp. 4-11.

Clark, K.M. (1996) *Fostering a Farewell to Arms: Preliminary Lessons Learned in the Demobilization and Reintegration of Combatants*, Washington, DC: Research and Reference Services, United States Agency for International Development.

Cliffe, L. and Davidson, B. (eds), (1988) *The Long Struggle of Eritrea for Independence and Constructive Peace*, Trenton, New Jersey: The Red Sea Press.

Cliffe, L., Bush, R., Lindsay, J., Mokopagosi, B., Pankhurst, D., and Tsie, B. (1994) *The Transition to Independence in Namibia*, Boulder, CO and London: Lynne Rienner.

Cock, J. (1994) 'Demobilization and democracy: the relevance of the 1944 "Soldier's charter" in Southern Africa today'. Paper presented at the University of Witswatersrand History Workshop Conference, 13-15 July 1994.

Codagnone, C. (1998) 'The new migration in Russia in the 1990s', in Koser, K. and Lutz, H. (eds) *The New Migration in Europe: Social Constructions and Social Realities*, Macmillan: London, pp. 39-59.

Coles, G. (1985) 'Voluntary repatriation: a background study', Unpublished paper prepared for the Round Table on Voluntary Repatriation convened by UNHCR and the International Institute of Humanitarian Law, 16-19 July 1985, San Remo.

Coles, G.J. (1989) *Solutions to the Problem of Refugees and the Protection of Refugees – A Background Paper*, Geneva: UNHCR.

Colletta, N.J., Kostner, M., and Wiederhofer, I. (1996a) *War-to-Peace Transition in Sub-Saharan Africa*, Washington, DC: World Bank, Directions in Development.

—— (1996b) *Case Studies in War-to-Peace Transition: The Demobilisation of Ex-combatants in Ethiopia, Namibia and Uganda*, Washington, DC: World Bank.

Collier, P. (1994) 'Demobilisation and insecurity; a study in the economics of the transition from war to peace', *Journal of International Development*, 6(3): 343-51.

Collinson, S. (1993) *Europe and International Migration*, London: Pinter.

Comisión Nacional de Derechos Humanos (1993) *Informe sobre el Menor Mexicano Repatriado desde Estados Unidos*, Mexico: Comisión Nacional de Derechos Humanos.

Cornelius, W.A., Martin, P.L. and Hollifield, J.F. (eds) (1994) *Controlling Immigration: A Global Perspective*, Stanford: Stanford University Press.

Crisp, J. (1984) 'The politics of repatriation: Ethiopian refugees in Djibouti, 1977-83', *Review of African Political Economy*, 30: 73-82.

—— (1987) *Voluntary Repatriation for Refugees in Developing Countries: a Bibliographical Survey*, Geneva: UNRISD.

Centre for Refugee Studies (CRS) (1993) 'Repatriation and development: developing a research agenda', Report of a one-day workshop, York University, (Ontario) 9 November.

Cunliffe, S.A. and Pugh, M. (1997) 'The politicization of UNHCR in Former Yugoslavia', *Journal of Refugee Studies*, 10(2): 134-53.

Cuny, F.C., Stein, B.N. and Reed, P. (1992) *Repatriation During Conflict in Africa and Asia*. Dallas, Texas: Centre for the Study of Societies in Crisis.

Current Digest of the Post-Soviet Press (1994) 'Kozyrev favors military presence in neighboring states', 46(3): 26-7.

Daley, P. (1991) 'Gender, displacement and social reproduction: settling Burundi refugees in western Tanzania', *Journal of Refugee Studies*, 4(3): 248-65.

Davenport, P., Healy, P.J. and Malone, K. (1995) 'Vulnerable in the village: a study of returnees in Battambang Province, Cambodia, with a focus on strategies for the landless', Lutheran World Service, UNHCR, Japan Sotoshu Relief Committee, unpublished report.

De Jong, C. and Gardner, R. (eds) (1981) *Migration Decision-Making: Multidisciplinary Approaches to Microlevel Studies in Developed and Developing Countries*, New York: Pergamon.

Demograficheskii Ezhegodnik Rossii (1995) Moscow: Goskomstat.

Department of Home Affairs (1996) *Deportation and Repatriation Statistics: 1996*, Capetown: Department of Home Affairs.

Dixon-Fyle, K. (1994) 'Prevention as the best solution', *Refugees*, 96: 22-25

Doherty, K. (1990) 'Namibia repatriation operation: lessons learned survey', Geneva: Regional Bureau for Africa, Namibia Repatriation Unit, unpublished report.

Douglas, M. (1966) *Purity and Danger: An Analysis of the Concepts of Pollution and Taboo*, London: Routledge.

Duffield, M. and Prendergast, J. (1994) *Without Troops and Tanks: Humanitarian Intervention in Ethiopia and Eritrea*, Lawrenceville, New Jersey: The Red Sea Press.

Dupree, N.H. (1989) 'Prospects for Afghan women after repatriation', *Refuge*, 9(1): 17.

Endale, Y. (1996) 'Ethiopia's mental health: trampled by armed conflicts', in Allen, T. (ed.) *In Search of Cool Ground: War, Flight and Homecoming in Northeast Africa*, London: James Currey, pp. 274-76.

Fadin, A. (1994) 'Post-SSSR kak rossiiskie Sudety', *Obshchaia Gazeta*, 14-20 October.

√ Fahlen, M. (1995) UNHCR Mission Report, Eritrea, 26 May.

√ Food and Agriculture Organisation (FAO) (1995) *Environment Eritrea*, 1(3), February.

Federal'nii zakon (proekt) (1997) 'O podderzhke rossiiskoi diaspory, pokrovitel'stve rossiiskim sootechestvennikam i repatriatsii' Moscow: Komiteta Gosudarstvennoi Dumy po delam Sodrushestva Nezavisimikh Gosudarstv I sviazam s sootechestvennikami.

Feldman, A. (1991) *Formations of Violence: The Narrative of the Body and Political Terror in Northern Ireland*, Chicago: University of Chicago Press.

Ferguson, J. (1990) *The Anti-Politics Machine. 'Development', Depolitization, and Bureaucratic Power in Lesotho*, Cambridge: Cambridge University Press.

Ferris, E. (1993) *Beyond Borders: Refugees, Migrants and Human Rights in the Post-Cold War Era*, Geneva: World Council of Churches Publications.

Filippova, E. (1996) in *Forum pereselencheskikh organizatsii Rossii (stenogramma i dokumenty)* Part 1, Moscow and Saratov: Koordinatsionnii sovet pomoshchi bezhentsam i pereselentsam i Assotsiatsiia vynuzhdennikh pereselentsev Saratovskii istochnik.

√ Fitzgerald, E.V.K. (1994) 'Economic aspects of the relief, rehabilitation, development continuum and external assistance', Oxford: Queen Elizabeth House, unpublished paper, 14th June, 1994.

√ Fosseldorf, H. and Medson, C. (1994) *Refugee Repatriation: a Selected and Annotated Bibliography*, Copenhagen: Danish Refugee Council.

Foucault, M. (1977) *Discipline and Punish. The Birth of the Prison*, London: Allen Lane.

— (1991) 'On Governmentality' in Burchell, G., Gordon, C. and Miller, P. (eds) *The Foucault Effect*, London: University of Chicago Press.

Frechette, A. (1994) 'Notes toward the development of a multi-disciplinary model for comparative research on integration', Oxford: Refugee Studies Programme, unpublished report.

Gannushkina, S. (1996) 'Kontseptsiia zakona o repatriatsii', Unpublished document.

Gasarasi, C.P. (1997) 'Development, refugee generation, resettlement and repatriation: a conceptual review', *Refuge*, 15(2):1-11.

Gebremedhin, N. (1995) 'Environmental aspects of resettlements', Government of Eritrea', Report to Donors Workshop, Asmara, Eritrea, 19-20 May, unpublished.

Glytsos, N. (1995) 'Problems and policies regarding the socio-economic integration of returnees and foreign workers in Greece', *International Migration*, 33: 155-73.

Gmelch, G. (1980) 'Return migration', *Annual Review of Anthropology*, 9: 135-59.

Goodwin-Gill, G. (1990) 'Voluntary repatriation: legal and policy issues', in Loescher, G. and Monahan, L. (eds) *Refugees and International Relations*, Oxford: Clarendon Press, pp. 225-91.

Goss, J. and Lindquist, B. (1995) 'Conceptualizing international labour migration: a structuration perspective', *International Migration Review*, 29(2): 317-51.

Grafova, L. (1995) *Obshchee delo Rossii*, Moscow: Koordinatsionnii sovet pomoshchi bezhentsam i vynuzhdennim pereselentsam.

Grafova, L., Filippova, E. and Lebedeva, N. (1995) 'Compact settlements of forced migrants on the territory of Russia, Open Society Institute, New York, unpublished report.

Gramajo Morales, H. A. (1995) *De la Guerra … a la Guerra. La Difícil Transición Política en Guatemala*, Guatemala: Fondo de Cultura Editorial.

Grankina, V. (1996) 'Sud'ba bezhentsev v rossii', *Nezavisimaia Gazeta*, 7 June: 3.

Gupta, A. and Ferguson, J. (1992) 'Beyond 'culture': space, identity and the politics of difference', *Cultural Anthropology*, 7(1): 6-23.

Habte Selassie, B. (1989) *Eritrea and the United Nations*, Trenton, New Jersey: The Red Sea Press.

Hall, S. (1990) 'Cultural identity and diaspora', in Rutherford, J. (ed.) *Identity, Community, Culture, Difference*, London: Lawrence and Wishart, pp. 222-37.

Harrell-Bond, B.E. (1989) 'Repatriation: under what conditions is it the most desirable solution?', *African Studies Review*, 32(1): 41-69.

Harrell-Bond, B.E. and Wilson, K. (1990) 'Dealing with dying: some anthropological reflections on the need for assistance by refugee relief programmes for bereavement and burial', *Journal of Refugee Studies*, 3(3): 228-43.

Harrell-Bond, B.E. and Voutira, E. (1992) 'Anthropology and the study of refugees', *Anthropology Today*, 8(4): 6-10.

Harrell-Bond, B.E., Voutira, E. and Leopold, M. (1992) 'Counting the refugees: gifts, givers, patrons and clients', *Journal of Refugee Studies*, (5)3/4: 205-25.

Hathaway, J.C. (1995a) '"Root causes" as refugee protection: a chimerical promise?', in Perrakis, S. (ed.) *Immigration and European Union: Building on a Comprehensive Approach*, Athens: Ant. N. Sakkoulas, pp. 117-22.

—— (1995b) 'New directions to avoid hard problems: the distortion of the palliative role of refugee protection', *Journal of Refugee Studies*, (8)3: 288-304.

Hernandez Castillo, R. A., Nava Zamora, N., Flores Arenales, C. and Escalona Victoria, J.L. (1993) *La Experiencia de Refugio en Chiapas. Nuevas Relaciones en la Frontera sur Mexicana*, Mexico D.F: Academia Mexicana de Derechos Humanos.

Hoile, D (1994) *Mozambique 1962-1993, A Political Chronology*, London: Mozambique Institute.

Human Rights Watch (1996) *Forced to Flee: Violence Against the Tutsis in Zaire*, Human Rights Watch Report 8(2), July.

—— (1997) *Uncertain Refuge: International Failures to Protect Refugees*, Human Rights Watch Report 9(1), April.

Hunt, J. (1992) 'The impact of the 1962 repatriates from Algeria on the French labour market', *Industrial and Labour Relations Review*, 45(3): 556-72.

Iaz'kova, A. (1996) 'Chuzhie v svoem otechestve', *Segodnia*, 5 July: 9.

Iaz'kova, A., Vardomskii, L. and Katsner, M. (1997) 'Gosudarstvo i migratsiia', *Nezavisimaia Gazeta*, 11 January: 6.

International Council for Voluntary Agencies (ICVA) (1988) 'Meeting with UNHCR on Repatriation of Afghan Refugees', Geneva: ICVA, unpublished report.

Informatsionno-analiticheskii Biulleten (1995) 7, Moskva: FMS.

International Organisation of Migration (IOM) (1995) *Report on the Implementation of the Direct Assistance Component of the IOM Comprehensive Activity Programme for the Russian Federation*, Geneva: IOM.

International Resource Group (IRG) on Disarmament and Security in the Horn of Africa (1994), Report of the IRG workshop on demobilisation in the Horn of Africa: Lessons from experiences in sub-Saharan Africa', Addis Ababa, 4-7 December 1994, unpublished.

Jackson, J. (1994) 'Repatriation and reconstruction in Zimbabwe during the 1980s', in Allen, T. and Morsink, H. (eds) *When Refugees Go Home*, London: James Currey, pp. 126-66.

Joseph, G.M. and Nugent, D. (eds) (1994) *Everyday Forms of State Formation. Revolution and the Negotiation of Rule in Modern Mexico*, London: Duke University Press.

Kabera, J.B. and Muyanja, C. (1994) 'Homecoming in the Luwero triangle: experiences of displaced population of Central Uganda following the National Resistance Army victory in 1986', in Allen, T. and Morsink, H. (eds) *When Refugees Go Home*, London: James Currey, pp. 96-104.

Kearney, M. (1995) 'The local and the global: the anthropology of globalization and transnationalism', *Annual Review of Anthropology*, 24: 547-65.

Kibreab, G. (1989) 'Local settlements in Africa: a misconceived option?', *Journal of Refugee Studies*, 2(4): 468-90.

—— (1996a) 'Prospects for repatriation of Eritrean refugees from the Sudan and responses of the international donor community,' in Allen, T. (ed.) *In Search of Cool Ground: War, Flight and Homecoming in Northeastern Africa*, London: James Currey.

—— (1996b) *Ready, Willing ... and Still Waiting: Eritrean Refugees in Sudan*, Uppsala, Sweden: Life and Peace Institute.

King, R. (1978) 'Return migration: a neglected aspect of population geography, *Area*, 10(3): 175-82.

Kingma, K. (1995) 'Demobilisation and reintegration of armed forces in Africa', Bonn: Bonn International Center for Conversion.

Korkeakivi, A. (1996) 'Commitments without compliance. Refugees in the Russian Federation', New York: Report of the Lawyers Committee for Human Rights, May, unpublished.

Koser, K. (1993) 'Repatriation and information: a theoretical model', in Black, R. and Robinson, V. (eds) *Geography and Refugees: Patterns and Processes of Change*, London: Belhaven Press, pp. 171-84.

—— (1996a) 'Recent asylum migration in Europe: patterns and processes of change, *New Community*, 22(1): 151-58

—— (1996b) 'Information and refugee migration: the case of Mozambican refugees in Malawi', *Tijdschrift voor Economische en Sociale Geografie*, 87(5): 407-18.

—— (1997a) 'Information and repatriation: the case of Mozambican refugees in Malawi', *Journal of Refugee Studies*, 10(1): 1-18.

—— (1997b) 'Social networks and the asylum cycle: the case of Iranians in the Netherlands', *International Migration Review*, 31(3): 591-611.

Koser, K. and Lutz. H. (eds) (1998) *The New Migration in Europe: Social Constructions and Social Realities*, London: Macmillan.

Kuhn, T. (1970) *The Structure of Scientific Revolutions*, Chicago: University of Chicago Press.

Larkin, M.A. (1992) 'Preface', in Larkin, M.A., Cuny F.C. and
  Stein, B.N. (eds) *Repatriation under Conflict in Central America*,
  Washington, DC: Hemispheric Migration Project, Georgetown
  University, pp. vii-xii.
Larkin, M.A., Cuny, F.C.and Stein, B.N. (eds) (1992) *Repatriation
  under Conflict in Central America*, Washington DC: CIPRA.
Lauriciano, G. and Waterhouse, R. (1994) 'Resettlement of
  Mozambican returnees: communities in transition: results from
  a field study of the resettlement and re-organisation of returnee
  communities to Magude District, southern Mozambique', June
  1994, unpublished report.
LeBeau, D. and Pemberton, W. (1993) 'Unpublished information:
  surveys and the social and economic characteristics of returnee
  and stayer groups', in Preston, R. (ed.) *The Integration of Returned
  Exiles, Former Combatants and other War-affected Namibians*,
  Windhoek: Namibia Institute for Social and Economic
  Research, pp. 5/16-5/89.
Lemarchand, R. (1970) *Rwanda and Burundi*, New York: Praeger.
Lemarchand, R. and Martin, D. (1974) *Selective Genocide in Burundi*,
  London: Minority Rights Group, Report No. 20.
Leys, C. and Saul, J. (eds) (1995) *Namibia's Liberation Struggle: The
  Two Edged Sword*, London: James Currey.
Limón, J. (1989) 'Carne, carnales and the carnivalesque:
  Bakhtinian batos, disorder and narrative discourse', *Amercian
  Ethnologist*, 16: 471-86.
—— (1994) *Dancing with the Devil*, Madison: University of
  Wisconsin Press.
Loescher, G. and Monahan L. (eds) (1990) *Refugees and International
  Relations*, Oxford: Clarendon Press.
Luckham, R. (1994) 'The military, militarisation and
  democratisation in Africa: a survey of the literature and issues',
  African Studies Review, (37)2: 13-75.
Makanya, S. (1993a) 'Preparing for repatriation: a survey of
  information needs of Mozambican refugees in Malawi', Harare:
  Save the Children Fund, draft unpublished report.
—— (1993b) 'Lessons from elsewhere: integration strategies in
  independent Zimbabwe', in Preston, R. (ed.) *The Integration of
  Returned Exiles, Former Combatants and other War-affected
  Namibians*, Windhoek: Namibia Institute for Social and
  Economic Research, pp. 3/1-3/19.
Malkki, L.H. (1992) 'National geographic: the rooting of peoples
  and the territorialization of national identity among scholars and
  refugees', *Cultural Anthropology*, 7(1): 13-45.

—— (1995a) 'Refugees and exile: from 'refugee studies' to the national order of things', *Annual Review of Anthropology*, 24: 495-523.

—— (1995b) *Purity and Exile: Violence, Memory and National Cosmology among Hutu Refugees in Tanzania*, Chicago: University of Chicago Press.

Marsden, P. (1996a) *Exile and Return: Report on a Study of Coping Strategies among Afghan Refugees in Iran and Returnees to Afghanistan*, London: The Refugee Council, June.

—— (1996b) *Living In Exile: Report On A Study Of Economic Coping Strategies Among Afghan Refugees In Pakistan*, London: The Refugee Council, December.

—— (1997) *Return and Reconstruction: Report On A Study Of Economic Coping Strategies Among Farmers In Farah Province, Afghanistan*, London: The Refugee Council: July.

Masungulo (1993) 'Mozambican refugees in South Africa', Maputo: Masungulo, unpublished report.

—— (1994a) 'Report on the present situation', 21 July 1994, Maputo: Masungulo, unpublished report.

—— (1994b) 'Report on information/registration campaign', May 1994, Maputo: Masungulo, unpublished report.

Mathis, C. (1997) 'Die Geschichte der Tamilien in der Schweiz, 1981-1996' Lizentiatsarbeit, Philosophische Fakultät I der Universität Zürich, Switzerland.

Mayotte, J. (1992) *Disposable People? The Plight of Refugees*, New York: Orbisa Books.

McDonald, M. and Gatehouse, M. (1995) *In the Mountains of Morazán*, London: Latin America Bureau.

McDowell, C. (1995) 'Criminalisation and deportation from Switzerland, 1991-1994', Case Study IV, in Quick, S., Chingono, M. and Preston, R (eds) *Social Applications of Refugee Law Repatriation in Safety and Dignity*, IRLP, University of Warwick, International Centre for Education in Development, Vol. 2, unpublished report.

—— (1996) *A Tamil Asylum Diaspora: Sri Lankan Migration, Settlement and Politics in Switzerland*, Oxford: Berghahn.

McDowell, C. and Cernea, M.M. (eds) (forthcoming) *New Approaches to Resettlement*, Oxford: Berghahn.

McMillan, J. (1985) *20th Century France. Politics and Society 1898-1991*, London: Edward Arnold.

McSpadden, L. (1996) 'Returning 'home'? The decision-making processes of Eritrean women and men,' in Giles, W., Moussa, H.

and van Esterik, P. (eds) *Development and Diaspora: Gender and the Refugee Experience*, Ontario, Canada: Artemis Publishers, pp. 216-37.

—— (1997) 'Life and death matters in Eritrean repatriation', in Johnston, B.R. (ed.) *Life and Death Matters: Human Rights and the Environment at the End of the Millennium*, Walnut Creek, CA: Alta Mira Press, pp. 241-64.

Mebtouche, L. (1990) 'Surinam: pilot project for repatriation and socio-economic re-integration of Surinamese refugees from French Guiana', Geneva: United Nations High Commissioner for Refugees, PTSS Mission Report, 90/17, unpublished.

Messina, C. (1994) 'From migrants to refugees: Russian, Soviet and post-Soviet migration', *International Journal of Refugee Law*, 6(4): 620-35.

Michugina, A. and Rakhmaninova, M. (1996) 'Natsional'nii sostav migrantov v obmene naseleniem mezhdu rossiei i zarubezhnimi stranami', *Voprosy Statistiki*, 12: 44-8.

Migratsiia bedstvie ili blago: materialy kruglogo stola po problemam vynuzhdennoi migratsii v Rossii (1996) Moscow: Institut etnologii i antropologii RAN/ Koordinatsionnii Sovet pomoshchi bezhentsam I vyhuzhdennim pereselentsam.

Miller, P., and Rose, N. (1990) 'Governing economic life', *Economy and Society*, 19(1): 1-31.

Mills, G. (1992) 'The process of integration of national armies in a post-conflict situation: lessons from other countries', Paper presented at a conference on 'Mozambique post-war: challenges and realities', Instituto Superior de Relações Internacionais, Maputo.

Minaar, A. and Hough, D. (1995) 'Illegals in South Africa: scope, extent and impact', Paper presented at IOM Conference, Pretoria, August.

Minear, L., Clark, J., Cohen, R., Gallagher, D., Guest, I. and Weiss, T.G. (eds) (1994) *Humanitarian Action in the Former Yugoslavia: the UN's Role 1991-93*, Washington, DC: Thomas J. Watson Jr., Institute for International Studies, and Refugee Policy Group, Occasional Paper no. 18.

Ministry of Foreign Affairs (Government of The Netherlands) (1996) *Migration and Development, Policy Paper*, The Hague: Development Cooperation Information Department.

Mollica, R.F. (1992) 'Repatriation and disability: a community study of health, mental health and social functioning of Khmer residents of Site II. Vol. I: Khmer adults. Vol. II: Khmer children', Harvard University, unpublished MA dissertation.

Moore, H. (1996) 'The changing nature of anthropological knowledge. An introduction', in Moore, H. (ed.) *The Future of Anthropological Knowledge*, London and New York: Routledge.

✓ Motumu, T. and Hudson, A. (1995) 'Rightsizing: the challenges of demobilisation and social reintegration in South Africa', in Cilliers, J. (ed.) *Dismissed*, Institute for Defence Policy, South Africa: Halfway House, pp. 112-29.

Médecins sans Frontières-France (MSF-F) (1994a) 'Report on Field visit to Mozambique by MSF South Africa from 22/03/94-26/03/94': Johannesburg: MSF, unpublished.

—— (1994b) 'Cross border visit to Mozambique, 6th June to 8th June 1994', Johannesburg: MSF, unpublished.

✓ Musemwa, M. (1995) 'The ambiguities of democracy: the demobilization of the Zimbabwean ex-combatants and the ordeal of rehabilitation, 1990-93', in Cilliers, J. (ed.) *Dismissed*, Institute for Defence Policy, South Africa: Halfway House, pp. 44-57.

Mysliwiec, E. (1988) *Punishing the Poor: The International Isolation of Kampuchea*, Oxford: Oxfam.

Newbury, M.C. (1988) *The Cohesion of Oppression: Clientship and Ethnicity in Rwanda, 1860-1960*, New York: Columbia University Press.

O'Donnell, D. (1994) 'Resettlement or repatriation: screened-out Vietnamese child asylum seekers and the Convention on the Rights of the Child', *International Journal of Refugee Law*, (6)3: 382-401.

Okulov, A. (1994) 'Bezhentsy i pereselentsy', *Posev*, 2: 817.

Open Society Institute (OSI) Forced Migration Projects (1996) *Crimean Tatars: Repatriation and Conflict Prevention*, New York: OSI.

Open Society Institute (OSI) (1997) *Forced Migration Alert*, 28, 12 May.

'O vnesenii izmenenii i dopolnenii v zakon Rossiiskoi Federatsii 'O vynuzhdennikh, pereselentsakh' (1995) *Sobranie Zakonodatel'stva*, 52, 25 December: 9317-27.

Parker, M. (1996) 'Social devastation and mental health in Northeast Africa', in Allen, T. (ed.) *In Search of Cool Ground: War, Flight and Homecoming in Northeast Africa*, London: James Currey, pp. 262-73.

✓ Phizaklea A. (1996) 'Structure and agency: conceptualizing forced migration in the Former Soviet Union', unpublished paper.

Pilkington, H. (1998) *Migration, Displacement and Identity in Post-Soviet Russia*, London and New York: Routledge.

Pottier, J. (1996a) 'Why agencies need better understanding of the communities they assist: the experience of food aid in Rwandan refugee camps', *Disasters*, 20(4): 324-37.

—— (1996b) 'Relief and Repatriation: views by Rwandan refugees; lessons for humanitarian aid workers', *African Affairs*, 95(380): 403-29.

Preston, R. (1992) 'Refugees in Papua New Guinea: government response and assistance, 1984-1988', *International Migration Review*, 26(2): 843-76.

—— (ed.) (1993a) *The Integration of Returned Exiles, Former Combatants and other War-affected Namibians*, Windhoek: Namibia Institute for Social and Economic Research.

√ —— (1993b) 'Studying integration', in Preston, R. (ed.) *The Integration of Returned Exiles, Former Combatants and other War-affected Namibians*, Windhoek: Namibia Institute for Social and Economic Research, pp. 2/1-2/15.

—— (1994a) 'States, statelessness and education: post-return integration of Namibians trained abroad', *International Journal of Educational Development*, 14(3): 299-319.

—— (1994b) 'Returning exiles in Namibia since independence', in Allen, T. and Morsink, H. (eds) *When Refugees Go Home*, London: James Currey, pp. 260-67.

—— (1995) 'Dialogue with reference to a study of the social application of refugee law concerning repatriation in safety and dignity', Coventry: University of Warwick, International Centre for Education in Development, unpublished report.

—— (1997) 'Demobilising and integrating fighters after war: the Namibian experience', *Journal of Southern African Studies*, 23(3): 453-72.

Prunier, G. (1995) *The Rwanda Crisis, 1959-1994: History of a Genocide*, London: Hurst.

√ Quick, S. (1995a) 'The return of Eritreans from Djibouti, 1980-1990', Case study VI, in Quick, S., Chingono, M. and Preston, R. (eds) *Social Applications of Refugee Law Repatriation in Safety and Dignity*, IRLP, University of Warwick, International Centre for Education in Development, Vol.2, unpublished report.

—— (1995b) 'Tigrayans returning from Sudan to Ethiopia in the mid-1980s', Case Study VII, in Quick, S., Chingono, M. and Preston, R. (eds) *Social Applications of Refugee Law Repatriation in Safety and Dignity*, IRLP, University of Warwick, International Centre for Education in Development, Vol.2, unpublished report.

Quick, S., Chingono, M. and Preston, R. (eds) (1995) *Social Applications of Refugee Law Repatriation in Safety and Dignity*, unpublished paper prepared for IRLP, University of Warwick, International Centre for Education in Development.

✓ Reid, A.K. (1992) 'Political studies in the voluntary repatriation of refugees', Deakin University, Australia, unpublished D.Phil. thesis.

✓ Reynell, J. (1989) *Political Pawns – Refugees on the Thai-Kampuchean Border*, Oxford: Refugee Studies Programme.

Richmond, A. (1994) *Global Apartheid: Refugees, Racism and the New World Order*, Oxford: Oxford University Press.

Riesco, M. (1995) 'Honour and eternal glory to the Jacobins', *New Left Review*, 212: 55-67.

✝ Robinson, C. (1994a) 'Something like home again. The repatriation of Cambodian refugees', Washington, DC: U.S. Committee for Refugees, unpublished report.

—— (1994b) 'Rupture and return: a study of Cambodian repatriation, displacement and reintegration in Battambang Province'. Occasional Paper No/007, Indochinese Refugee Information Center (IRIC), Institute of Asian Studies, Chulalongkorn University.

Rogers, R. and Copeland, E. (1993) *Forced Migration: Policy Issues in the Post-Cold War World*, Medford, Massachusetts: The Fletcher School of Law and Diplomacy, Tufts University.

Rogge, J. (1994), 'Repatriation of refugees: a not simple "optimum" solution', in Allen, T. and Morsink, H. (eds) *When Refugees Go Home*, London: James Currey, pp.14-49.

✓ Rosaldo, R. (1989) *Culture and Truth*, Boston: Beacon Press.

✓ Roseberry, W. (1994) 'The language of contention', in Joseph, G.M. and Nugent, D. (eds). *Everyday Forms of State Formation. Revolution and the Negotiation of Rule in Modern Mexico*, London: Duke University Press, pp. 355-66.

Sayer, D.(1994) 'Some dissident remarks on hegemony', in Joseph, G.M., and Nugent, D. (eds) *Everyday Forms of State Formation. Revolution and the Negotiation of Rule in Modern Mexico*, London: Duke University Press, pp. 367-78.

✓ Schaffer, J. (1995) 'Repatriation and reintegration: durable solutions?' Oxford: Refugee Studies Programme, unpublished paper.

Schulz, M. and Wähnung, S. (1989) 'Namibia: emergency, rehabilitation measures for returnees', Geneva: United Nations High Commissioner for Refugees, PTSS Mission Report, 89/95, unpublished.

Schwarz, T. (1996) 'Post-Soviet migration and ethno-political tension: conceptualizing the interaction', unpublished paper.

Scudder, T. (forthcoming) 'Resettlement' , in Biswat, A. K. (ed.) *Handbook of Water Resources and Environment,* New York: McGraw Hill.

√ Sepulveda, D. C. (1995) 'Challenging the assumptions of repatriation', *Courier,* 150: 83-85.

Shacknove, A.E., (1985) 'Who is a refugee?', *Ethics,* 95(2): 274-84.

Shevtsova, L. (1992) 'Post-Soviet emigration today and tomorrow', *International Migration Review,* 26(2): 241-57.

Shikangalah, S. (1995) 'The development brigades: the Namibian experience', in Cilliers, J. (ed.) *Dismissed,* Institute for Defence Policy, South Africa: Halfway House, pp. 70-71.

√ Simon, D. and Preston, R. (1992) 'Return to the promised land: the repatriation and resettlement of Namibian refugees, 1989-1990', in Black, R. and Robinson, V. (eds) *Geography and Refugees: Patterns and Processes of Change,* London: Belhaven Press, pp. 47-63.

Slater, D.(1995) 'Challenging Western visions of the global: the geopolitics of theory and North-South relations', *European Journal of Development Research,* 7(2): 366-388.

Smith, C. (ed.) (1990) *Guatemalan Indians and the State 1540-1988,* Austin: Texas University Press.

Stein, B.N. (1986) 'Durable solutions for developing country refugees', *International Migration Review,* 20(2): 264-82.

Stein, B. (1992) 'Policy challenges regarding repatriation in the 1990s: is 1992 the year for voluntary repatriation?', Paper commissioned by the Program on International and U.S. Refugee Policy, The Fletcher School of Law and Diplomacy, Tufts University, February, unpublished.

—— (1994) 'Ad hoc assistance to return movements and long-term development programmes', in Allen, T. and Morsink, H. (eds) *When Refugees Go Home,* London: James Currey, pp. 50-70.

—— (1997) 'Reintegrating returning refugees in Central America' in Kumar, K. (ed.) *Rebuilding Soceities after Civil War,* Boulder, CO: Lynne Rienner Publishers, pp. 155-80.

Stein, B. and Cuny, F. (1990) 'Patterns of spontaneous voluntary repatriation and its implications for policy and program', Briefing paper, presented at meetings on 'Repatriation under conflict: the Central American case', Washington DC: Center for Immigration Policy and Refugee Assistance, Georgetown University, December 1990, unpublished.

Stepputat, F.(1992) 'Beyond relief? Life in a Guatemalan refugee settlement in Mexico', University of Copenhagen, Ph.D. dissertation

✓ —— (1994) 'Repatriation and the politics of space: the Mayan diaspora and return movement', *Journal of Refugee Studies*, 7(2/3): 175-85.

—— (1997) 'Postwar Guatemala: encounters at the frontier of the modern state', in Wilson, F. and Frederiksen, B.F. (eds) *Livelihood, Identity and Instability*, Copenhagen: Centre for Development Research.

Stewart, F. (1993) 'War and development: can economic analysis help reduce the costs?' *Journal of International Development*, 5(4): 357-80.

Stockton, N. (1996) 'Rwanda: Rights and Racism', Unpublished paper, Oxford, 7 December 1996.

Suhrke, A. and Zolberg, A. (1989) 'Beyond the refugee crisis: disengagement and durable solutions for the developing world', *Migration*, 5(89): 69-119.

Sword, K. (1992) 'Responses to geopolitical change: refugee flows in the post-Communist era. A report on the Third Annual Meeting of the International Research and Advisory Panel, January 1992', *Journal of Refugee Studies*, 5(2): 87-105.

Tamas, K. and Gleichmann, C. (1993) 'Returned exiles on the Namibian labour market', in Preston, R. (ed.) *The Integration of Returned Exiles, Former Combatants and other War-affected Namibians*, Windhoek: Namibia Institute for Social and Economic Research, pp. 11/1-11/39.

Tapscott, C. (1994) 'A tale of two homecomings: influences of the economy and state on the reintegration of repatriated Namibian exiles, 1989-1991', in Allen, T. and Morsink, H. (eds) *When Refugees Go Home*, London: James Currey, pp. 237-50.

Tavares, D. (1993a) Caracterização, expectativas e representações sociais de militares desmobilizados (Huambo). Lisboa: OIKOS/ADRA.

—— (1993b) Caracterização, expectativas e representações sociais de militares desmobilizados na província de Malange. Luanda: ADRA/ICCO/Oxfam.

—— (1993c) Caracterização, expectativas e representações sociais ° de militares desmobilizados na província de Huíla. Luanda: ADRA/ICCO/Oxfam.

—— (1994) 'Representações sociais e expectativas de futuro de desmobilizados de guerra em Angola'. Lisboa: III Congresso Luso-Afro-Brasileiro de Ciências Sociais.

Terekhov, V. (1994) 'Bezhentsy i emigranty: Kak predotvratit' katastrofu?', *Nezavisimaia Gazeta*, January 12: 6.

Thorn, L. (1992) 'From rice truck to paddy field: a study of the repatriation and reintegration needs of vulnerable female heads of household and other vulnerable individuals living in the Cambodian refugee and displaced persons camps along the Thai-Cambodian border', Geneva: United Nations High Commissioner for Refugees, unpublished report.

Tishkov, V. (ed.) (1996) *Migratsii I Novie Diaspori v Postsovetskikh Gosudarstvakh*, Moscow: Institut ethnologii i antropologii RAN.

√ Toren, N. (1978) 'Return migration to Israel', *International Migration Review*, 12(1): 39-54.

Troeller, G.G. (1991) 'UNHCR resettlement as an instrument of international protection: constraints and obstacles in the arena of competition for scarce humanitarian resources', *International Journal of Refugee Law*, 3(3): 564-78.

Turner, V. (1967) *The Forest of Symbols: Aspects of Ndembu Ritual*, Ithaca, NY: Cornell University Press.

Turton, D. and Ghai, D. (1993) 'Refugees returning home: Report of the Symposium for the Horn of Africa on the Social and Economic Aspects of Mass Voluntary Return Movements of Refugees 15-17 September 1992, Addis Ababa'. Geneva: UNRISD, unpublished.

United Nations Co-ordinating Unit for Humanitarian Assistance (UCAH) (1994) 'Strategies for a demobilization and reintegration program in Angola under the Lusaka Protocol', Luanda: United Nations Co-ordinating Unit for Humanitarian Assistance, unpublished report.

—— (1995) 'Final report. The identification of social and economic expectations of soldiers to be demobilised' Luanda: United Nations Co-ordinating Unit for Humanitarian Assistance, unpublished report.

United Nations Development Programme (UNDP) (1993) Overview of Disaster Management, New York: UNDP Disaster Management Training Programme Materials.

√ United Nations (UN) (1996) 'United Nations consolidated appeal for Bosnia-Herzegovina, Croatia, Federal Republic of Yugoslavia, Former Yugoslav Republic of Macedonia. January – December 1997'. New York and Geneva: United Nations, November 1996, unpublished report.

√ —— (1997), 'United Nations consolidated appeal for Bosnia-Herzegovina, Croatia, Federal Republic of Yugoslavia, Former Yugoslav Republic of Macedonia. Implementation report: 1 January – 31 May 1997'. New York and Geneva: United Nations, July 1997, unpublished report.

United Nations High Commissioner for Refugees (UNHCR)
(1990) 'Inter-agency mission on repatriation of Cambodian
refugees and displaced persons', Geneva: United Nations High
Commissioner for Refugees, unpublished report.
—— (1993a) *The State of the World's Refugees: the Challenge of
Protection*, London: Penguin Books.
—— (1993b) 'Report on mission to South Africa', 13-22 August
1993, Johannesburg, unpublished report.
—— (1993c) 'Guidelines for refugee status determination of
Mozambicans in South Africa, Point 5', December 1993,
Johannesburg, unpublished report.
—— (1993d) 'Background to the Mozambique Repatriation
Operation', Johannesburg, unpublished report.
—— (1993e) 'Mission Report: Visit to Gaza Province/Districts
bordering South Africa, 24-28 October 1993', Johannesburg,
unpublished report.
—— (1994a) 'Returnee aid and development', UNHCR
EVAL/RAD/15, May, unpublished report.
—— (1994b) 'Policy and methodological framework for Quick
Impact Projects (QIPs) as a means of facilitating durable
solutions through integration', 30 June, unpublished report.
—— (1994c), 'Recommendations of the OAU/UNHCR Symposium
on Refugees and Forced Population Displacements in Africa',
Sub-Committee of the Whole on International Protection,
EC/1994/SCJP/CRP.7/Add.1, September, unpublished report.
√ —— (1994d) 'Addis Ababa – 8 September 1992' in *Repatriation:
Special Report*, Geneva: UNHCR, September 1994 Geneva,
unpublished report.
—— (1994e) 'Report from Mission to South Africa 10-20 February
1994', Geneva: UNHCR Regional Program Officer for Women
and Children, unpublished report.
—— (1995a) *The State of the World's Refugees: In Search of Solutions*,
Oxford: Oxford University Press.
—— (1995b) Executive Committee, Sub-Committee on
Administrative and Financial Matters, 32nd Meeting,
EC/1995/SC.2/CRP.4, January, unpublished report.
—— (1995c) *Mozambique 1993/1995 Review*, Johannesburg:
UNHCR Public Information Unit.
—— (1995d) 'Briefing note', 2 October 1995, Maputo: UNHCR
Field Office South: Mozambique, unpublished report.
—— (1996a) 'Mozambique: an account from Lessons Learned
Seminar on Reintegration, 24-25 June 1996'. UNHCR: Geneva,
unpublished report.

—— (1996b) 'Mozambique, repatriation and reintegration of Mozambican refugees', Status Report, 1 April 1996, Maputo: UNHCR Mozambique, unpublished report.

—— (1997a) 'Rebuilding a war-torn society: a review of the UNHCR reintegration programme for Mozambican returnees', *Refugee Survey Quarterly*, 16(2): 47-50.

—— (1997b) 'Information notes: Bosnia and Herzegovina and regional reports, no. 5, May/June 1997', Sarajevo: United Nations High Commissioner for Refugees, Office of the Special Envoy, unpublished report.

—— (1997c) Statement to the Intergovernmental Consultations on Asylum, Refugee and Migration Policies in Europe, North America and Australia, Washington, 6 May 1997.

United Nations High Commissioner for Refugees (UNHCR)/United Nations Development Project (UNDP) (1995) 'A framework for inter-agency initiative to promote a smooth transition from humanitarian assistance to sustainable human development', Geneva: UNHCR and UNDP, unpublished report.

UNHCR Regional Bureau for Europe (1996) 'The CIS conference on refugees and migrants', *European Series*, 2(1), January 1996.

United Nations Childrens Fund (UNICEF) (1994) 'Mozambican refugees in South Africa: focus on vulnerable groups', April 1994, Johannesburg, unpublished report.

United Nations Institute for Namibia (UNIN) (1986) *Namibia: Perspectives for National Reconstruction and Development*, Lusaka: United Nations Institute for Namibia.

United Nations Office for the Coordination of Humanitarian and Economic Assistance Programmes Relating to Afghanistan (UNOCA) (1988) *First Consolidated Report*, Geneva: UNOCA.

—— (1989) *Second Consolidated Report*, Geneva: UNOCA.

—— (1990) *Third Consolidated Report*, Geneva: UNOCA.

—— (1991) 'Operation Salam Programme for 1991: humanitarian and economic assistance programmes relating to Afghanistan', Geneva: UNOCA, unpublished report.

—— (1992) Operation Salam Programme for 1992: humanitarian and economic assistance programmes relating to Afghanistan, Geneva: UNOCA, unpublished report.

United Nations Research Institute for Social Development (UNRISD) (1995) *States of Disarray: The Social Effects of Globalization*, Geneva: UNRISD.

—— (1996) 'WSP Research Update 2', Geneva: War-Torn Societies Project, unpublished report.

United States Committee for Refugees (USCR) (1993) 'No Place like home: Mozambican refugees begin Africa's largest repatriation'. Washington, DC: USCR, December 1993, unpublished report.

—— (1997) *World Refugee Survey*, Washington, DC: USCR.

Van Gennep, A. (1960) *The Rites of Passage*, Chicago: University of Chicago Press.

Vickery, M. (1990), 'Refugee politics: the Khmer camp system in Thailand', in Ablin, D. and Hood, M. (eds) *The Cambodian Agony*, London: M.E. Sharpe, pp. 293-331.

Vincent, R.J. (1986) *Human Rights and International Relations*, Cambridge: Cambridge University Press.

Vines, A. (1995) *Renamo: from Terrorism to Democracy in Mozambique*, London: James Currey

Vishnevskii, A. (1994) 'Neizbezhno li vozvrashchenie?', *Znamia*, 1: 177-87.

Voutira, E. (1991) 'Pontic Greeks today: migrants or refugees?', *Journal of Refugee Studies*, 4(4): 400-20.

—— (1996) 'Mainstreaming gender in humanitarian emergencies: problems and prospects', Paper presented to the 5th Meeting of the International Research and Advisory Panel, Eldoret, Kenya, April.

—— (1997) 'Population transfers and resettlement policies in inter-war Europe: the case of Asia Minor refugees in Macedonia from an international and national perspective', in Mackridge, P. and Yiannokis, E. (eds) *Ourselves and Others: The Development of a Greek Macedonian Identity since 1912*, Oxford: Bergman.

Wagner, P (1994) *A Sociology of Modernity. Liberty and Discipline*, London and New York: Routledge.

Warner, D. (1994) 'Voluntary Repatriation and the Meaning of Return to Home: A Critique of Liberal Mathematics', *Journal of Refugee Studies*, 7(2/3): 160-74.

Watson, C. (1996) *The Flight, Exile and Return of Chadian Refugees: a Case Study with a Special Focus on Women*, Geneva: UNRISD.

Webster, J.B., Ogot, B.A. and Chrétien, J.P. (1992) 'The Great Lakes Region, 1500-1800,' in Ogot, B.A. (ed.) *General History of Africa. V: Africa from the Sixteenth to the Eighteenth Century*, Paris: UNESCO. pp. 776-827.

Weiss Fagen, P. (1995) *After the Conflict: a Review of Selected Sources on Rebuilding War-torn Societies*, Geneva: UNRISD, Programme for International Security Studies.

Wilson, K. (1994) 'Refugees and returnees as social agents: the case of Jehovah's witnesses from Milange', Allen, T. and Morsink, H. (eds) *When Refugees Go Home*, London: James Currey, pp. 237-50.

Wilson, K. and Nunes, J. (1994) 'Repatriation to Mozambique: refugee initiative and agency planning in Milange District, 1988-1991', in Allen, T. and Morsink, H. (eds) *When Refugees Go Home*, London: James Currey, pp. 167-236.

Wilson, R. (1991) 'Machine guns and mountain spirits. The cultural effects of state repression among the Q'eqchi' of Guatemala', *Critique of Anthropology*, 11(1): 33-61.

World Bank (1993) 'Demobilisation and reintegration of military personnel in Africa: the evidence from seven country case studies', New York: World Bank Discussion Paper IDP-130, Africa Regional Series, October 1993, unpublished.

Zaionchkovskaia, Zh. (1996) 'Russkii vopros', *Migratsiia*, 1:7-11.

Zetter, R. (1988) 'Refugees, repatriation and root causes', *Journal of Refugee Studies*, 1(2): 99-106.

—— (1991) 'Labelling refugees: forming and transforming a bureaucratic identity', *Journal of Refugee Studies*, 4(1): 39-62.

—— (1994) 'The Greek-Cypriot refugees: perceptions of return under conditions of protracted exile', *International Migration Review*, 23(2): 307-22.

Zinkin, P. (1993) 'Disability and rehabilitation in post-war Namibia, in Preston, R. (ed.) *The Integration of Returned Exiles, Former Combatants and other War-affected Namibians*, Windhoek: Namibia Institute for Social and Economic Research, pp. 7/1-7/29.

Zur, J. (1993) 'Violent memories: Quiché War Widows in NW Highland Guatemala', London School of Economics, Ph.D. dissertation.

INDEX